Sindia,

the Final Voyage

"Ocean City's famous shipwreck"

HARRY ALLEN WENZEL

Sindia,

the Final Voyage

Yellowtail Snapper Publishing
Harleysville, PA
USA

Allan MacKenzie, Master - S.V. Sindia - 1901

DEDICATION

Angus Alexander MacKinnon lived along the shore of the Firth of Clyde in the coastal town of Troon, Scotland. He was born in Glasgow and raised on the wee Hebridean Island of Eriskay until the age of twelve, at which time he moved back to Glasgow for secondary education. He retained his native language, Scottish Gaelic, and demonstrated an excellent command of English, both verbal and written. He was formerly employed with British Petroleum and served as fifth, fourth, then third engineer officer on steam turbine supertankers. Angus was enamored with the days of sail. In his retirement he spent volumes of time researching maritime history and documenting and photographing modern day vessels arriving at the port of South Ayrshire, for the Clyde Maritime Portal.

The roots of the MacKinnon clan extend to a long line of mariners. His father, a mariner for forty years, held a master's certificate and captained his own ship. While delving into his ancestry, Angus spoke of the presence of whalers. He unselfishly provided me access to many hours of his time, allowing me to learn from his knowledge and expertise, while acting in the capacity of a research assistant, advisor, and ultimately valuable friend.

Angus was born on December 4, 1942 and passed away on August 15, 2015. He was laid to rest at the place of his birth, the Isle of Eriskay (Old Norse for Eric's Isle), located in the Outer Hebrides, northern Scotland.

CONTENTS

Author's Preface
Acknowledgements
Introduction - Bureau Veritas of Paris
               The Wreck Register and Chart for 1899
               Merchant Sailing Vessels
               Beaufort Wind Force Scale

Chapters

APPENDICES

"While a historian stands firmly planted in the present and looks back into the past, a historical novelist has a more immediate task: to set readers in the midst of bygone events and lead them forward, allowing them to live and feel the wonderment, fear, hope, triumph, and pain as if they were there."

James Alexander Thom, Author
"The Art and Craft of Writing Historical Fiction"

AUTHOR'S PREFACE

Why write a story about a sailship and a Scottish sea captain --- a story culminating in an event that happened over one hundred fourteen years ago? This story has never been written. Angus MacKinnon, a Scotsman and my research assistant, touched upon a second important reason for writing this story. "This story needed to be told."

Many years ago as a boy, I vacationed with my family in Ocean City, N.J. I spent the entirety of each day playing on the beach, collecting shells, and surfing the waves with my inflatable canvas raft. Each evening my family walked the boardwalk. The air would cool and it was refreshing to inhale the salt ladened sea breeze blowing in from the ocean. Mom wore a buttoned sweater and I donned a sweatshirt as we strolled along the wooden boards. We passed the Flanders Hotel and then, standing in front of the Copper Kettle, vacationers were greeted with a small sign displaying a message, ticker tape format, parading across a screen in red letters. "Good fudge isn't cheap, cheap fudge isn't good, buy Copper Kettle Fudge." College students stood behind large glass windows, alongside huge copper kettles, filled with pounds of thick liquid fudge. They twirled and whipped the fudge laden wooden paddles, preparing the mixture for the oven.

Our walk continued to 13th Street on the boardwalk and it was there that I saw him. We walked through the door of the Smuggler's Shop and a world of sights and sounds from the sea emerged. The smuggler was standing behind the cash register. His hair was sandy in color and his moustache and beard were groomed to perfection. He resembled a Scottish sea captain having just docked his ship at port.

Glass display cases were filled with scrimshaw. Beautiful, expensive carvings on whalebone. The detail was amazing: delicate craftsmanship, pictures of sailships, whales, sailors, harpoons, braided rope and anchors, all depicting scenes from an era long gone.

Mom and I walked around surveying his store -- chantey songs were playing throughout. The seamen turning the capstan on a cargo carrying sailship would sing chanteys, enabling them to ease the strain of the workload during a day's toil. The smuggler printed a message on a card listing the location where his treasure was found. A collection of varied seashells from islands and places around the world caught my eye. And then there was *Iron Mike*, a display depicting a large canvas deep sea diving suit used for man's foray into undersea exploration.

My dad would wait for us, resting on a wooden bench situated on the boardwalk facing the ocean, a plastic container of Johnson's caramel popcorn in hand. A couple of minutes later and a few blocks south we visited Sindia. The metal sternpost of the square-rigged windjammer was the sole remnant from the shipwreck in 1901. The remainder of the ship lay in ruin, undisturbed beneath the sand on the beach. My imagination was stimulated with thoughts and questions. What did the sailship look like? How large was the vessel? Who were the crew? Where did they come from? What happened? The questions remained unanswered for many years to follow.

In October 2013, the idea of researching the history and writing the story took seed. A visit to the Ocean City Historical Museum and a search for the origin and fate of the captain and crew began. There was virtually nothing available on the background of the captain, with the exception of one lone sentence hidden in the obscurity of a newspaper article, written years following the shipwreck. A former survivor and cabin boy, David Jackson, commented at a Sindia Day commemoration, "He was a nice old man from the north of Scotland."

My journey began. This story is constructed from many hours of historical research. There are a few elements of fiction created for the purpose of enhancement. Most of the chapters are filled with events, including the identity of actual people who were alive at the time, and whose lives became the fabric of local history. In some cases the identity of the real character could not be found and additional characters were created to complete the story and provide detail to bring the account to life.

You are about to read a historical novel written with a depth designed to inform and educate the curious. Without this work, many details hidden in history would remain in obscurity. Step into the shoes of Master Allan MacKenzie and walk through a portal in time. Weigh anchor, op the riggin, and hoist and set your sails mate! I hope you enjoy the journey. It's a fascinating story. It's the story of Sindia, the Final Voyage.

Harry Allen Wenzel
July 10, 2016

ACKNOWLEDGEMENTS

My thanks to Jeff McGranahan, Executive Director, and Noel Wirth, Trustee and Secretary of the Ocean City Historical Museum, for providing access to historical files and pictures of artifacts, and a valuable resource depicting the history of Ocean City's Life-Saving Service; to David Swope, Trustee, Secretary, and researcher at the Museum of New Jersey Maritime History, Beach Haven, for research pertaining to New Jersey's preponderance of shipwrecks; to David Boone of the Independence Seaport Museum, Philadelphia, for research assistance with shipwrecks and an informative sailmaking display; to David McVeigh, Sales and Marketing Mgr. at Harland and Wolff Heavy Industries, Ltd. of Queens Island, Belfast, Northern Ireland, for his research of ships purchased by Thos. & Jno. Brocklebank, Ltd.; to David White of the Liverpool Nautical Research Society, for reference to a book about Anglo-American Oil Sailors; to Maureen Freed, for genealogical research pertaining to the MacKenzies; and to Arielle Eckstut and David Henry Sterry, co-authors of "The Essential Guide to Getting Your Book Published," a valuable book to be studied by all authors.

EDITOR
BOOK COVER DESIGN AND ILLUSTRATION

Stephen J. Edgcumbe, writer and editor, for editing services.

Lee Carol Wenzel, design and creation of the book cover. Literary, proofreading, and copyediting.

Tony Troy, illustrator and artist, Ocean City, N.J.

The cover picture is a likeness of Master Allan MacKenzie, drawn from an old photograph, most likely 1901, by Tony Troy. There are only two photographs of the captain known to exist in the U.S.A., displayed in the Ocean City Historical Museum. The second photograph surfaced in the spring of 2016.

Born in Liverpool, England, Tony began his career drawing portraits on the streets of London, Paris, Copenhagen, Munich and Florence. He was later invited to exhibit his portraits by the prestigious Royal Society of Portrait Painters of Great Britain, and the Pastel Society of Great Britain. His experience includes paintings of the aristocracy of Great Britain.

INTRODUCTION

THE BUREAU VERITAS OF PARIS

A report was published in the year 1877 (one year prior to the launch of Sindia) listing the merchant navies of the world. The leading countries were ranked by number of ships followed by total tonnage. Worldwide up to that date, there were a total of 58,208 registered ships. The top four countries are listed below.

United Kingdom	20,265	5,807,375 tons
United States of America	7,249	2,390,521 tons
Norway	4,749	1,410,903 tons
Italy	4,601	1,292,076 tons

THE WRECK REGISTER AND CHART FOR 1899

The Board of Trade, London, issued its annual report of "Shipwreck Statistics" for the year 1899, one year prior to the departure of Sindia from Liverpool to New York, then to Shanghai and Kobe.

Throughout the year there were a total of 5,040 shipping casualties, 4,434 involving British and Colonial vessels, and 606 attributed to vessels of foreign registry. All were a result of incidences occurring in and around the coast of the United Kingdom. The definition of a casualty included collision, foundering (sinking), stranding and missing vessels. The loss of life totaled 520 for the same year.

Included in the "Shipwreck Statistics" for the previous ten year period is a total ship casualty per year, according to their definition.

❖ 1890	-	4,344
❖ 1891	-	4,198
❖ 1892	-	4,710
❖ 1893	-	3,499
❖ 1894	-	4,951
❖ 1895	-	4,917
❖ 1896	-	4,620
❖ 1897	-	5,277
❖ 1898	-	4,964
❖ 1899	-	5,040
Total		46,460

MERCHANT SAILING VESSELS

There were a total of ten sailing vessels (SV) built by Harland and Wolff at Queen's Island, Belfast, Ireland, for Thos. & Jno. Brocklebank, Ltd. of Liverpool, England, with launch dates between 1863 and 1888. The tonnage of the first was 1,352 and the dimensions and weight of each grew every time a new ship was designed and built for the owner. The last ship was 3,072 tons.

On the nineteenth of November in the year 1887, there was launched at Belfast by Harland and Wolff, a windjammer, a four-mast square-rigged steel *barque* of 3,067 tons, the first of two sister vessels (the other named *Holkar*) built for Brocklebank for their East India trade. The hull of the vessel was identified as Ship No. 204. The length between perpendiculars of the ship was 326' 3," the breadth 44' 10," and the depth 26' 8." The four masts supported a total of thirty-two canvas sails and when fully unfurled, this magnificent vessel displayed a total sail capacity of approximately 35,000 square feet.

The official number identifying the ship was 93757 assigned by Lloyd's Registry, and the Port of Registry was listed as London, England. The ship bore the name <u>*Sindia*</u>. In the year 1901, Sindia, along with Holkar, were the largest windjammers under sail on any ocean of the world. Sindia was sold by the Brocklebanks to the Anglo-American Standard Oil Co., Ltd., of London in 1900.

By 1889 the construction of sailing vessels for commercial cargo carrying purposes was in a state of transition. Harland and Wolff built a total of eight more ships for Brocklebank between 1889 and 1906. These latter vessels were designated cargo ships and were powered by steam reciprocating engines. The initial ship was registered as 4,014 tons and thereafter each ship increased in size. The last cargo ship propelled by steam built for the Brocklebank firm weighed 7,653 tons.

BEAUFORT WIND FORCE SCALE

Developed By

Sir Frances Beaufort, United Kingdom Royal Navy 1805

Force	Wind (Knots)		Appearance of Wind Effects Conditions on the Sea
0	< 1	Calm	Sea surface smooth
1	1-3	Light air	Ripples, no foam crests
2	4-6	Light breeze	Small wavelets, crests, no breaking
3	7-10	Gentle breeze	Large wavelets, scattered whitecaps
4	11-16	Moderate breeze	Small waves 1-4 ft. many whitecaps
5	17-21	Fresh breeze	Waves 4-8 ft., whitecaps, spray
6	22-27	Strong breeze	Waves 8-13 ft., whitecaps, spray
7	28-33	Near gale	Sea heaps up, waves 13-19 ft.
8	33-40	Fresh gale	Waves 18-25 ft., crests begin break
9	41-47	Strong gale	23-32 ft., sea rolls reduced visibility
10	48-55	Storm	29-41 ft., heavy rolls, low visibility
11	56-63	Violent storm	Very high waves, 37-52 ft.
12	64+	Hurricane	Waves over 45 ft., driving spray

"There comes a moment in time when the storm blows cold punishing winds and rain; a hollow dry sickness forms and envelopes the entirety of a seaman's being. With my sight impaired, fingers numbed, hands bloodied, and arms aching without reprieve, I struggled to fight the weather to keep the ship's wheel on the card. My belly spewed forth as the remnant of a wave washed my fear toward the taffrail, over the stern. It was then that I recalled the admonishment of Captain MacKenzie, many months before. "Whatever you do, don't show them the white feather." There were thirty-three of us --- I was the helmsman."

Mitchell Graeme
December 14, 1901

CHAPTER
1

PECK'S BEACH
C. 1700

One wave after another crashed upon the shore as the whaleman continued his work for the day. He paused from his toil momentarily to take in the beauty of his surroundings. A series of seven he thought as he watched the spray from the wave fold backward over the crest, while the rest of her fell toward the shoreline. His experience at sea was extensive and he spent most of his time circumnavigating around this particular island and waters further south. He watched, mesmerized, for more than several minutes, as one by one each wave crested then fell upon the wet sand. They came in a series and he understood that from years of observation from his whaleboat. His livelihood depended on his knowledge of the sea, including his ability to maneuver his boat from the ocean into the inlets.

He was the only one present on this day. The greenish hue enveloping each wave was a thing of beauty nature had created for his personal enjoyment. The smell of the salt air filled his lungs as he drew in slow deep breaths. The waves, accompanied by the constant chatter of the herring gulls, were the only noises on this particular autumn day.

The barrier island was well known to him. He had plenty of time to explore the seven mile stretch of beach that lived here. The island was separated by a large inlet on the north side. A Dutch map dated 1698 labeled the inlet the Great Egg Harbor. He visited the inlet on the south side, and it was not as wide and looked completely different from its relative to the north. There was another barrier island south of the stretch of shoreline that became his favorite. The tide ebbed into the ocean allowing each wave to collapse with regular continuity. He picked this island as his favorite working place and Mother Nature provided him a bountiful harvest of flounder and sea bass for food. In a few weeks the bluefish would make their presence known from northerly places as they would slip by the island on their way south.

He was working on the northeastern end laden with thick patches of woods. Portions of the island located below the cedar grove were strewn with sea-grasses, bayberry, sassafras and other herbs. The sea turtle inhabited the beaches and laid eggs in the sand dunes in abundance. The herbs were harvested and sold to Holland and other neighboring European communities. A surveyor with ownership rights to the island planted the harvest and drove his cattle across the inlet to the south, using the island for grazing purposes.

Turning his shoulder to the south he realized his sole presence had been interrupted by a small group. He was no longer alone. It happened before and they knew each other. They had other opportunities to become acquainted but they couldn't speak with one another. Communication was limited to a few words. Gestures and hand signals helped to improve the inability to speak with each other. They were friendly but timid in nature, expressing caution in their approach. Although contact between them was limited, a watchful trust of one another was present. It grew with each encounter.

There were eight in total, four males, two females and two children, most likely seven to ten years old. The males wore pants sewn out of deerskin. Their long-sleeved shirts were made from the same material but darker in color. Two of them wore colorful beads laced on a cord and draped around their necks. The women wore similarly shaped tops and the neckline was cut to fit loosely. They wore one-piece skirts around their waists. Two of the men wore bands around their foreheads, tied in a knot in the back. A single feather standing upright protruded from the band on one but not on the other. A one feather placement identified his position within the cluster. The other men wore their hair shoulder length, bundled together to form a singular thick dark braid that hung near the neck.

Fishing nets woven by hand and weighted around the perimeter were thrown into the surf in an effort to bring in a catch. Small fish were harvested intermittently. He reasoned they and their ancestors were coming to the island long before he set foot upon the sand.

There was a name given to these coastal residents and the name fit the description of who they were. The *Unalatchtigo* meant people who live by the ocean. They were Lenape's and word spread along the trade routes confirming they were part of the greater Delaware Nation, a people who settled the vast area from New York south, and eastward into Penn's woods and New Jersey. Their native tongue suggested their ancestral beginnings were from far-away northern places and could be traced to the Algonquian tribe.

John Peck was a whaler and he was busy making provisions to store his catch. The Unalatchtigo not only understood his business, they participated in the same endeavor. They were a respectful people. He knew he could leave his provisions and upon return find them undisturbed.

He was well acquainted with the habits of the North Atlantic Grey Whale. They were a coastal whale migrating along the northeastern portion of the royal colonies, extending up to the southeastern border of Canada. They ventured close to shore and their migration pattern took them from winter breeding and calving grounds into the southeastern royal colonies to summer foraging grounds.

John harvested the meat for sale and consumption and the blubber was used to create a high-grade lamp oil. He cut the blubber into blocks called horse pieces and then sliced them into "Bible leaves" before being boiled in pots. There were a dozen applications for the oil harvested from his rendering operation.

He was one of a number of whalers who occupied the mainland near the beaches. Their whaleboats, carved from cedar, were thirty feet long and manned by a crew of six. In addition to the oarsmen there was a rudder-man and a harpoons-man. The tools of their trade were handmade into a head spade, a cutting spade, a bone spade, and the harpoon lance.

Some of his partners inhabited the upper, middle or lower seaside and the upper, middle or lower bayside areas. Arthur Cresse owned 300 acres along the middle seaside. He was a descendant of a pilgrim family from the Mayflower. Captain Ezekiel Eldredge owned 200 acres along the lower bayside, William Goldin owned 600 acres along the upper seaside and Samuel Matthews owned 175 acres along the lower bayside.

There were other whalers who worked together to help with the harvest: Nathaniel Short, Ebenezer Swaine and two brothers known to be John and

Caleb Carman. All of them frequented the waters surrounding Cape May County. It was Caleb, known for his reputation as one of the best whalers, who formed a business relationship with Peck and together they spent much time in the vicinity of the island.

Peck and his crew would navigate the whaleboat through a passage between the northeastern end of the island and into the bay areas. At low tide mounds of sand would appear and the shapes reminded him of monstrous eggs. The grey whale could be found breeding and calving in the accompanying shallow areas of the back bay. The hunting was plentiful and his prospects for harvest became greater in these areas.

This was John's place of business and this was the shoreline that he knew well. The whalers and fishermen were acquainted with one another as they worked in harvesting groups. They came from Long Island and parts of New England, looking for more favorable conditions to engage in their trade. Some founded Portsmouth Town, located southwest along the bayside. One day a memorial stone was set in place so future generations would remember the location of the town founded by them.

As the waves rolled by so did many years. In time the people who came to hunt or enjoy an occasional picnic would refer to ferrying across the bay to Peck's Beach. The island was one of a few in a long stretch of beaches, and it became part of a greater portion of land designated as the King's Royal Colony, New Jersey.

CHAPTER

2

WHITEHAVEN

There were more than 100 vessels built and sailing from the small coastal town by the middle part of the 18th century. Large quantities of locally mined coal deposits fueled the construction of ships, providing the means to transport the mineral in large quantities, thereby increasing trade with Ireland.

Reverend Daniel Brocklebank and his spouse, Sarah, moved from the small village of Wigton to nearby Torpenhow. The move was prompted by an offering made to Reverend Brocklebank; he accepted a post to become the priest in charge of Torpenhow Parish Church, founded in the county of Cumberland, England.

Together they raised five children; the eldest child John, was followed by Thomas, Ralph, Margaret, Eleanor and Daniel, who was born in 1741. In the year 1755 at the age of fourteen, Daniel (Jr.) made way to Whitehaven, where he accepted an apprenticeship as a carpenter to a shipbuilder. Daniel spent the following fourteen years at Whitehaven, devoting his efforts to become proficient in the trade of shipbuilding.

By the year 1769, Daniel, at age twenty-eight, married Miss Anne Cuppage in Whitehaven. The couple remained in the growing coastal town for one year while Daniel formulated plans to build a new career in New England. Coastal settlements near Whitehaven lacked the quantity of timber to keep pace with the growing demand for new ships. Some of the timber used for ship construction was imported from the colonies. Daniel knew of the stories of vast forests populating the eastern coast of the colonies; the source for lumber he would secure for his own enterprise.

SHEEPSCUT, MAINE 1770

The winter was harsh and the annual snowfall exceeded the previous winter's tally by twenty-one inches. Daniel picked this locale to establish a small enterprise to begin his operation and build his first ship. Over the next five years he and his men built a total of five vessels. The fifth, Castor, played an important role in the life of the Brocklebanks for some years to come. Completed in 1775, Castor was a twenty gun brig of 220 tons.

Spring arrived and Daniel determined it was necessary to return to England. He became increasingly impatient with the colonists who criticized King George III and his desire to levy new taxes on the colonies. He would gather a crew and set sail for Whitehaven. They would navigate south of Nova Scotia off the coast of Newfoundland, catch a large quantity of fish due to provisions being light, and cross the great ocean. Many nautical miles and thirty-three days later they would enter the Irish Sea, sail northward passing the eastern side of the Isle of Man, arriving home.

The seed of rebellion grew as word spread among the colonists; they complained of taxation without representation. The opinions offered by Thomas Paine fostered disagreement with the directives coming from the Crown. Disenchantment could be felt from Boston south through New York to Philadelphia. Benjamin Franklin cranked his press, printing words expressing freedom and the fuel for a fire of rebellion was being lit. The colony of Virginia joined the chorus with expressions of liberty and freedom from Patrick Henry and Thomas Jefferson. All were English and with one accord vocalized their disagreement with the king and their mother country.

Daniel reacted to the fires of revolution being stoked by colonists and set about the work of privateering. His Majesty King George III granted a Letter of Marque to Daniel Brocklebank. In essence, the letter became a license to outfit the Castor as an armed vessel to attack and capture merchant ships owned by the enemy, and commit acts that in times of peace, would be classified as piracy.

Years passed and in 1785 Daniel established his shipbuilding business. He was a master mariner and he was knowledgeable about the ways of the sea. During the following seven years he focused on building a yard capable of producing the finest wooden ships for any master to command. By 1792 his work was well known, he was recognized as one of the best.

He was a visionary and energetic. He set about his goal of building his fleet, while taking advantage of existing opportunities and developing new ones to create a merchant shipping business.

Time advanced and the passing years produced the inevitable change in the seasons of life. The Brocklebank family mourned the loss of Daniel in the year 1801. The ship Cumberland, built in 1800, was the 40th and last ship to be designed and constructed by the patriarch of a future family dynasty. Cumberland's dimensions were 100' in length, 28' 2" in breadth, and 18' 6" depth. The tonnage was 340.

The firm's business responsibilities were inherited by his two sons, Thomas, at the age of twenty-six, and John, age eighteen. The years continued to elapse and by 1809, the sons changed the firm's name to Thomas & John Brocklebank. Customers increased as did shipping routes and their merchant ships sailed as far away as South America. The two sons combined their business acumen and continued their endeavors; seven years later, in 1816, their fleet totaled seventeen ships. As the year came to a close, the Dryad, a 231-ton brig, was the 77th ship built by the Brocklebank family.

England stood at the threshold of pioneering more trade routes and the brothers were eager to be a part of an expanding empire. In 1819, the brothers decided it was strategic to locate to Liverpool to build the shipping company. Several years passed and during the summer of 1822, an office was opened and Thomas was chosen to manage the business affairs. John remained in Whitehaven, continuing the ship-building business. Seven more years passed and merchant trade was established with China.

CHAPTER
3

THE HIGHLANDERS AND THE SEA

The *Abhainn Nis* (Scottish Gaelic) is twelve miles long and flows from the northern end of *Loch Ness* through *Loch Dochfour*, meandering in a northeasterly direction through the village of Inverness. The English translation for the Gaelic name is simply River Ness. The river discharges into *Beauly Firth* (a sea bay, inlet or strait). Lowland Scots use the word firth to denote various coastal waters. The town of Inverness received its name from the Scottish Gaelic, *Inbhir Nis*, or "Mouth of the Ness." The confluence of these bodies of water became important to neighboring residents in the 1800's. The Beauly Firth, when followed eastward, leads into a large bay that ultimately becomes one with the North Sea. The area was of prime importance for the resident fishermen making a living off the sea, either harvesting from its bounty or furthering their abilities to manage the passage of merchant vessels sailing these waters.

John Macrae was a schoolmaster and in this particular year would fulfill a responsibility as an enumerator. He was readying to complete the census-taking for Parish No. 98 in a single day. Scotland was divided into a series of enumeration districts based largely upon the existence of parishes. The night before taking the census he was given a schedule for every household in his district. On the following day he would be responsible for completing and collecting the census schedules for this parish.

The address 48 Grant Street was located on a short thoroughfare three blocks from the River Ness. Grant Street became part of a residential district and a number of small two-storied homes lined the street. It was typical of a small Scottish town in the nineteenth century.

The homes were relatively small in size, one and one half stories, usually constructed of block and plastered over. A center chimney protruded through the roof as a convenient and effective method to supply heat for the family during winter. Many a roof was constructed of slate. Some of the homes were built with reddish colored clay block. The yard was small with a short white fence circumventing the perimeter. A few blocks away commercial buildings were constructed of stone, often light gray in color. Some of the stones were varying shades of light pink and off-white, with stone lintels supporting the window frames.

The enumerator knocked on the door of 48 Grant Street, the home where the MacKenzie family resided. John and Janet were the parents of five children, two girls and three boys. The members of John's house were noted and listed by Mr. Macrae accordingly.

Name	Age	DOB
John MacKenzie	35	1806
Janet MacKenzie	30	1811
Mary Anne MacKenzie	11	1830
George MacKenzie	9	1832
John MacKenzie	7	1834
Isabella MacKenzie	4	1837
Allan MacKenzie	16 mos.	1839

John MacKenzie was a ship's captain and his wife a homemaker. His ancestral roots could be traced to the village of Clackmannan years prior. He believed there was an opportunity to own his own fishing boat, complete with crew, so they moved close to the waterways leading to the North Sea. Grant Street provided convenient access with a short three block walk to the banks of the River Ness.

John ruled his family with a stern hand yet he knew how to soften his approach toward Mary Anne and Isabella. The three boys would be taught a trade, the logical choice, to live off the sea. If the sea wasn't their calling they would gravitate toward farming or serving an apprenticeship in the local textile industry.

The youngest, Allan, was born on November 22. One month later, John and Janet arranged for their third son to be baptized on December 21. The MacKenzie's embraced their faith with sincerity. The Church of Scotland was the home to all Presbyterians and being highlanders, the family roots were recorded and could be traced through local parish records. Through their leadership and living by example, John and Janet would undertake all of the necessary responsibilities to ensure their children were raised to embrace their faith. It was one that would carry them through life's trials and tribulations sure to follow. They, along with many northern Scots, perpetuated the long line of family tradition, embracing the Presbyterian way of life and culture. They would do their best to build a future for their children.

∞

Twelve years passed since the '41 census and Allan was now thirteen. Schooled at home by his mother, he reached the appropriate age whereby it was imperative he build his own career and pathway for productivity. If you were a MacKenzie, your home was the sea. Grant Street was a place to rest your tired muscles and a place to remember the precious times each would enjoy growing up in a family of seven.

George, at twenty-one, and his younger brother John, at nineteen, helped their father with the family fishing business. Allan put to sea with them by the time he was twelve. The dangerous risks and the toil of living a fisherman's life in the North Sea was embedded in him. Although he was young his father recognized specific talent and acumen that was bestowed upon the youngest of his family. He was intelligent and quick to grasp seafaring terms and responsibilities. His brothers observed his fearlessness that at times, although older, surpassed their own. It was up to John, the father of the three young men, to rely on his connections to prepare a way to advance the careers of his sons.

∞

In 1852 there were few options to hire on as a crew member of a merchant vessel in the hope of learning the trade. The first step to be secured was an apprenticeship. John MacKenzie used his influence plus a negotiated sum of pounds to persuade Harris Stevens, Captain of the Hugh Crawford, to hire his son, Allan, as an apprentice. The Seaman's Agreement signed by John for his son designated his son's position as "Boy." The MacKenzie's were a known commodity around the village of

Inverness and his father's reputation was respected. John still had to pay the agreed upon sum for the privilege of engaging his son as an apprentice. He would learn to work on a sailship while living his life at sea.

Captain Stevens was a historian and he knew the past of the Hugh Crawford quite well. The ship was a 366-ton fully rigged vessel. Built in New York in 1809, the original name was Orbit. The owner used the ship for trade between America and Liverpool. In 1813 the British captured the ship and renamed it Hugh Crawford. Twenty-seven years prior, the ship was privately chartered to carry free emigrants to New South Wales, making three such voyages between 1825 through 1827. The ship was also used to transport cargo and passengers between London and Hobart Town to Sydney, Australia, in the early 1800s.

In the month of July 1852, Allan at the age of twelve, set sail on his first merchant voyage. During the next few years he would secure voyages of short duration-up to two months. Between assignments on merchant ships he was expected to assist his father and brothers with the family fishing business.

He entered the corps as the lowest grade seaman; it was up to him to work diligently and intelligently if he were to rise in the ranks. And so he did. Allan invested his time and efforts wisely. Patience was required to learn all of the parts and workings of a sailing vessel. The terminology seemed never ending. The transition of working in a family fishing business paled in comparison with serving an apprenticeship with a crew on the Hugh Crawford.

∞

By 1855 Allan established a connection with the captain of the ship, Johns, because the port of registry for the ship was Inverness. In the following two years he would deepen his experience, studying and learning the technical aspects of seamanship. There was the business of being uprooted from family and thrown into the mix of a group of men who were crowded together, onboard a sailship, out at sea with land nowhere in sight. Cold and dampness ruled supreme. Living in wet conditions was the norm as waves routinely crashed over the deck, refusing to remain with the body of water they were sailing upon.

Menial tasks were assigned and it was often difficult to perform basic duties. But they had to be done and it often became an opportunity for Allan to persevere and prove his potential worth. The poor pay was not a motivator to continue but the pride of being a descendent from clan MacKenzie, as his grandfather suggested, was another matter. Allan was taught at a very early age a MacKenzie lived by a motto and to break the creed would meet with a stern rebuke. The look from the eyes of his father would be fixed in his memory for some time to follow. It was expected that all matters and tasks in life would be approached with integrity supported by a hard work ethic. Upon the completion of the task you could look back with an element of pride for what you accomplished and then, only look for a second and move on.

His supervisors were those who rose to the rank of able bodied seaman or junior officers. The makeup of the crew was a mixture of all sorts of human specimen. Some even displayed characteristics unhuman. There were often crude personalities with little regard for the manner or usage of the spoken word. Allan quickly realized it was difficult for a master to recruit a crew both with character and the capability to sail the world's oceans in weather fair and foul.

On one of his trips through the English Channel following the European trading coast, Allan recalled the likes of Ed, an Englishman of stubborn and disagreeable personality. Ed was running away from the law, and from an irate husband of a wife, and he lacked discipline of any kind. It was a damp, foggy, and downright miserable day, when Allan watched the captain rearrange old Ed's skull, banging him upside the head with a wooden belaying pin. The sailors spoke of times when the boatswain "let the cat out of the bag," administering a flogging to discipline a wayward seaman with his "*cat-o-nine-tails.*"

During the earlier years of sail, many of the ships' masters carried small firearms for protection, a last resort to quell all sorts of mayhem or even a possible mutiny. On some ships, life at times was defined as survival of the fittest. The first law any seaman learned: the captain was the law. He would maintain order and discipline. There would be no routine consumption of drinks containing alcohol and playing cards was left at the port. Reasons for argumentation among crew would be minimized if possible. The lives of all on board depended on the captain's decision-making. Observation was an effective teacher and Allan realized if he was to rise to the rank of master, he must maintain law and order.

∞

Allan tallied the duration of his service on Hugh Crawford and the Johns to be four years and two months, lasting between July of 1852 and May of 1857. He signed on as "Boy" and advanced to "Apprentice" between the ages of thirteen and seventeen. Upon reaching the age of eighteen he secured an agreement to work with the captain of the Enterprise. The port of registry for this ship was also Inverness. It was a short engagement; however, from June through August of 1857 his employment and experience qualified him as "Ordinary Seaman."

It was difficult to locate work and when opportunities surfaced it paid to be at the right place at the right time. The following year, at nineteen, Allan signed on with the Countess of Lawdon, registered in Banff. The Agreement and Account of Crew stated the employment would last from June to August in 1858. Banff was located in northeastern Scotland on the Banff Bay in the County of Aberdeenshire.

The board governing merchant trade recognized Allan as an AB (able bodied seaman). His years of service began in July of 1852 to November of 1863, a total of eleven years and seven months. He was responsible to keep a list for his personal record and the Board of Trade, London, maintained a detailed account as well. There were insurance and liability matters to be addressed and there must be a record if a seaman met the unfortunate fate of burial at sea.

Ship's Name	Port of Registry	Rank	Service Date (s)
Hugh Crawford	London	Boy	1852-1855
Johns	Inverness	OS	1855-1857
Enterprise	Inverness	OS	1857
Countess of Lawdon	Banff	AB	1858
Gertrude	London	AB	1858-1859
Wanata	Liverpool	AB	1859-1860
Vespasian	Liverpool	AB	1860-1861
Bothnia	London	AB	1861
Koh is oroon	Bermuda	AB	1861-1862
Florine	Liverpool	AB	1863
Royal Charlie	Banff	BS	1863

OS – ordinary seaman
AB – able bodied seaman
BS – boatswain (bosun)

Between voyages Allan returned to Inverness to help his brothers with their fishing business. Their father placed the business in the hands of his sons after he had become a merchant sea captain. Allan's next ship was Gertrude with the port of registry of London. The barque departed in November of 1858 and remained at sea until her return in September 1859.

∞

A period of four years passed and Allan would continue helping his brothers with their fishing business. On reaching the age of twenty-four, the call to sea beckoned and he was presented with more opportunities. The Florine was registered in Liverpool so he made way to England in search of furthering his career. The months between May to August of 1863 were spent as an AB, working short cargo carrying missions along the coast of Europe.

Once Florine returned to port Allan was introduced to the master of the Royal Charlie. The size of the vessel he served on increased in dimension. The ship weighed 460 tons; the length of the ship was 118' 5," the breadth 28' 3" and the depth of the hull 19.' The port of registry was London but it was the history of the ship that intrigued the young seaman.

The ship was built for Mr. S.G. Fry at the Port of Sunderland in 1851. The first master was W. Escott and the maiden voyage departed London for New Zealand. Three years later, 1854, Florine was used as a passenger ship, transporting over one hundred people from Southampton to Port Adelaide, Australia. Nine years later Allan, at twenty-four, signed on in September of 1863. His position would last two months.

While working from the port of Sunderland he learned how the master made the final choice in crew selection. He observed how to employ efforts to recruit men known by the first, second, or in some cases, the third mate. The main ports of Liverpool, London, Newcastle and Glasgow, groomed seamen who were known to be of better reputation and were desirable as crew. During a voyage to Calcutta he learned how easily the ship and the entire crew were vulnerable to the elements. The weather as well as poor navigation was always a threat. There was starvation, lack of water, fever brought on by disease, and man-made hazards. In time Allan would graduate to the level of junior ordinary seaman and through his steady efforts, the designation of senior ordinary seaman followed swiftly.

The time following his last engagement would be spent preparing for testing to become officially recognized in a higher capacity by the Board of Trade, London. In the month of January in the year 1864, Allan listed his address as 62 Telford Road, Inverness. It was necessary for the applicant to list all of their service on ships up to the point of the examination. Allan prepared his list of six ships dating back to July 1852, up to and including his last sail on Royal Charlie. He had accumulated a total of ten years of service at sea.

On the sixteenth of January at the Port of Sunderland, he passed the examination for second mate. The certificate of competency issued by the board registered him as #30124. The chief officer of the Royal Charlie, being impressed with Allan's cut and intellect, encouraged him to pursue obtaining the first mate designation quickly. Allan set to the task of reviewing and studying the required information and sat for the examination on March 19, 1864. Two months elapsed since the passage of the first exam. While at the Port of Sunderland at the age of twenty-five, he fulfilled the examination requirements set by the Board of Trade and was issued a certificate of competency as first mate.

The life of a seaman appeared romantic; however, it was anything but attractive. Many deprivations impacted every waking hour. The work was hard and fraught with risk. Living conditions were wet and the food turned foul like the weather after the first few weeks at sea. The sunny days brought brilliant bluish hues to the sky as they became the greatest reward. Saint Anthony, the Scottish patron saint for mariners was credited for those days. The seaman would draw in slow deep breaths of nature's fresh salt air and exhale with pleasant satisfaction. King Neptune was targeted for blame when the weather turned foul, extremely foul.

The following months became a process of building on experience and knowledge. Allan applied his intellect to reading and studying charts, creating a memory of images within his mind, with reference points for locating areas and objects of interest or peril, all specifically designed to navigate skillfully and successfully. He became versed in sounding depths, studying bodies of water for hazardous signs, and reading weather patterns. He was consumed with understanding weather since his powers of reasoning would require decisive navigation. He was determined to ensure the safety of the crew and the owner's investment in the cargo and the vessel.

The newly designated first mate rose to the position where he became a valuable asset to the ship's master. The youngest of the MacKenzies positioned himself to fulfill duties on the largest of sailing vessels at a very young age. During the next six years he would avail himself of any opportunity to participate in a voyage, especially one that would enable him to increase his knowledge and skill. He did so by transferring to the port of Liverpool, England.

Allan was teachable and he listened and learned well. He was consistent in his approach and demonstrated an attitude inherited from his forefathers. It was traceable to his younger years, born out of a family life constructed in the highlands. He was grounded and determined and often reflected on the teaching planted firmly by his father and grandfather. Time was a commodity that could not be overlooked by the young seaman and he continued on a path toward accomplishment. At the age of thirty-two the Board of Trade at Liverpool granted a new certificate to young MacKenzie. On October 21, 1870, his Master's Certificate of Competency was approved and the young seaman was certified to captain his own ship.

CHAPTER
4

PECK'S BEACH
C. 1849

The task of trading goods between foreign lands increased and the number of ships carrying the products and natural resources grew with demand. Navigational routes were established as instrumentation and increasing knowledge was shared between ports and ship's masters. The Atlantic was ferocious as any sea could be, placing many an obstacle in the path of the crew of a clipper navigating these waters.

The North Atlantic would swell and flex muscle during the summer months of June, July and August, when thunderstorms formed on land from places such as Pennsylvania, Delaware, Virginia and points south. They combed through the forests and fields then turned on the low lying area of New Jersey and blew out to sea.

Summer would fold into autumn and the South Atlantic would serve as a catalyst, breeding storms with warm moist tropical air blowing off the coast of South Africa. The mixture of warm air and moisture provided ideal conditions to generate hurricanes. The storms propelled through the open waters of the South Atlantic and spun northward for hundreds even thousands of miles. Sometimes the storms would veer toward the territory known as Florida. Other times they were pulled with the intensity of a strong magnet, careening northward as they slammed into the coastal Carolinas and Virginia. On occasion a storm persisted, finding its way up the coast, intent on slamming into the low-lying coastal areas of New Jersey.

The threat of violent storms diminished after October however, the nor'easter would present another peril for ships found in the ocean off the east coast during the winter months. Dangerous seas ruled by King Neptune presented other obstacles for many a mariner. Inlets were subject to erosion, exposing sandbars. Unpredictable currents and wave action were present in the Great Egg Harbor and Barnegat Inlets. Many ships were driven dangerously close to the coastline and the colony of New Jersey became a graveyard for ships.

As time passed, the seven mile stretch of island was worn with pathways, imprints from daytrippers making periodic pilgrimages to picnic and fish along the seagrass lined shores. The Unalatchtigo disappeared more than a quarter of a century earlier and the seascape was changing. The North Atlantic Grey Whale was absent from waters beyond the breakers and the back bay breeding areas were barren, no longer producing off-spring.

In 1849 a life-saving station was established on the island. The location for the station was determined to be the east side of the island, about one mile from the Great Egg Harbor Inlet. By 1856 a second life station was located on the south side of the island and Peck's Beach Station #2 was built. Protection was paramount since the occasional swimmer was to be guarded. Ship groundings and wrecks presented an ever present danger. It became the responsibility of the life-saving service to answer many a call from a ship, stranded or foundering and in trouble.

Recruits manned the two stations and ranks and positions were attained by each member. The keeper of the station was in charge of the crew and the equipment. The surfmen were assigned positions of rank according to their ability and skill, all tested and measured periodically. They wore a patch on the sleeve of their uniform to denote rank. A surfman with the number one on his sleeve was next in line to be keeper of the station. He had to be ready in case the keeper was unable to fulfill his responsibilities.

The surfmen donned storm clothes and a rain hat when beginning their stretch of beach patrol in bad weather. Their watch didn't stop when nightfall set in, since darkness brought heightened risk for passing ships. Unlucky crew may not sail safely to their intended port. The surfmen carried a walking staff, a patrol clock, and punch key, a case containing Coston signal flares, and a patrol lantern. It was said of the life-saving members their goal was to exhibit professionalism and fitness.

The elements were brutal on some evenings and a halfway house was built, consisting of a shed where one surfman met another, as they covered their route, day after day, night after night. They would exchange a metal badge called a "check" to confirm they reached the boundary of their round.

In the evening of March 30, 1863 a brig flying under the flag of England stranded at Corson's Inlet, a body of water separating Peck's Beach from an island to the south. The length of the brig was 98' 6," the beam was 21' 1" and her draft was 11' 1." The surfmen witnessing the grounding lit a Coston flare for signaling. The flare burnt for two minutes before going out. The crew of the ship saw the brilliant red light, emanating from the flare placed in a wooden holder in the surfmen's hand. The captain ordered a return shot from a flare to signal they were in trouble and would await a rescue attempt.

CHAPTER
5

BOWMORE, ISLE OF ISLAY
1876

Shona Graeme lay in her bed, the pain intensifying once again. She was a very beautiful woman of Scottish descent. Her father, a farmer, was born near the village and his father before that. Her hair was auburn and her skin was fair. Her warm blue eyes displayed the finishing touch bestowed upon a beautiful mother to be of twenty-eight years. Her appearance was the expression of the long line of Scots who were her forbearers. Her father and mother were insistent that their family of two sons and three daughters worship together, each Sunday morning at *Eaglis Cill an Rubha*, the Scottish Gaelic name for Killarow Church, founded in 1767 in the county of Argyll. It was springtime in the year of her first pregnancy.

The pain intensified and the contractions grew shorter. She thought there was time but the intensity of the pain suggested this would be the day. She would give birth to their first child for her beloved husband. Ross left her side momentarily while he ran to the gate, hinged on the white picket fence running along the south side of their croft. Keitha was the only midwife in this part of the kingdom and he scrambled to secure her services as his beloved Shona was preparing to deliver their child.

She turned her head toward the kerosene lamp sitting on the table next to her bedside. Another contraction ensued, subsiding almost as quickly as it came. Her prayer book was resting near the quill used by her hand the day before. Her father gave the book to her for Christmas three years before.

The pain intensified once again and she became anxious, as if something may not be right. Time passed slowly and another contraction ensued. The blistering pain shot through her spine causing her to reach for her abdomen. The contractions gained and intensified to the point where the pain was unbearable and she fell into a state of unconsciousness. A brief darkness unfolded as she lost sight of her surroundings. Her room, lit by the sun, unfolding to a pathway through the window to the colorful wildflowers beyond, was no longer visible.

Her mind drifted, yet she was aware she was carrying Ross's child. It was at this point she became acutely aware of a transforming shining light. It began with a flicker. As the light intensified it displayed spectacular brilliance, all in a matter of seconds. It was unlike any other source of light she had ever seen or experienced. Was she awake, was this a dream? Instantaneously her fear metamorphosed into confusion. There was no spoken word, yet through the brilliance of the light there was a manifestation, causing her spirit to be calm and at peace.

The presence of a being became clear and Shona was spoken to through the light. Her eyes pierced through wondrous shades of silver and white mixed with varying hues of blue, green and yellow. The colors intertwined and illuminated as never envisioned before. Color abounded, beautiful crystals she thought. She told herself this was humanly impossible to see something so intense, overpowering, yet sedating to the soul.

A face appeared and it was enshrouded within the light. She saw eyes, the forehead of a person, hair, but the painting of her visitor was diffused, lacking clarity. There was no introduction, no knowledge of who this visitor could be.

"Who are you?" Shona inquired.

Words were spoken with softness and reverence and she understood clearly.

"He sent me." Her mind paused in thought. "He, who is he?"

"He has been with you for many years. He saw you before you were born and he formed you while you rested in your mother's womb."

Shona lay silent, motionless, absent of pain. The messenger spoke once more as the light emanated and moved.

"It was he who spun the fabric of your life as he wove you into a beautiful young woman."

"And what is your name?" Shona called.

The messenger responded and it was at that moment a name was placed within her mind. Shona awoke, tired, listless, yet aware she was lying in her bedroom. Her window appeared and the bouquet of abundant wildflowers sprung forth once again. The kerosene light sat on the lampstand next to her bed and her prayer book lay alongside. She wrote the name spoken to her on the inside of the back cover after the last page. She closed her eyes and took in fresh breaths of air, slowly, patiently, at peace.

The Graeme's were excited about the birth of their first child, and pleased the event came at the time when nature gives birth to spring. The fields were washed in thick blankets of yellow, pink and lavender blue. Ross hurried to the bedroom to check on his beloved Shona and to hold her hand and comfort her.   Keitha didn't knock as she pushed the front door to their cottage aside. She was a midwife for many of the births for the past twenty years in and around the village. The lines in her forehead served notice she had worried through birthing complications on a number of occasions. She wore a gray dress with a royal blue apron tied about her waist. Her hair was black, mixed with strands of gray. Next month she would turn fifty years old.

Shona groaned as her abdomen was enveloped in tortuous agony; Keitha entered the bedroom. Ross positioned himself next to her pillow as he watched the midwife begin preparation for the expected delivery. Another protracted loud groan and Keitha knew this birth may not be one that is normal. Her fears were confirmed as she positioned her hands to feel for the baby's head. The birth would be breech unless she could intervene successfully and soon. Keitha lifted her head and Ross knew by her expression, no words need be spoken to describe Shona's condition. Worried, she ordered Ross out of the room, to Anna McCall's house to secure her assistance.

CHAPTER
6

BROCKLEBANKS

Nigel Harris, reporter, was an accomplished writer with a keen mind for business. The editor of the Liverpool Daily Post assigned him a task to research and write about the rise of the merchant shipping magnates in the United Kingdom. He strolled down the cobblestone walkway looking for number 20 Bixteth Street; his ten o'clock appointment would find him interviewing Thomas Fisher Brocklebank.

It was a cool October day in the year 1887. The office door opened; Mr. Harris was immediately impressed with the stature and dress of Thomas F. Brocklebank. He stood nearly six feet, his silver hair contrasting well with his black wool frock coat. He wore a Victorian white dress shirt and the collar was adorned with a black silk puff tie. His trousers were made of brushed cotton dyed slate gray. Wire rimmed glasses provided the finishing touch of what obviously was a stately looking businessman. He must have arrived moments before as a charcoal gray flat top hat sat on a chair. The owner invited the writer to take a seat in a comfortable chair in front of his lavish wooden desk.

The exchange of customary pleasantries per British etiquette followed. Nigel asked Mr. Brocklebank to describe where and how the business all began. He paused for a few seconds, reached for a cigar, offered one to Nigel, and pondered for a few seconds more.

"Our company is one of, if not the oldest merchant shipping firm in the world," he began. The founder was my grandfather, Captain Daniel Brocklebank."

"And how far back in time was that?" Nigel inquired.

"My grandfather left the colonies in 1775. But before that he completed an apprenticeship in Whitehaven. He applied his knowledge and experience, establishing himself as a master mariner and shipbuilder."

"Which colony was this, sir?"

"He managed his shipbuilding business from Sheepscutt, Maine, in 1770."

"A very long way from Liverpool," Nigel observed.

"He was a loyalist, Mr. Harris, and he believed in the sovereignty of the Crown. When it became evident a revolution was near, he decided it was time to set sail for home. His journey took him back to Whitehaven, sailing on the fifth brig he built, the Castor."

"You referred to your grandfather as captain, what was his next step?"

Nigel settled into the chair. The fascination of sailing the ocean and the entrepreneurial aspect of shipbuilding intrigued him.

"War broke out between England and the colonies and he became a privateer."

Nigel pondered, this is very interesting, and he could collect a wealth of material, a second story.

"My grandfather decided to establish his ship building business at Whitehaven ten years later. One of his strengths was his ability to foresee the future. He was an expert in tactical planning, a visionary," continued Thomas. "By the onset of 1792 his plans and specifications for shipbuilding were well known and his advice was sought after among his peers."

"How many ships did he build, over what period of time?" asked Nigel.

"In the ten year period between 1785 and 1795, he amassed a fleet of eleven wooden vessels totaling 1,750 tons," confirmed Thomas.

"May I defer to another subject for a moment?"

"Certainly!"

"My understanding is your father, John, died as a result of an unfortunate accident?" Nigel curiously continued.

"He was killed as a result of a fall from his horse. The year was 1831. A small child ran into the path of his horse, he fell while trying to avoid the child. That was also the year I moved to Liverpool to assist with the family business affairs."

Thomas lit his cigar; Nigel wrote profusely then turned another page.

"I applied myself and learned well; therefore, my uncle appointed me to the role of Chairman of the Mersey Docks and Harbor Board in 1843."

"Did your company continue to grow?" Nigel inquired.

"By the following year we had built a total of fifty vessels since our firm began."

"What precipitated the move to Liverpool?"

"We decided it was wise to close the Whitehaven shipyard in 1865. Wooden ships were becoming outdated by new technology, being replaced by steel hulled sailships."

"Who is your shipbuilder?" Nigel curiously inquired.

"Harland and Wolff of Belfast became the frontrunner in the production of merchant sailing vessels at this time."

As Nigel thought about his next question, his mind shifted from the past, looking toward the future. The world of shipping was growing geographically and this would require new ship manufacturing methods and technologies. Harland and Wolff were at the forefront of the development of new technology and orders to build new and larger ships were increasing.

∞

The firm of Thos. & Jno. Brocklebank, Ltd. grew as a result of a demand for products that could be found in far-away places such as India. The British East India Co. established trade routes dating back to 1599. Others followed for the purpose of engaging in trade with India. The stage was set for the establishment of more trade with systems of exchange in place. The sought after products were an array of spices, sugar and tea. Minerals such as coal and iron were also mined. There were other products sought after by the residents of the United Kingdom for furnishing their homes. While Britain invested in infrastructure, building railroad lines, shipping companies invested in vessels.

The interview continued.

"Our trade routes to India date back to the early 1800s," commented Thomas.

"And then a change occurred?" Nigel asked.

"In 1813 the East India Company's trading monopoly was broken up; we entered trade with India."

"Did this alter your plans with other trade routes?"

"We have always maintained our trade routes with North and South America as well as the West and East Indies."

"Tell me about the sail plan; do your captains use the Suez?"

"The Suez Canal officially opened in 1869; however, our company continues operating sailships to India via the Cape of Good Hope. You need to interview one of our captains. They could tell you much about trade routes. In fact, the information would add to your story," offered Thomas.

Nigel nodded in agreement.

"Would you review your trade routes for me please?"

"They could be separated into the following categories."

Whitehaven - Liverpool - West Indies
Whitehaven - Liverpool - Brazil, Chile, Ecuador, Peru
Whitehaven - Liverpool - Canadian Maritime Provinces
Whitehaven - Liverpool - Calcutta, Dutch East Indies
Whitehaven - Liverpool - Colombia, Bombay, Karachi

"When did you begin service to Bombay?"

"The year was 1833. Move forward in time, by 1874 we had fourteen sailships leaving Liverpool for Calcutta at intervals of three weeks."

"What about China?" Nigel quizzed.

"A London to China route was established in 1860. We had a few departures for China and in addition we had a couple for Melbourne."

Nigel, thinking in terms of days at sea, redirected his questions.

"Could you provide me with an estimation of days at sea, measuring the length of a voyage to your service ports?"

"We run tea clippers to Hong Kong on average 113 days; Shanghai would be near 133 days. Windjammers will take more time as they are not as fast as the clippers."

"Can we return to shipbuilding?" Nigel asked.

"Of course!"

"Tell me about the vessel, Thomas Brocklebank?" Nigel inquired.

"The ship was our 147th, named after my uncle and built by the Brocklebanks in 1847."

"What about the specifics, the dimensions and so forth."

"Tonnage was 629, the length 129' 8," beam 27', and draught 21' 3." The ship was in service twenty-two years in the Calcutta trade. During the past twenty-five years we have engaged Harland and Wolff to fill the construction and outfitting of our shipping vessels," Thomas shifted his focus momentarily. "All ships were three or four-mast barques, I might add."

"Can you provide me with a listing including name, description and delivery date?"

Thomas pulled a book from the shelf, turned a few pages, and slid it across the wooden table. As Nigel perused the list he noticed a number of foreign names and concluded there must be a story behind each one.

Thos. & Jno. Brocklebank Fleet, Deliveries – 1863 – 1885

Ship No.	Name	Delivery Date	Tonnage
19	Alexandra	1863	1,352
27	Baroda	1864	1,364
45	Candahar	1866	1,418
46	Tenasserim	1866	1,418
87	Belfast	1874	1,957
89	Majestic	1875	1,974
182	Zemindar	1885	2,120
183	Talookdar	1885	2,120

As Nigel perused the list Thomas requested he compare the delivery dates and the tonnage of each ship. Brocklebanks purposely directed Harland & Wolff to build a series of four sister ships from 1863 to 1885. The pairs were Alexandra and Baroda, Candahar and Tenasserim, Belfast and Majestic, and Zemindar and Talookdar.

Nigel noticed the *Baroda* was a peculiar name and decided it was worthwhile to investigate further. The added information would serve to broaden his article and tell the story to his readers.

"The name Baroda comes from a state located on the western side of India," Thomas offered. "We decided it would enhance business relations if we named a number of our ships after someone, or a place in the country where we are trading," he continued. Thomas paused, "Unfortunately we lost Baroda last year."

"What happened?"

"She sank in the Mersey, near South Battery, third collision in one week. The other vessels were the Ajax and Qui Vive."

Nigel began to realize the risks associated with merchant marine shipping are not all relegated to violent storms and the ocean.

"Can I have the particulars on Baroda?"

"She was another windjammer, built by Harland & Wolff in 1864, tonnage was 1,364, length 225,' beam 36' 5," draught of 23' 9." She was iron-hulled and sailed with a crew of thirty-two."

"Was the Baroda inbound or outbound?"

"Inbound, she was loaded full with a cargo of wheat and linseed. The ship left May 22 under the command of Master Healy bound for Calcutta."

"The ship sails round the world and sinks near her home port!" Nigel shook his head in bewilderment. "How does a ship sink in the Mersey?" Nigel continued.

"Baroda was in tow by the tug, Kingfisher. Another iron-ship, the Buceleuch, was in tow, outbound, by the steam-tug Ranger. Baroda was struck on the starboard side by Buceleuch and she sank in twenty minutes."

It was time to explore more subjects.

"There must be a story associated with Candahar?" Nigel pressed on.

"Candahar is located in Afghanistan. The primary trading products include wool, felt, grains, pomegranates and tobacco. Candahar is also a range of hills located in Burma. They act as a separation barrier between this country and Thailand."

"No doubt you encounter problems with ships no matter the port of location?" Nigel inferred.

"Candahar was loaded with cargo at Melbourne. Captain McLean left the Thames at night, month was October 1875. They were running down the channel and struck the Kingsbridge, the ship sank in three minutes. Ten hands were lost also."

Nigel shook his head.

"I had no idea there were so many risks."

"Candahar suffered damage as well, had to return to Falmouth for repairs. It was a narrow escape, the captain wrote. Speaking of ship's masters, Allan MacKenzie is here in Liverpool, and available. You should consider including him in an interview." Thomas offered. "He commanded Candahar on one voyage to San Francisco in 1875, followed by multiple voyages to Calcutta during the years 1876 – 1880."

Nigel, fascinated with the stories, listened eagerly.

"The *Tenasserim* is a ship with a story that I can't forget." Nigel raised his head, Thomas was in thought.

"The ship was built in 1866. The Post ran an article about the disaster on November 26, 1878. They titled it, *"Dreadful Tragedy on a Liverpool Ship."*

"What happened?"

"They were returning from Calcutta when the chief officer and a boy were murdered."

Nigel, surprised, momentarily remained silent, thinking of an appropriate follow-up question.

"Life presents all sorts of risk; tell me sir, how many of your ships have been lost at sea?"

"We have endured a total of twenty-one lost vessels since 1775, the year of our founding by Captain Daniel Brocklebank."

Nigel paused for a moment before sensing it appropriate to continue with another question.

"The next ship, Belfast, is obvious because of its name and that brings us to the clipper, Majestic, a sailship weighing 1,974 tons, the largest of our vessels purchased thus far."

Nigel, beginning his next question, was interrupted by Thomas.

"The Majestic is a fine clipper with a sleek hull and among one of the finest beauties."

The statement aroused Nigel's interest.

"The ship was designed with a shapely bow and fine lines. Captains have talked about the ship cleaving the waves, enabling her to glide through the water. The ship weighs 2,800 tons, fully loaded, and she's outfitted with 11,000 yards of canvas." Thomas thought further. "Captain MacKenzie was credited with the fastest run from New York to San Francisco. The year was 1884, the total days at sea was 98. Do you want the specs on the Majestic?"

"Interesting! Of course," responded Nigel.

"The Majestic was the 176th ship owned by the Brocklebank firm. We have record of every ship dating back to Captain Brocklebank."

Nigel was impressed with the meticulous record keeping employed by the Brocklebank firm.

"She was built in 1875 by Harland & Wolff. Iron hull, usually manned by a crew of forty. The length is 273' 4," beam 40' 2," draught 24' 2."

"Will you continue purchasing more ships since it has been two years since the launch of the *Talookdar*?"

"There are more on order. We received a cablegram indicating the Sindia will be launched in Belfast next month. If all goes according to plan, we should take delivery of the vessel around February next year."

Nigel, sensing Thomas was about to move on to another subject, hurried to ask a follow-up question.

"What about the name Talookdar?"

"Oh yes, the name represents a position held only by specific men in India. They were responsible to collect rents from the occupants of land after governmental claims were paid. There is a deeper explanation, of course."

Nigel, although inquisitive, felt it best to move on.

"Zemindar, we've neglected the source for this name!" he exclaimed.

"The term refers to a system of taxing and tax collecting, all part of the culture, law, and business of conducting trade with India."

"With your permission Mr. Brocklebank, can we take a wee bit more time to discuss Sindia?"

"What do you wish to know?" Thomas nodded in agreement.

"Let's begin with the source of the name."

"We desire to continue the tradition of honoring the culture and land of India, a key trading partner of the firm. The name given each ship is deliberate."

Nigel raised his head and asked again.

"Explain the origin of the name."

"This is what I can tell you based on my conversation with John."

Nigel turned another page to scribble notes.

"There will be a figurehead displayed below the bowsprit of Sindia. The person depicted in the figurehead lived between the years 1750 to 1795. We know this as evidenced by the type of turban worn on his head."

"Very interesting!" Nigel thought.

"The *Maharaja Mahadji Scindia* was the most powerful Indian of his time. We decided on the figurehead after deliberating various options." Thomas continued. "The Brocklebank business contacts include the *Shrimant Rajmata Maharani Scindia of Gwalior*. This is what led us to name the ship Sindia. We have been told that Scindia can also be interpreted, slipper bearer. Maharaja is a term for king and Gwalior is a province."

He watched Nigel as he busily took notes.

"There was a time when the Scindias were leaders of the *Mahratta*, a tribe of central Indian horsemen," Thomas continued.

Nigel peered above his glasses, the look in his brown eyes questioning, as he reacted in silence to the explanation, both lengthy and informative.

CHAPTER

7

SHIPWRIGHTS

They met in Ireland prior to 1861. On this particular cloudy and cool day they strode out of the Belfast City Hall after filing legal documents to form Harland and Wolff, a shipbuilding company. Gustav Wilhelm Wolff, co-owner, was born in 1834 and migrated from Hamburg, Germany, to Ireland. Edward Harland, co-owner, was born in 1831, a native of the area. Gustav, having attained the age of twenty-seven and Edward, at the age of thirty, formulated a plan to combine their knowledge, business experience, and capital to expand into a shipbuilding business.

They agreed to locate their new enterprise at an island in Belfast. The city was surrounded by hills and was located along the northern coast of Ireland. The sea outside the boundaries of their new domain was a beautiful blend of blue. The clerk in the town hall explained that the city's name was derived from two words, *Beal Feirste*, meaning mouth of the sandy ford. This was the crossing point where the Farset and Lagan Rivers met. The island wasn't formerly named until after a visit by Queen Victoria in 1849.

In the year 1863, their company had completed the construction of the 450-foot-long Hamilton Dock and the Abercorn Basin. The demand from governments to build warships and the increase in trade routes along the coast of Europe, extending to South America, India and China, required the best and latest technology from a shipbuilding company. Two companies responsible for purchasing many of Harland and Wolff's ships were the White Star Line, and Thos. & Jno. Brocklebank, Ltd., located in Liverpool.

HULL NO. 204

The autumn of 1887 abated to winter and the celebration of Christmas in England became a memory of the recent past. Four decades later the city streets still displayed remnants of a Victorian era described by Dickens in his novel about the yuletide season. Nigel's supervisor was willing to send him to Belfast to further his opportunity to expand on his Brocklebank interview and forthcoming story. The construction of the Sindia was completed on November 19 and the new owner contracted with a master and crew to deliver the ship to Liverpool.

Nigel was standing alongside her at slip number 2 at the South Yard. His senses awakened as he took in the impressive view of a newly constructed merchant ship. To say he was excited would be an understatement as he had been invited to participate in the maiden voyage from Belfast to Liverpool. He couldn't wait for the captain to order the sails set so he could add to his story.

Moments later, Edward Harland joined Nigel and shook his hand while placing a brown envelope in the other. The contents included an official ship's description containing the dimensions and particulars for the outfit of the topside and decking below. A signed letter incorporating a portion of the ship's plans would enable him to write a good story. The Sindia was scheduled for delivery in Liverpool by February 6.

The four-mast windjammer was an impressive sight. Nigel wanted to experience what it would be like to sail the seas. It was a journey that would be lived by him and savored by the seamen that would take command of her at the appointed time.

"She's the largest sailship of her kind," offered Edward. "Her hull is built of steel and her gross tonnage is 3,067. Other ships built for the same purpose are 2,120 gross tons." Nigel was impressed with the dimensions.

Edward continued, "The length of her hull is 326' 3" and the beam is 44' 10." Her depth is 26' 8" and the freeboard amidship is 28' 6."

Nigel stood in awe while Edward Harland surveyed his company's completed product. His pride tucked away inside, he credited his employees with the accomplishment of building another ship, registered in their records as hull number 204. The mainmast towered nearly 200 feet above the deck of the ship. Edward pointed to and counted the braces that would hold a total of thirty-two sails to be rigged to the masts. They proceeded along the wharf inspecting the stern of the ship moving toward the bow. The view from the bow of the vessel was most impressive to Nigel.

"The figurehead!" he exclaimed.

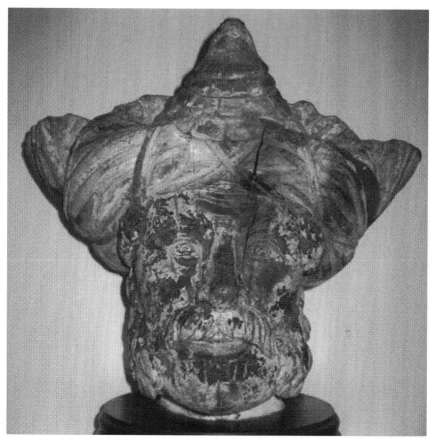

The original head of the figurehead below Sindia's bowsprit

Nigel was observing with awe and excitement what others would react to with curiosity, as he stood gazing at the massive figurehead fixed to the hull directly beneath the bowsprit.

"This ship will be one of the last of the windjammers," Edward commented. "We are building steamships now and are preparing for an increase in demand. Steam propulsion will eventually replace the wind."

"How was the name windjammer derived?" Nigel inquired.

"Take a look at her bow. Notice the pointed shape to the hull. The Sindia is designed to cut through the wave as she sails the ocean, compared to plowing through the water. We took the design of the bow from the tea clippers."

Nigel studied the angle of the bow.

"By clipping the wave you separate the water to the side as opposed to a plowing movement. Do this with a tea clipper and you increase speed and improve the efficiency of the vessel's movement."

"But Sindia is a windjammer?" Nigel quizzed.

"Yes, the windjammer has the hull shape of the tea clipper, but there are differences. The windjammer is crowded with larger sails, thus jamming the wind upon them. It takes a lot of air pressure to move a 3,067-ton fully loaded cargo ship. The windjammers will sail at nearly half the speed of the tea clippers."

The two of them stepped on the gangplank and proceeded to the main deck for the remainder of Nigel's tour. The size and immensity of each of the four masts was the first thing that impressed him. As they stood amidship Nigel counted a total of fourteen rope lines tied to belaying pins on each side of the ship. The ropes ascended skyward, attached to the sails, held by braces on the mainmast. As they approached the foremast Nigel counted an additional fourteen ropes also attached to the sails. Two life boats were fixed to cradles sitting on top of a large platform constructed on the main deck. There was a doorway leading into the platform large enough for a man to enter while standing upright.

They turned to walk toward the stern. Nigel again counted fourteen rope lines leading to the mizzenmast sails. They passed two more lifeboats anchored in the same fashion atop a second platform. Upon reaching the jiggermast he counted a series of twelve rope lines attached to the sails on the jiggermast. He began to visualize the amazing feat that unfolds when seamen are working the rope-lines of each mast, adjusting sail; who knows, perhaps with a storm in process and the waves created by the ocean spilling onto and sweeping across the deck.

In his excitement his mind was preoccupied with the event of the next day; he would be the first passenger on Sindia. They were ready to sail for Liverpool for delivery to the Brocklebank firm. What would it be like to work a ship under full sail at sea? He was creating a scene he could write;

seaman performing an amazing feat, working the rope lines attached to each brace, adjusting sail per the first mate's orders. The wind picked up and whipped through the shipyard as Edward motioned.

"It's time to visit slip number four. There is something you need to see."

After a walk of five minutes, Nigel approached a vessel very similar in appearance to Sindia. Men were walking about the deck carrying tools and moving equipment, all designed to help them complete the task of building another ship.

"Her name will be Holkar," he offered. "And by design, she is a sister ship to Sindia. The dimensions are nearly the same; 326 feet in length between perpendiculars and her breadth is 45 feet."

"And her gross tonnage?" Nigel asked.

"Approximately 3,072 tons, five tons heavier than her sister, Sindia. We hope to launch on February 11 and follow-up with preparations for delivery to Brocklebanks by April 30."

∞

The weather for Monday, February 6, 1888, was one of the few days with full sun in Liverpool. By mid-afternoon the temperature climbed into the mid-forties. Some of the employees at the Brocklebank shipping firm were invited to board a horse drawn carriage for the seven block ride to the docks alongside the Mersey River. Within the hour they were greeted by a majestic sight. The Sindia was making a grand entry to port; Nigel Harris stood proudly at the wheelhouse alongside the helmsman. A tug was waiting nearby to guide her into the dock where she would moor awaiting her maiden voyage.

The ship was massive. Protruding through the deck were four distinct tall masts. Thomas Brocklebank's eyes were drawn to the bow where the tallest, the mainmast, built in three sections, supported six individual yards. The three sections of each mast ascending skyward were the mainmast, the topgallant mast, followed by the royalmast. A seaman was standing on top of the second yard watching over the ship and the festivities of navigating to port.

The mainmast supported six square-rigged sails. The bottom sail, the course sail, was unfurled as were the topsail and the lower topgallant. His eyes peered above the first three sails since he could see three additional braces supporting the upper topgallant then the royalsail. Atop the mast was the brace for the skysail. It was an impressive sight.

The foremast was next and it was the second tallest mast though not much shorter than the mainmast. Thomas counted six braces fixed to the foremast. The next four braces supported another set of lower and upper topgallants; the royal sail and the skysail were tied to the braces.

A crowd of onlookers gathered for the past twenty minutes. The arrival of a new ship or any ship for that matter, large enough to draw the attention of nearby merchants and townspeople, was always a welcome sight.

The third tallest mast, the mizzenmast, displayed six braces supporting another set of square-rigged sails. The crojack was tied to the brace. The ship's master gave the order to come about with minimal sail to facilitate navigation for the helmsmen and reduce speed. The fourth mast, the smallest of the set, was the jiggermast. The spanker and upper spanker were secured to the braces along with the gaff topsail.

Comments and chatter could be heard from the gathering crowd as they watched the magnificent ship come closer to port. There were four rigging lines stretched from the mainmast extending to the ship's bow. Attached to each line were the inner, outer and flying jibs. Between the mainmast and the foremast were three additional rigging lines descending in a downward direction from the foremast to the mainmast. The main royal staysail, the main topgallant staysail and the main topmast staysail were secured.

Thomas was struck with the immensity of the masts and accompanying sails. This was a picture he had seen before; however, the Sindia was the largest sailship purchased by his company to date. He counted three more rigging lines, each attached to the mizzenmast and sloping downward to the foremast. The last three topsails were attached to each of the lines. He could visualize the beauty of thirty-two white canvas sails, all set, propelling his newly acquired merchant ship on the southern blue Atlantic Ocean.

The rigging crew at Harland and Wolff fixed three flags, per protocol, one on each of the three largest masts. The ensign was the flag of Britain. The second flag flown below the ensign bore the name Sindia and the third flag, attached to the jack staff, was the Brocklebank house flag, signifying the owner of the vessel.

CHAPTER
8

THE INTERVIEW

The art of developing questions and segmenting topics of information obtained from his interview and sailing experience aboard the Sindia was underway. Nigel had many questions stimulated by his own imagination. What about the crews selected to man a ship? Who were the masters of each ship? Where were they trained and how and by whom? What did the foreign ports look like? The world of a seaman was as large as the ocean they sailed on. The ship's captain, his officers, and crew were favored with seeing it all. But there was a price to pay for the benefits they received. Questions without answers! He was determined to find the answers to improve his story. Nigel resolved to write a bloody good one to present to his boss, and ultimately the readers of the Liverpool Daily Post.

Several weeks had passed and he wrote to Thomas Brocklebank since he was eager to continue his endeavor. The reply contained a recommendation that he allow Thomas sufficient time to arrange a meeting with a ship's master. This was the only realistic plan to ensure Nigel would have the most accurate information available.

Days swept by and then on a Friday morning, Nigel was pleasantly greeted by an envelope placed on his desk.

Attention: Mr. Nigel Harris c/o Liverpool Daily Post, from the firm of Thos. & Jno. Brocklebank, Ltd.

Dear Mr. Harris. Per your request, Mr. Thomas Brocklebank has arranged a meeting for the purpose of an interview.

Meeting Date - Monday, March 11, 1888 - 10:30
Location - Thos. & Jno. Brocklebank, Ltd.
20 Bixteth Street, Liverpool
Ship Master - Allan MacKenzie

The midmorning sun spilled into the room as he opened the door, entering the shipping firm's office. He introduced himself to the office manager, Mrs. Hepburn. The hinges of an old wooden door creaked as a man stepped out of the office. Nigel studied him. He looked fit for an aging sea captain. His frame was muscular, spun out of years of toil on the finest of ships. Nigel's instincts told him immediately: it was he, Allan MacKenzie.

A brief introduction and the securing of a pot of tea was all they required to begin the interview. The captain stood five-feet nine-inches tall. He wore a black brushed cotton Livingston sack coat, the kind many men wore in this day for casual and recreational purposes. He looked stately in his attire. The coat displayed a soft dark black finish. It was stylish with a high button front that was unfastened at the top to let his vest show through. There were three buttons sewn on each cuff, the back of his coat was unvented. His highland vest was also black and there were four pockets sewn onto the exterior. Black brushed cotton pants depicted the about-town business attire. A stand-up collared white dress shirt was tucked in and he wore braces attached to the front and back buttons on his trousers. His hair was dark, streaked with gray, and his eyes were steel blue. He spoke politely, yet a wary firmness surrounded his elocution. He was a gentleman; his diction portrayed one used to giving orders with the expectation there would be no delay in following the directive. This was clear.

Formalities dispensed with, Nigel was anxious to follow his outline.

"How does one become certified by the Board of Trade as a ship master?" Nigel began.

The captain provided his list of service at sea while designated an ordinary or able bodied seaman. A second list covered his years of service as a mate or bosun, up to the point where he received his second mate certificate. The documents were placed on the brown oak table for Nigel's inspection.

Allan MacKenzie's Service at Sea

Ship's Name	Port of Registry	Rank	Service Date (s)
Mary Stewart	Banff	Mate	1864
Englishman	Glasgow	Mate	1865
Erromanga	Glasgow	Mate	1865-1866
Currency	Glasgow	Mate	1867
Witch of the Teign	Teignmouth	Bosun	1868-1869
Cossack	Liverpool	Mate	1869
White Jacket	Newcastle	1st Mate	1869-1870

Nigel perused the list of ships, his eyes stopping at the third from the top.

"Erromanga is a very interesting name; describe the ship please!"

The captain removed papers from his satchel; leafed through them one by one, then paused and responded.

"Built in Sunderland in 1856; she weighed 309-tons --- the ship's length was 116,' breadth, 25' and the depth, 16'2."

"Where did the name come from?" inquired Nigel.

"The owner named the ship after the Pacific Island of Erromango."

"Your experiences are many. You must have visited some amazing places."

"You could say they are stored inside my mind, Nigel. Yes, there are some truly amazing pictures I can recall when needed."

"And when do you need them, captain?"

Allan MacKenzie's blue eyes were penetrating; he reached for his packet of Black Twist tobacco on the desk next to his clay pipe.

"When any of us need them --- when we miss home and seek moments of tranquility! Erromango, for example, is a beautiful South Pacific island located east of Caledonia. It's a very large island located within the Vanuatu Archipelago. The inhabitants are local natives."

"Why would a ship dock at Erromango?"

"There's plenty of sandalwood; the Chinese for instance, treasure this wood for its aromatic scent."

Nigel pondered.

"And you were twenty-nine when you served as bosun on the Witch of the Teign?"

Captain MacKenzie confirmed this with a nod while reaching for another document.

"Here it is; built in 1857 at Teignmouth. The owner was Hutchings. The tonnage was 265, length 115,' breadth 21'4" and depth of the hull, 14' 7." Hutchings was involved in South American trade."

"Your service on the Cossack lasted nearly one year?" Nigel inquired.

"Interesting story! J. Griffith of Griffiths & Co. was the master and the owner. The Cossack weighed 111 tons, built in 1856; the length was 76'8," breadth 21'4" and the depth, 11'4," one of the smallest ships of my service."

The last entry on the list was White Jacket, tonnage of 1,148, the length of 191'2," breadth of 36'7" and depth of 23.'

"Service on the White Jacket brings us to the year 1870!"

"The year when my experience at sea led to a turn of events," the captain responded.

"White Jacket was built in New Brunswick in 1859 and the port of registry was Newcastle. The master on that voyage was Johnson. We were employed by the owner, H. Milvain."

"Looks as though you were at sea for almost a year?"

"Yes, our sail plan took us to India and back, returning to Liverpool by the end of September 1870."

"And at the age of thirty-two you passed the examination for the master's certification?"

The captain grinned. "Correct! I was at sea for eleven months and twenty-eight days. One month after returning to port I went home."

"Where is your home, captain?"

"In my youth and years as a young man, it was the highlands, Inverness. But at that time of the exam, I resided at 107 Duke Street, Liverpool. There I prepared for the examination."

"Obviously you passed?"

"On October 14 of 1870 I passed the three parts, navigation, seamanship and commercial code signals. By the 18th my results were sent to the Registrar General of Seamen."

Captain MacKenzie pulled an official document from his satchel and placed it on the desk in front of Nigel. Adjusting his glasses, Nigel read.

MASTER'S CERTIFICATE OF COMPETENCY

"Master in the Merchant Service"
Issued by the Lords of the Committee of Privy Council for Trade per
Merchant Shipping Act of 1854

"Your list of service on merchant ships is long and impressive," Nigel commented. "Describe the composition of the crew; where and how do you find them?"

"The demand for skilled seamen has grown significantly," Captain MacKenzie responded. "The rapid growth in merchant ship building has outpaced the availability to equip each vessel with the required skilled seamen. Literally, at times, we hire whoever we can find."

"Have you seen the Sindia?" responded Nigel.

"Aye --- I had an opportunity to walk about the ship and do my own inspection."

"May I ask for what reason?"

"The Brocklebank's requested I take command on the maiden voyage."

"Congratulations, is the destination the Calcutta trade?"

"It is; departure is next month."

Nigel, desiring to pinpoint questions to enhance his story, glanced at the list of Allan MacKenzie's service with the Brocklebank firm.

Allan MacKenzie's Service with Thos. & Jno. Brocklebank, Ltd.

Ship's Name	Yr. Built	Tonnage	Year of Service	Trade Route
Cormorin	1855	803	1874	Calcutta
Candahar	1866	1,418	1875	Calcutta
Candahar			1876	Calcutta
Candahar			1877	Calcutta
Candahar			1878	Calcutta
Candahar			1879	Calcutta
Candahar			1880	Calcutta
Khyber	1880		1881	Calcutta
Khyber			1882	Calcutta
Khyber			1883	Calcutta
Majestic	1875	1,974	1884	San Francisco
Zemindar	1885	2,120	1885	Calcutta
Zemindar			1886	Calcutta
Zemindar			1887	Calcutta

"How many men will you require to sail Sindia efficiently?"

"Thirty to thirty-five," responded the captain. Officers would total six to seven. The rest of the crew would be ordinary and able bodied seamen plus a few apprentices."

Nigel, head down, continued taking notes.

"The crew must follow commands and perform strenuous and sometimes dangerous tasks on the ship. Some of them will have no prior experience and a few, no doubt, will have never sailed the seas."

Nigel sipped from his cup, steam passing over his eyes, squinting as he looked at the captain.

"Liverpool to Calcutta," he mused. "That's a long journey --- over one hundred days at sea! Could try one's patience for sure," he suggested.

Captain MacKenzie leaned back in the stained wooden chair and lifted his cup from the table.

"Many are prepared for the life at sea, others will not manage so well. A South Atlantic voyage means rough seas. Ice storms and freezing temperatures are common. They are sometimes malnourished and some come to us in health less than satisfactory," he added. "There is more; the seamen we speak of are referred to as rigging monkeys. They climb the lines in all kinds of weather, fair and foul, adjusting sails and making repairs.

You have to serve as a crew member changing sail on a windjammer to understand that accidents happen. They get used to living in small spaces. Minimal food allotments are common and it smells due to aging of oils."

"Don't think I could do it," Nigel responded.

"Water must be rationed! Grog (hot rum, water and possibly a spice) is only served to the crew for special occasions. The cook is responsible for keeping track of the stores; food, water and other provisions."

"So the drunken sailor is a myth?" Nigel mused.

"Drunken while at sea, a myth, of course," the captain responded. "Unless they choose to break the law and bring liquor on board. Sometimes captains are forced to employ ex-convicts and the unemployable, the unskilled. Strong drink causes fighting and seaman will forfeit three days' pay if caught with alcoholic drink on my ship. The captain will be challenged to fight the elements. It's to the detriment of everyone's safety if he has to fight the crew."

"Has the despicable act of crimping been dispensed with?" Nigel probed.

The point of Nigel's question could cause a tremor to run up and down the spine of captains and mates of good reputation. A seafarer's life was filled with hardship and danger in the middle part of the 19th century. Lowlife, the worst of the dregs of society, the devil's footman, would prey upon many a sailor. Crimps were a brotherhood of international dockside degenerates, preying upon masters and shipowners, but mostly targeting unsuspecting sailors for personal financial gain.

Upon signing the Account and Agreement of Crew, a seaman was obligated to fulfill the duration of the voyage; otherwise, to jump ship would find them guilty of and in violation of the law. Crimps would cozy up to a seaman leaving his ship dockside after completing a voyage. His wallet was filled with the wages from the entirety of his voyage. They found themselves away from home in a city where they had no family or contacts, left to fend for them and find temporary housing accommodations. The crimp, with pre-established housing resources, would set up the seaman with a place to bunk, and take him on a tour of Liverpool's gambling houses, brothels and ale houses. A large bill, including a price for the crimp's services, was presented to the seaman, usually draining him of his wages from the previous voyage. Out of money or worse yet, in debt, the seaman would find himself in a position where his only alternative was to re-sign on another long voyage.

The seaman wasn't the only target exploited by the crimp. Some ship masters were unable, due to a bad reputation, to secure a fit crew for each voyage. Crimps, through threats of violence, even murder, would establish themselves as a go-between, to find a crew for the master's next departure. Sometimes they drugged the seaman, slipping something into his drink, other times he was hit on the head from behind, only to wake up in the fo'c'sle of a sailship heading out to sea.

"Your use of the word despicable is accurate," responded Captain MacKenzie. "I would tell you crimping has been greatly diminished since the mid part of the century. There's more to the story. Entrepreneurs such as Ralph Brocklebank have greatly improved the shore life of a seaman."

"In what manner," asked Nigel?

"The Brocklebanks have been at the forefront, building good working relations with their masters, mates and crew. Ralph was the driving force behind the establishment of the Sailor's Home, here in Liverpool."

Nigel swallowed, realizing how good his life was considering the life allotted to others. He, on the other hand, frequented upscale eating establishments down at Albert Dock. The captain's comments caused a moment of reflection. He cocked his head, thinking of a question in a different area.

"Tell me about your requirements for skilled labor."

"We have need of a carpenter and a cooper. The carpenter is helpful in repairing things on the ship that break or fall into disrepair. Many times the repairs are made at sea but some are made at port."

Nigel continued his notetaking.

"There are times when he makes a coffin too. The cooper can make barrels for holding provisions and there is sometimes a need for metalwork as well."

"What about the sails?" Nigel asked.

"The canvas is manufactured in Arbroath," responded the captain.

"There's a critical position to fill on a sailship. We must have a sailmaker to repair and fabricate additional sails. They tear, and worn sails require repair. They rub against the ropes and spars and require constant attention. We use roughly 300 pounds of canvas per sail."

"What about the treatment of wounds?" Nigel asked.

"We don't have a licensed surgeon on board. It's my duty to stock the medicine chest before leaving port. Men will get sick due to the hard living conditions, and sometimes I must separate the sick from the healthy."

Nigel stared at the captain, contemplating life on a huge sailship.

"We have occasional emergencies to manage once we put to sea, Nigel. There is little room to ere; if we do, we might suffer severely."

CHAPTER
9

THE VISION
1879

Decades passed since the days of the whalers and change was coming to Peck's Beach. Countless waves had crested and fallen on the sands of the shore during those passing years. Patterns developed when waves reacted to the forces of Mother Nature. They grew largest during the times when the wind blew from the southeast or the northeast. It was common to see the wind force waves to crest at five feet without the presence of a storm.

Mother Nature played a game with the waves and blew the wind in from the west creating land breezes. The westerly wind forced each wave to crest and the cap was cut off the top, blowing spray backward into the sea. The spray would shoot three to five feet in the air and glisten when the sun brought forth its rays.

The worst storms were birthed off the coast of Africa. They swept westward across the Atlantic turning northward toward the coastline of North America. The time most feared by coastline residents occurred during the months of October or November. By December, King Neptune could anger with a huff as if to stir the ocean to obey his command and blow in a nor'easter. The waves would intensify and crash ferociously onto the beach. In some of the storms the waves forced the ocean to penetrate the back bay region and the moon was unable to draw the salt water out to sea on a changing tide. It was during the flooding of low lying areas when the many eggs made of sand were reshaped at low tide. The raging sea would calm over a couple of days, and the sand on the shoreline would shift and reshape the island into newly formed patterns.

The Unalatchtigo no longer graced the beach. Men with fair skin, Europeans, continued their migration and settled the areas formerly occupied by their native neighbors. The Lenape, the ones who loved to hunt and fish, living near the tributaries and inlets, moved away. Their new trail took them west; they found themselves combined with other natives from distant lands, settling in Oklahoma.

The ensuing years brought hunters and people who would ferry across the Great Egg Harbor to picnic and day trip on Peck's Beach. The newer and more recent visitors were unaware of a missing sight and sound. One that created a picture of massiveness and beauty, a demonstration of power found only in the sea. The North Atlantic Grey Whale no longer breached close to the beach. They were absent from their back bay sanctuary. Massive, growing to a weight of forty tons, the picture painted by nature over many years was altered. They had been hunted to the point of depletion, their appearance no longer visible.

One day four men hired a ferry to cross the harbor to set foot on Peck's Beach. Their visit was prompted by stories of the beauty and serenity that prevailed on the windswept beaches. A variety of shore birds occupied the beaches and hunted the coastal waterways. Osprey, egrets, herring gulls and plovers populated the island.

The visitor's came from Pleasantville. The Lake family consisted of Ezra B. Lake, James Lake, S. Wesley Lake and a relative, William Burrell. The group of men represented a blend of people with theological training and business acumen. Together they pursued a vision. They were ordained ministers in the Methodist Church and they were looking for a site to develop. They would market their idea as a place for rest, refuge and replenishment. They had previous experience with real estate development at nearby Absecon Island including Atlantic City. Their visit and observation confirmed what they had hoped; Peck's Beach was ripe for development as a site of inspiration for the future.

Certain members of the Lake family were married to women from the Somers family, then owners of Peck's Beach. They negotiated an agreement with the Somers family to purchase the entire tract. The island known as Peck's Beach now stood at a threshold and was destined to be governed by a newly established association. The new owners, as developers, were preparing to establish a camp meeting seaside resort.

CHAPTER
10

BOGH MOR
(BOWMORE)
1888

The stones in the wall were brown and gray, piled upon each other at a height near two feet. The wall served as a perimeter; built by the members, it circumvented the church. The wind blowing from the south was riding the back of Mother Nature as she brought fresh air from the Irish Sea, past Gartbreck, before moving through Bowmore.

Killarow Church was small. The round building stood on a bluff overlooking the village and the blue sea. Whitewashed with cement on the outside, the cone shaped roof was supported by a massive pillar erected in the center. Small rectangular windows were placed at intervals, one above another. There was a saying that the devil would not be able to find a place to hide in a round church.

Toward the rear of the churchyard he stood, graveside, wearing black boots, dressed in pressed black trousers, cream colored shirt and black coat. His hair was dark brown, clean shaven, tears streaming down his face to the point where his vision was impaired. For the moment, the ability to see was useless. He was looking through his heart that day. People who knew him recognized it was a broken heart filled with ache. The dreams of a future he planned to build lay before him, neatly tucked inside a casket, six feet down.

Lavender wildflowers cut in the field outside the window next to his home, lay upon her casket. The minister concluded with these final words.

"Rest in peace Shona Graeme," he beckoned softly.

Keitha, stood nearby, head down, sobbing. Anna McCall, her assistant, stood by her side, an arm placed around her shoulder. An angel watched over a young mother to be, dying in childbirth. Ross Graeme, eyes clearing, glanced into the brilliance of the blue sky over the western coast of Scotland.

"He's a fine looking young man," the voice interrupted.

Ross, startled, awoke from his daydream. His mind, taken back in time twelve years prior, he now heard the voice of his father-in-law, Ronan Garrow. Ross fulfilled a promise made to his wife Shona. Years passed whereupon she lay on her death bed. The tremendous ache in his heart from an earlier life had subsided for the most part, yet it was moments like this that brought back the memory of his youth and his love. Their plan was to farm and raise a family of children and live forever in happiness. It was a fine plan, one which they both desired to the fullest, yet one cut short. An unexpected complication during her first birth ended with her death, but the child survived.

Ross fulfilled Shona's request when he opened her prayer book on that fateful day. Twelve years before, he turned to the inside of the back cover to retrieve the name of the baby to be. Keitha told her it was a boy. And so Ross had registered his son with the name Mitchell Graeme, per the dying wish of his beloved Shona.

His grief materialized into a determination to raise his son in a manner which he knew would be approved by Shona. There was little means outside of farming to cover living expenses, so he chose to accept the offer extended by the boy's maternal grandparents to reside with them near Glasgow. Ronan and Caitir Garrow were the parents of two sons and two daughters, Shona being the younger. Ross knew it would be for the best to accept their offer to occupy two of the rooms in their upstairs home.

The family was dedicated to supporting their son-in-law in his effort to raise their grandson, absent of his mother's love. Ross built a carpentry business around Glasgow while providing for his son's education. Mitchell would grow up to be an educated man with position. He would learn a trade that would provide him recognition, worthy of the surname Graeme.

Mitchell spent his formative years learning the value of hard work through different positions obtained in Glasgow. He applied himself and learned lessons from the books as well. By the time he turned eleven years he displayed an interest in the sciences. Ronan followed up on a few contacts, paving the way for his grandson to gain entrance to school. The day had come. Mitchell would be provided an opportunity to advance his studies in mathematics, geology and science, including the study of the sea.

CHAPTER
11

BUILDING A SHIPPING COMPANY
1900

The Brocklebank firm was established nearly 130 years ago, their name was recognized as the leading shipping company in many parts of the world. Thomas Fisher Brocklebank was appointed a partner in the firm; charged with executive officer duties and responsibilities. His cousin, Ralph Brocklebank, was brought into the business in 1843. Between the two they demonstrated keen ability to manage the affairs of the business. Ralph was appointed to Chairman of the Mersey Docks and Harbor Board in the same year. He was a likeable gentleman and veered toward the politically and socially active side of British society. In time he was appointed a baronet by the British Crown.

The shipping firm continued to grow over many years. In 1900, they ordered a steam propelled merchant vessel, the Marwari I, to be delivered to Liverpool. They had gone through a process of reducing their fleet to four sailships and two steamers. The passage of time produced technical innovation and the science of shipbuilding changed significantly. The Whitehaven facility was closed decades ago as a result of a management decision to concentrate their resources at Liverpool. The partners answered a call; the future involved locating, developing and grooming new trade routes, thus replacing shipbuilding. The seed was planted for years and others were scouring the market to find ships fabricated with newer technology. The Brocklebanks turned to Harland and Wolff to accommodate their requirements for new ships.

The Sindia sailed since 1888; Captain Allan MacKenzie commanded the ship on the maiden voyage to Calcutta. The ship made thirteen trips following that year, two of which were to New York. The remainder was voyages to Calcutta to support the East India trade. Thousands of nautical miles were sailed, delivering merchandise and products for the many customers of the firm. Sindia was the largest barque in their fleet.

Another sailship, hull number 205, built by Harland and Wolff, was christened *Holkar* in February 1888. In August, 1889, hull number 218, the *Ameer* was added. The Ameer was built with steam propulsion, becoming the firm's first cargo ship. Growing business demands and increased trade routes propelled the firm to buy a series of steamships. They added hull number 219, the *Gaekwar,* in March of 1890. The *Pindari,* hull number 245, was delivered toward the end of 1891. The same year closed with the delivery of hull number 246, the *Maharatta.* The investment of capital by the Brocklebanks depleted as they added four steam propelled ships to their fleet.

The name of each ship was selected with the intent to honor people and places instrumental in enhancing their business trade. The Holkar were a people who grew into a dynasty in central India. The Ameer depicted an independent ruler or chieftain, and the Gaekwar was the title of a ruler in the state of Baroda, India. The Pindari were a people who originated in the Maratha State in India. Their history involved plundering and pillaging to supply the *Marathas.* Then there were the *Mahratta,* whose name denoted a member of an agricultural caste of the State of Maharashtra in India.

Business empires were built on vision and capital investment. They grew or declined when change dictated the need for the owners to respond to new discoveries, to meet the increasing demands altering their plan. Thos. & Jno. Brocklebank, Ltd. reached the apex by 1900. Other companies were competing by securing vessels to fit shipping and transportation needs.

In 1888, an American company, Esso, initiated new business in London and chose to operate under the name Anglo American Standard Oil Co. Ltd. of London. The newly formed company was legally designed to operate as a British affiliate of Standard Oil Trust. Their original source of business included the shipment of lamp oil to the United Kingdom. Later, the business evolved into the sale and transfer of harness oil, steam cylinder oil, spindle oil and various greases. The opportunity developed to supply the needs of British manufacturers from stock oils supplied in America.

The Brocklebanks adopted a cautious approach, watching the development and growth of steam propelled cargo ships over two decades. They took slow deliberative steps, studying and evaluating the advantages and disadvantages of shipping cargo using steam propulsion. It was during the year 1889 that the shipbuilding magnates at Harland and Wolff delivered the S.S. Ameer. The net tonnage of the ship was 4,000 and when fully loaded, the gross tonnage increased to 6,450. The cargo vessel was propelled by a triple expansion engine and could reach ten knots and maintain this momentum with consistency. In this year the Ameer would be one of the largest vessels to use the Suez Canal for passage, avoiding the dangerous seas rounding Cape Horn.

The Marine Superintendent employed by the Brocklebanks was Captain William Ray. His length of seamanship dated back to October 11, 1859, when he completed his apprenticeship with Brocklebanks. Another captain, William Ellery, began his career on December 17, 1856 as a seventeen year old apprentice, onboard the 256-ton barque, Hindoo, bound for Pernambuco, Brazil.

It was imperative to develop a feasible plan to facilitate the transition of trading with a fleet of sailships to cargo carrying steamships, all over a number of years. The maiden voyage of the Ameer would serve as a training ground for existing shipmasters under the Brocklebank employ. Prior to the maiden voyage, several senior captains were chosen to participate in steamship cruises owned by other companies. The Ameer was scheduled to depart from the Mersey on her maiden voyage to Calcutta on October 27, 1889. Several highly respected senior captains with a crew of more than thirty men were chosen to represent the Brocklebank compliment of seamen, guiding Ameer to Calcutta.

Captain William Ray	Master
Captain William Ellery	First Mate
Captain Allan MacKenzie	Second Mate
J.G. Simpson	Third Mate (Master's Certificate)
J. Cook	Fourth Mate (Master's Certificate)
Chief Engineer	
Engineer Officers	
Two Stewards	

Two Cooks
One Donkeyman
Fourteen greasers, firemen and trimmers
Twelve Able Bodied Seamen

A new century blossomed with opportunity by 1900. Mr. John D. Rockefeller guided the development and growth of the Anglo American Standard Oil Co. of London, Ltd. An increase in trade with China and growth in shipments of kerosene and oil-based products required an aggressive procurement of barques for shipping products. Mr. J. McDonald, Mgr., set about the business of locating and purchasing three- and four-masted ships to keep up with the demand. As 1900 closed, Mr. McDonald added eleven fine ships to the Anglo American fleet.

Name of Ship	Description	Tonnage	Yr. Built
Drumeltan	4-mast iron barque	1,909	1883
Kentmere	4-mast iron barque	2,525	1883
Lindhurst	4-mast steel barque	2,311	1886
Johanna	4-mast steel barque	1,756	1891
Juteopolis	4-mast steel barque	2,842	1891
Alcides	4-mast steel barque	2,704	1892
Lawhill	4-mast steel barque	2,942	1892
Calcutta	3-mast steel barque	1,694	1892
Glendoon	3-mast steel barque	1,981	1894
King George	3-mast steel barque	2,242	1894
Falls of Ettrick	4-mast steel barque	2,264	1894

Mr. Rockefeller, continuing to operate in expansion mode, set about laying plans with three ship builders, Hamilton, Russell, and Rodger, to deliver new vessels to his already fine fleet of oil sailors.

Name of Ship	Description	Tonnage	Yr. to be Built
Comet	4-mast steel barque	3,014	1901
Nonpareil	4-mast steel barque	3,014	1901
Brilliant	4-mast steel barque	3,765	1901

Daylight	4-mast steel barque	3,765	1901
Arrow	4-mast steel barque	3,090	1902
Eclipse	4-mast steel barque	3,090	1902
Alacrita	steel ship	1,974	1903
Radiant	steel ship	1,974	1903

Thomas Brocklebank received a Western Union Cablegram from Mr. J. McDonald representing the interests of John D. Rockefeller and the Anglo American Standard Oil Co. They were in need of another sailship and displayed an interest in the purchase of Sindia to facilitate their merchant shipping business.

The Western Union Telegraph Company, Inc.

Attention: Mr. Thomas F. Brocklebank
Thos. & Jno. Brocklebank, Ltd.
20 Bixteth Street
Liverpool, England

Reference: Sindia

Message: Need sailship to fill trade route plans. Interested in barque, Sindia. Respond of your interest to market same if intentions fit your plan. Will arrange for surveyor to appraise value.

Respectfully: J. McDonald, Manager
Anglo-American Standard Oil Co. of London, Ltd.
22 Billiter Street
London, England

Thomas and John met to discuss the business implications of reducing their fleet by one. The last time their firm witnessed a fleet reduction was ten years prior, 1890, when *Talookdar* sank, as a result of a collision. She was launched on August 22, 1885 and her hull number was 183, the eighth sailing vessel to be built by Harland and Wolff for the Brocklebank firm. The ship's tonnage was 2,120. It was a depressing day, only five years after her initial launch; the Talookdar would sail no more.

The advantages and disadvantages of the offer were weighed and the decision reached to pare the shipping company's fleet; their largest sailship of 3,068 gross tonnage would be sold. Harland and Wolff were busy constructing steam powered vessels for the future and Thomas and Ralph reasoned the proceeds of $200,000 would be well employed in new technology.

The movement and shipping of petroleum-based products moved to the forefront of Mr. McDonald's priorities. His next objective was to secure the services of a sea captain to fulfill the responsibility of master of the Sindia. Her voyage under new ownership would include a sail from Liverpool to the port of New York, then to the other side of the world.

The Western Union Telegraph Company, Inc.

Attention: Mr. Thomas F. Brocklebank
Thos. & Jno. Brocklebank, Ltd.
20 Bixteth Street
Liverpool, England

Reference: Ship's Master

Message: In contact with Lloyd's, Re: securing ship master. Records indicate Allan MacKenzie, certificate C30124, extensive experience. I would appreciate your reference regarding same.

Respectfully: J. McDonald, Manager
Anglo-American Standard Oil Co. of London, Ltd.
22 Billiter Street
London, England

The Western Union Telegraph Company Incorporated

Attention: Mr. J. McDonald, Manager
Anglo-American Standard Oil Co. of London, Ltd.
22 Billiter Street
London, England

Reference: Master – Allan MacKenzie

Message: None the finer have sailed the seas commanding our
ships.

Master 1889-1890 Sindia / in the company's service
1870-1889.

Respectfully: Thomas Brockelbank
Thos. & Jno. Brockelbank, Ltd.
20 Bixtieth Street
Liverpool, England

Within a few days, Mr. McDonald found his potential master. It was time to determine his availability and willingness to employ under the Anglo-American Oil Co.

CHAPTER
12

SEAMEN

Allan MacKenzie became the first choice to fill the position of ships' master by J. McDonald. As manager he checked with the Board of Trade and knew that Captain MacKenzie was certificated at the age of thirty-two at the Port of Liverpool in the year 1870. While checking with Lloyd's of London Register of Ship Captain's and Mates, he confirmed Captain MacKenzie was employed in the Brocklebank's service during the years 1870 through 1889. He made note of his master's certificate #30124. He was confident he had found his man and telegraphed his recommendation to company headquarters in New York City.

The following advertisement was placed in the Liverpool Daily Post by Mr. McDonald, fulfilling his next step and responsibility.

SEAMEN WANTED FOR EMPLOYMENT

ABLE BODIED, ORDINARY SEAMEN AND APPRENTICES

Departure Date   December, 1900

Vessel   SV Sindia - Ensign - Britain

Departure Port   Liverpool - Duration - 14 months

Destination   New York - China - Japan

Owner   Anglo-American Standard Oil Co. of London, Ltd.

The newly chosen captain was informed that Sindia was in transit from Dundee, Scotland. The ship had recently completed service delivering merchant goods to Calcutta. Captain Heyburn was in command of the ship, arriving at the port of Dundee in June. The new owner, Anglo American Standard Oil, issued instructions to sail Sindia to the port of Liverpool in time for a winter passage to New York Harbor.

He closed the door to the office on Monday morning and requested to meet Master Allan MacKenzie. He wore a dark brown Inverness cloak and swagger, and looked the part of a ship's officer from Dundee. The length of the coat covered his body down to his calves. It would be impossible for a drizzle or downpour to penetrate the exterior and make him cold. His black trousers were made of one hundred percent cotton canvas and adorned with silver buttons spaced six inches apart around the circumference of his waist.

George Stewart was born in Dundee of Fairfax County in northern Scotland on June 30, 1866. *Dan-di*, the Scottish Gaelic form, was a small town located on the north bank of the Firth of Tay, a tributary leading into the North Sea. Many of the residents sought employment in the mills, manufacturing products from jute for which they were famous. They called it the "golden fiber" because of its silky shine. The product was used in manufacturing industrial yarn and netting and Brocklebank ships unloaded jute more than once per year.

He was thirty-four years of age and had been to sea many times since his first venture on the OE None, when they departed Liverpool on February 3, 1882. He was sixteen years of age at the time. The assistant asked him to take a seat in the corner office at the west end of the building.

"Mr. Stewart," greeted Captain MacKenzie as he strode through the door toward the desk.

He was nearly the same height as the captain. His hair was dark and his eyes were brown. His left arm was tattooed with his initials, GS. George Stewart was twenty-seven years younger; the captain was old enough to be his father. His frame was lean and he was of a slight but muscular build.

After exchanging pleasantries, it was time to focus on the requirements to fill the positions of officers for the voyage to the Far East.

"Captain, I served under Master Heyburn aboard the Sindia leaving Middlesbrough for Calcutta. We returned this past June 2nd. I sailed Sindia from Dundee, departing on September 26 to dock in the Mersey in time for this engagement. George Wilkie filled the role of my chief officer and we sailed with a mix of Scots and English. Many of them desire to make the sail to Shanghai."

The captain studied Mr. Stewart's face and demeanor before inquiring.

"Tell me about the crew, how many are certified seamen?"

"We have enough to fill half of the positions with a solid crew."

"Any misfits to be dealt with?" asked the captain.

"No issues of significance to be dealt with sir."

Mr. Stewart glanced at Captain MacKenzie's penetrating steel blue eyes.

"How many crew members will you employ?" Mr. Stewart inquired.

"Aside from the officers, we need twenty-six!"

"We have sixteen, we can round up ten more. I'll make inquiries at the Sailor's Home," responded Mr. Stewart.

The captain, reaching for a writing instrument inquired, "You have a sailmaker?"

"He's one of the best! Luke Addison comes from Arbroath; learned the trade early and well. He can maintain the worn canvas and replace the old with newly fabricated sail."

Some of the seamen were experienced and provided documentation of licensing with references. The captain's goal was to locate as many of these as possible. It was the other category that beggared him and that was the source of the challenge. Often the applicants had no work experience and for that matter, listed no sea experience. These would be the lot that would be ill-prepared for the conditions they would encounter once the ship left port.

The boatswain would be a critical choice as he was responsible to pass directives and enforce the officer's orders over the crew. Any command passed down from the ship's master to the first and second mates would be a directive to be followed immediately. The job required the crew to act harmoniously, synchronizing their efforts.

"Let's inspect your documents," requested the captain.

Mr. Stewart reached inside his right breast pocket and produced the merchant marine articles from a brown leather satchel. George was issued a Certificate of Competency #027439 when he lived at 8 Victoria Square in Dundee. The documents were spread on the wooden desk for the captain's inspection and acceptance. Manuscripts such as these told the life history of a seaman. It was often a long story that started with the beginning of their journey and ended with their most recent voyage.

George Stewart put to sea at the age of sixteen on February 3, 1882. The first of two pages containing "His List of Testimonials and full Statement of Service" spoke of his life at sea.

George Stewart Service at Sea

Ship's Name	Port of Registry	Rank	Service Date (s)
OE None	Liverpool	Boy	1882
"	"	OS	1883-1884
"	"	OS	1884-1885
British General	Liverpool	OS	1885-1886
London	Dundee	2nd Mate	1888-1889
Doris	Dundee	2nd Mate	1889-1890
"	Dundee	2nd Mate	1890-1891
Woodbark	Dundee	1st Mate	1891-1892
Thetis	Dundee	1st Mate	1892

His first engagement lasted nine months and fifteen days and his service record listed him as, "Boy." How familiar to Captain MacKenzie as he had gone through the same experience years before. On January 9 of '83 George signed on for his second excursion. He accumulated sufficient experience to be designated an ordinary seaman. He served on two square-riggers and the second voyage lasted for one year, six months and three days. Following a third voyage of nine months he signed on with the ship, British General, a 1,756-ton square-rigged sailship. The date was November 20, 1885, and the length of her sail lasted for a year and eleven days to January 12, 1886. After his first four voyages he had accumulated service at sea totaling four years, one month and twelve days.

By the year 1887 George passed the examination and was awarded a Certificate of Competency as a Second Mate. It was January 21 and he listed his address as 8 Sea Wynd, Dundee. His next three sails were aboard the ship, London, followed by two deployments on the ship, Doris, both registered from the Port of Dundee. He served as second mate on each voyage between May of 1888 and September of 1891, all of which were registered foreign service.

The captain was interested in his service on Thetis as the port of destination was Valparaiso. This was a major Chilean stopover for merchant seamen, sailing between the Atlantic and Pacific, navigating through the Strait of Magellan. He also visited Iquique, a northern port of commerce in the same country.

Captain MacKenzie perused through the listing of the service of his soon to be first mate and chief officer, for the deployment of Sindia to New York Harbor. George Stewart was awarded the designation of first mate, prior to his service on the ship, Woodbark, registered at Dundee, having departed on December 14, 1891, returning October 24, 1892.

Economic times were often beset with turbulence and survival was foremost in everyone's mind. It was a common practice for one with a master's certificate to sign an Account and Agreement of Crew as a first or second mate, in order to obtain employment and an income. By doing so they were serving in a lower capacity under the command of another master.

George Stewart continued on his path of learning seamanship including passing the navigation examination. On February 1, 1894, he passed his examination and the Board of Trade, London, issued him a Certificate of Competency as a Master. The document was signed by Mr. Ingram B. Walker, one of the Assistant Secretaries to the Board of Trade.

The captain knew George obtained his master's certificate less than six years prior, and was happy to have a man of his experience and certification willing to fulfill the responsibility of first mate. Sindia would embark on her maiden voyage under new ownership with not one but two certified ship masters.

Two days following their meeting, another George, this one with the surname of Wilkie, walked through the door to the office of the Anglo American Standard Oil Co. As he opened his mouth, the captain, sitting back in his chair, shrugged and mused, we've got another from *Dandi* who wants a job at sea. The accent was distinguishable; most Scots knew there was a peculiar way of pronouncing words when one hailed from the port north of the Firth of Tay.

George Wilkie was twenty-one years of age, born on May 31, 1879. He stood five-feet, nine-and-one-half inches. His hair was brown and so were his eyes. Under identifying marks he listed a tattoo with his initials GW, on his left forearm. He, like George Stewart, was also born in Dundee in the County of Fairfax.

David Jackson signed on as a cabin boy, making the trip to Liverpool on the Sindia with George Stewart and George Wilkie. Jackson was the third one born and raised in Dundee. George Wilkie filled in the paperwork listing his home address as 43 Dens Road, Dundee as of June 4, 1900. Two months prior, on April 6th, he passed the examination and received the certification as a second mate, #035250.

George Wilkie produced his file containing the list of testimonials with his signed application and agreement. He also left home at the age of sixteen to begin his service as a seaman.

George Wilkie Service at Sea

Ship's Name	Port of Registry	Rank	Service Date (s)
Dundee	Dundee	App	1895-1899
Dundee	Dundee	AB	1899-1900
Sindia	London	2nd Mate	1900

During the years 1895 through 1899, he assumed the role of an apprentice on the ship, Dundee. His certificate of competency issued by the Board of Trade was #86368, registered from the port of Dundee. He was elevated to able bodied seaman during a second engagement beginning September 13, 1899 through August 4, 1900.

Captain MacKenzie, having secured the services of a bosun, delegated the responsibility of filling the remaining crew to George Stewart, George Wilkie and the ship's bosun, Thomas Wright. Several applicants were readily dismissed when it was discovered they were ex-convicts. Grappling with the law didn't automatically disqualify them if the ship's officers found themselves hard up to find enough to man the ship. This particular voyage found enough men between sails and others needing wages, so they could scratch the undesirables from their list.

George Stewart looked at Tom Wright and laughed aloud after a disagreeable beggar named Collins closed the door behind himself. George poured coffee from the pot and shook his head in amazement.

"He's running from a pile of debt and some woman's irate husband."

The two were looking for mental stability and an array of skills that would be helpful after they put to sea. The voyage would take them to sea for days that rolled into months. The seamen would bunk below deck in dark, damp, crowded quarters. The berths would be eighteen inches across with little head room to toss and turn during a nights rest. The work would be strenuous with risk to life and limb. Those that could not stand the snoring of others found themselves lulled into sleep from a day's work that tired their muscles and penetrated their bones.

The master and mates wished to avoid the need to discipline any of the crew, yet they knew the moment would present itself in due course. The master of the merchant vessel was the dictator of the sea. He said what he meant and what he said would be obeyed. To do otherwise, seamen would find themselves in a most unfortunate set of circumstance.

On occasion a missing wooden belaying pin was found to be detached from the pinrail. Under normal circumstance the pin was used to hold rigging tied with rope in sailor's fashion. The pin was a handy device when masterfully employed as it produced the required impact, literally, intended by the officer. The purpose was to correct the misguided behavior of the seamen at the moment.

Many a risk would be present once the Sindia set sail. It was the responsibility of Master Allan MacKenzie and his chief officer to make the voyage as uneventful as possible. The weather would be foul at times, the seas rough, and navigation would change from good to impossible. The food would begin to spoil several weeks into the voyage and the potential of starvation, lack of water, even fever and disease might frequent their ship. Manmade circumstance brought on by irritability and loss of control of temper would jeopardize the safety of the ship and the crew. The master would administer justice, his way, and the seaman causing the problem would be dealt with, if required, harshly at times.

CHAPTER
13

THE CREW

A few days passed and the first and second mate completed the Account and Agreement of Crew, to be presented to the captain for approval. The document, once finalized, would be filled in according to form, signed by the captain, and sent to Mr. J. McDonald, Mgr. at the Anglo American Standard Oil Co. of London, Ltd.

A knock on the door and a brief introduction and Allan MacKenzie was face to face with Mitchell Graeme.

"And you have come for what purpose?" the captain inquired.

"The advertisement for the crew list for the Sindia," he replied.

"What are your skills?"

"I'm interested in furthering my apprenticeship. One day I'll be a quartermaster."

The captain cocked his head and nodded.

"Last name is Graeme, another Scot!" the captain noted.

"Aye!"

"And where ye from?"

"Glasgow, but I was born on the Isle of Islay (I-la), the small village of Bowmore."

Mitchell, like all others, focused on his penetrating steel blue eyes. The captain sized up his outward appearance while assessing his inward fortitude. He suspected this is someone who was capable of spending countless hours behind a ship's wheel in all sorts of weather, fair and foul.

"Who are your father and mother?"

"Ross and Shona Graeme."

"What is your father's occupation?"

"Farming, but when we moved to the mainland, carpentry occupied his time."

"Did your previous apprenticeship require service at sea for an extended sail?"

"Only for a short duration --- along the coast of England and France."

"We'll be out for the better part of a year lad --- your parents will miss you!" Captain MacKenzie reacted.

"My father is kept busy back home, my mother died, captain."

"What happened?"

"Child birth, sir."

The captain's eyes softened a wee bit, his face turning toward the sun shining through the window.

"How many siblings?"

"Just me, sir."

Captain MacKenzie secured the information he sought after.

"Let's take a look at your Statement of Apprenticeship --- referral letters, do you have any to present?"

Mitchell pulled the leather bound packet from his breast pocket and delivered the summation of his brief life's work into the hands of the captain. While studying the paperwork the captain continued with his questioning, one building on another. Mitchell handed him a letter from Reverend Adam Burnes.

"Church of Scotland?"

"Yes sir."

"The reverend appears to know you well. Am I to believe you are a disciplined young man?"

"Aye."

The captain reasoned he could predict the character of the man standing before him. His constitution was forged in his early years, no doubt from the wise upbringing by his father, grandfather and grandmother. The small communities dotting Scotland's countryside were known for their strong religious beliefs and practices. Absent of a mother in Mitchell's life, the captain assumed correctly. The parting words voiced by Caitir Garrow to her grandson were, "Remember your faith and prayers, every day." The captain's crew list was complete.

AGREEMENT AND ACCOUNT OF CREW
FOREIGN – GOING SHIP
Issued by the Board of Trade, London

NAME	AGE	CAPACITY	TOWN/ COUNTRY
Allan MacKenzie	61	Master	Inverness
George Stewart	34	First Mate*	Dundee
George Wilkie	21	Second Mate	Dundee
Thomas Wright	43	Boatswain	Bristol
Ewan Rowland	51	Steward	Liverpool
Luke Addison	52	Sailmaker	Arbroath
Boyd McAndrew	54	Carpenter	Greenock, Scotland
Martin Page	50	Cook	Merseyside
Mitchell Graeme	24	Apprentice	Glasgow
John Morley	27	Able Bodied	Rugeleys Staff
Frank Hudson	39	Able Bodied	N. York, England
Richard Parker	30	Able Bodied	Whitehaven
David Jackson	16	Cabin-boy	Dundee
John Dillon	36	Donkeyman	Claw, Wales
John Massie	22	Able Bodied	Aberdeen, Scotland
Louis Bank	23	Donkeyman	England
James Long	20	Apprentice	Whitehaven
John Cannon	22	Ordinary Seaman	Manchester
Thomas Brown	41	Able Bodied	Liverpool
Alex Kinnaird	21	Able Bodied	Peterhead, Scotland
William Webb	50	Able Bodied	N. York, England
Paul Nolan	36	Able Bodied	Clark, England
Edward Reed	21	Able Bodied	Liverpool
Albert Brother	22	Able Bodied	Liverpool
Thomas Newman	34	Ordinary Seaman	Liverpool
Ian Quay	42	Able Bodied	Dundee
Thomas Matthewsen	39	Ordinary Seaman	Liverpool
Thomas Burke	46	Able Bodied	Liverpool
John Farmer	25	Able Bodied	Liverpool
T. Christiansen	24	Able Bodied	Flensberg, Ger.
Thomas Fitzpatrick	41	Able Bodied	Dublin, Ireland
J. Rolvsson	42	Able Bodied	Norway
Sveinung Erickson	45	Able Bodied	Tonsberg, Norway
John Brown	32	Able Bodied	Norway

*Geo. Stewart holds a Certificate of Competency of Master

The third page of the agreement included multiple columns designed to capture specific information listed by the ship's captain. They included the amount of wages, paid weekly, a signature line of the official before whom the seaman engaged services, and particulars of discharge. Each of the crew knew and understood the risks associated with signing on as a member of the crew of a foreign-going merchant vessel. Under "particulars of discharge," the agreement listed several categories to be filled in by the captain. They included, discharge, death or desertion.

Seaman Thomas Matthewsen, from Liverpool, was the last to sign the agreement. He glanced at the rows setting forth each of the crew's wages, prior to placing his signature in the first column.

Particulars of Engagement

Signature of Crew	Capacity	Wages	(Wily)	
Allan MacKenzie	Master	Unlisted		
George Stewart	Mate	9	2	0
George Wilkie	2nd Mate	5	2	0
Thomas Wright	Boatswain	3	2	0
Ewan Rowland	Steward	5	2	0
Luke Addison	Sailmaker	4	2	0
Boyd McAndrew	Carpenter	6	7	0
Martin Page	Cook	4	12	0
Remainder of Crew	AB, OS	3	2	0

The three columns under wages were specified in payment of pounds, shillings, and pence distributed to each of the crew, weekly or upon discharge.

CHAPTER
14

NEW YORK BOUND

The departure date was confirmed with Anglo-American as December 18, 1900. J. McDonald provided a cargo list to fill most of the ship's hold awaiting their arrival in New York Harbor, thereabout January 17. The contents included containers of lamp oil owned by the Anglo-American Standard Oil Co. of London, Ltd., with insurance procured through Lloyd's of London.

Captain MacKenzie sat at his desk pouring over charts. He calculated the distance between Liverpool to New York Harbor to be near 3,100 nautical miles. His sail plan would have to navigate the westerlies, a consistent wind stream that blows in a southwesterly direction from the United States across the Atlantic to Europe, between the 30 to 60 degree latitude. He knew the wind pattern increased in strength during the winter.

Knowledge from his sailing experience and reports of other masters, suggested the winds would produce stronger ocean currents as they approached the shore of New York. Their course placed them in the path of headwinds for the entire crossing and his estimates were based on a speed of four knots. They would modify their sail plan and adapt tacking patterns once at sea. If they could average ninety or more nautical miles per day, they could sail to New York within thirty-five days.

The longshoremen met at the wharf on Friday the 15th to load the goods for shipment to New York, for the benefit of several British companies. Two days earlier, thirty-two men were filling the hold with their personal provisions with enough stores of food and water for a long voyage.

Families of the men met at the wharf to say goodbye and bid farewell as they set to sea. They would not return for approximately one year. John Massie was a twenty-two year old able bodied seaman from Aberdeen. His home town was located on the northeast coast of Scotland. The Dee and Don rivers connected at Aberdeen before they emptied into the North Sea.

"Are you ready for the long journey ahead, apprentice?" John called to James Long, two years his junior, and his first service on Sindia.

The ship's master, Allan Mackenzie, stood on the flybridge. First Mate George Stewart requested all of the crew to gather on the main deck as the captain wished to address them. Members of the family and friends of the crew stood by silently, portside, watching the men assemble. Many of them sailed with the captain on a previous voyage and they knew of his reputation earned throughout his years of service with the Brocklebank firm.

Ewan Rowland, steward, confirmed all of the stores were in their proper place and Tom Wright, bosun, confirmed the crew was counted. Mr. Stewart supervised as the tug made preparation to guide Sindia into the Liverpool Bay. The sound of the tugs' engine spilled over the bow as the first mate ordered crew to remove all ropes securing the ship to the wharf. There was an immediate jar and the ship was underway, heading in a northerly direction. The tug would guide Sindia through the Mersey River until they set sail.

Within a half hour they were nearing the western point and the mouth of the Liverpool Bay was in sight. The captain of the tug slowed the speed preparing to separate from the barque. The first and second mates and the bosun were ready to coordinate their crew to set sail. It had been a long time since either had crossed the Atlantic. A half hour later they approached the mouth of the bay leading directly into the Irish Sea. The day was cloudy and winds were fair. Captain MacKenzie stood atop the deck near the helmsman, shouting to his first mate.

"Mr. Stewart, have 'em lay aloft."

Mr. Stewart bellowed forth, "Starboard and port watches, lay aloft!"

The rigging monkeys scrambled up the lines secured to the foremast, the mainmast, and the mizzenmast. The windjammer was outfitted with six square-rigged sails on each of three masts. As the men reached the yards they secured footings, awaiting orders to loose the lines on each of the three skysails.

Mitchell, manning the ship's wheel, watched the flurry of men, scrambling up ratlines, hanging from the spars sixty to one hundred feet above, extending out over the sea. Thomas Wright broke in with a sea chantey song. The laborious and dangerous work on a sailship was eased and energy levels increased by singing a chantey. The crew joined in the chorus following the bosun's lead.

Bosun: "O blown the man down, bullies blow the man down."

Crew: "Weigh-oh, blow the man down, O blow the man down in Liverpool town..... Give a man time to blow the man down."

Bosun: "As I was a walking down Paradise Street, a saucy young bobby I happened to meet."

Crew: "Weigh-oh, blow the man down, O blow the man down in Liverpool town..... Give a man time to blow the man down."

By the time Tom Wright concluded several stanzas, Mitchell joined in on the final chorus.

Bosun: "O bobby, O bobby, you do me great wrong, I'm a Brocklebank sailor man, just home from Hong Kong."

Crew: "Weigh-oh, blown the man down, O blow the man down in Liverpool town..... Give a man time to blow the man down."

Mitchell was at sea --- he would be at sea for a long time --- Glasgow and his early beginnings in Bogh Mor were distant memories.

John Dillon, from Claw, and Louis Bank, were experienced donkeymen. The donkey boiler was powered by low-grade oil; spewing smoke, it was ready to produce steam to power two winches to raise the heavy sails. A metal cable was attached to the winch and the sails. It was a dirty job and the smoke from the boiler engine overpowered the smell of fresh salt air. The upper and lower topsails were heavy and, when wet, became impossible to be raised by seamen. So John and Louis made sure the donkey boiler was fired and operable, awaiting the captain's order to hoist the upper and lower topsails on each mast.

Residents on the western point excitedly watched the four-masted barque, drifting in the bay, while the crew prepared to hoist some of the thirty-two sails. It was a beautiful sight; although seen before, the residents never tired of watching ships set sail. One of the old timers described many a blighter set to sail at the pointe, yet it was always a fresh picture for the eye to catch on any given day. An old mariner standing by his grandson was perched on a wharf looking out to the bay. His right arm was around his grandson's shoulder, pointing as they watched the sails, one by one, snap, in response to the wind.

John Cannon of Manchester scurried up the ratline to the crow's nest. He was on the first watch as the ship lurched forward in the mouth of the bay. The view of the sea from the nest looked much different when aloft 150 feet. Starboard, John saw only water and plenty of it. The view of coastal England would remain portside for a long time as they would round the pointe by the bay. The first town spotted was Rhyl and afterward they passed Conway.

At North Pointe, he shouted "Amlwch" (Welsh-Amlock) as it appeared.

"Mr. Stewart," called Captain MacKenzie. "Have Luke Addison come to the aft deck."

Given the ship's position, the captain wanted to confer with his sailmaker. They would assess the conditions of the sea and the wind pattern, and then determine which sails to be set for their west by southwest tack through the Irish Sea.

Mitchell, standing erect with wheel in hand, would remember the first time he saw the sailmaker for the rest of his life. Luke was five-feet, seven-inches tall and stood firm, like a broad leafed tree. He would not bend easily in a strong breeze. It was a cold gray December morning. He was clad in heavy worsted trousers held up with brown leather braces including a belt. A woolen Guernsey, home knitted with a cable stitch pattern could be seen beneath a thick tweed waistcoat. His hair was red mixed with brown, and when he opened his mouth, his accent was as thick as the fog frequenting the Liverpool waterfront.

"Mr. Stewart," beckoned Captain MacKenzie once again. "Have the lookout notify you at the sight of Holyhead."

Dead reckoning was required for the moment, changing the course of the ship westward to the coast of Ireland.

"You wish to discuss sails captain?" Luke inquired.

"Our course is set for the Irish Sea, waves are moderate height."

"Aye, I've been studying conditions since the eighth bell captain. The wind is blowing at twelve to fifteen, she can take more sail."

Captain MacKenzie ordered Mr. Stewart. "Set the lower and upper topgallants."

The winches hoisted the four-course, the main, and the mizzensails. Luke, standing next to the taffrail, watched as the canvas caught wind, stiffening with the breeze. Mitchell adjusted the wheel as Sindia responded.

CHAPTER
15

THE HELMSMAN

Martin Page, cook, sounded two bells of the afternoon watch; John Farmer replaced Ewan in the crow's nest. He spotted the village of Holyhead, his eyes scanning the port bow. A shout below to Mr. Stewart was the only requirement to summon Captain MacKenzie to the flybridge. With computations complete, orders were given to the helmsman, Mitchell Graeme, to adjust the course to 210 degrees heading in a southwesterly direction. Their sail would take them across Saint Georges Channel off the coast of Ireland below Dublin.

Early afternoon breezes increased as the soft glow of the winter sun warmed the air. The winds blew near fifteen knots across the channel. Luke bounded up the ladder to the fore deck, to check on any changes in the sea and wind patterns. Captain MacKenzie, having finished his mid-day meal, would be on deck for some time.

"We can set the inner, outer and flying jibs. The lower and upper spankers can be set too," Luke advised.

Captain MacKenzie nodded in agreement and motioned Mr. Stewart to give the command. The top mast staysails, the topgallant staysails and the royal staysails were lowered on the fore, main, and mizzenmasts.

Mitchell, ship's wheel in hand, watched the flurry of activity as the port watch followed the command. This was his first trip on a four-masted barque, the largest of her day, and he was at the threshold of a journey of a lifetime.

The sun glistened as the sails caught the breezes Mother Nature created.

The flag bearing the symbol of the owner of the ship, attached to the foremast, flew 190 feet above the ocean. It was a two-colored square cloth with an emblem depicting a bird, wings spread, announcing the ship was the property of the Anglo-American Standard Oil Co. of London, Ltd. A triangular shaped, single colored flag, with the name Sindia, flew atop the mainmast. Mitchell's eyes turned to the British ensign snapping in the wind from the jiggermast. His ship's sails were set, displaying nearly 35,000 square feet of canvas.

One hour later after a knock on the captain's door, he was staring into the steel blue eyes of the veteran master. This was the first time he was invited into the captain's quarters, located below the ship's stern. He hoped this would not be the last invitation. Allan MacKenzie was a highlander; Mitchell was born on Islay, one of the largest islands of the Inner Hebrides. They looked like, sounded like, and were, Scotsmen. The difference, Mitchell spoke with an accent of the Hebrides; his English pronunciation revealed he was taught Scottish Gaelic since birth.

The cabin was shaped in a semi-circle. The walls were a medium tint, highlighting the North American oak planks, richly fitting the rest of the décor. Books, mostly navigational, filled a built-in shelf above a table. Lamps lit with kerosene hung on the walls, both port and starboard sides.

"My first time inside the quarters of a captain," Mitchell confided as he surveyed the surroundings.

"Take a seat, let's talk," the captain paused. "You're a bright lad; it was obvious the day of our interview. You will make a fine quartermaster."

Mitchell, silent, his interest peaked.

"You could go beyond this level if you have the desire."

Mitchell wanted to open the door to talk about many subjects.

"I would like to learn everything about celestial navigation, captain. I find it intriguing; a ship's master can determine and set the course of a huge ship, studying the heavens and calculating points from stars in the sky."

Captain MacKenzie pulled a book with a brown cover from the shelf.

"You will find what you're looking for within these pages, start with the Sumner line," the captain instructed. "The principle was developed by Thomas Hubbard Sumner, a sea captain of the 19th century. He was born in Boston and set out to become an architect; went to Harvard but the sea called him, it beckons anyone with the interest to serve at sea."

The captain proceeded to describe a young man, intelligent and full of promise, yet he enrolled as a common sailor on a ship engaged in China trade. Within eight years he was appointed captain of his own ship. Captain MacKenzie opened the book to a chapter, a slip of paper was wedged between the pages.

"You can read the detail on your own time, Mitchell. This chapter describes the development of the Sumner line used by every captain who sails the seas. The story begins with his voyage in 1837 when he sailed from Charleston to Greenock."

Mitchell, raised near Glasgow, knew of the town located along the Clyde River. The Sindia, the previous day, navigated through the Channel of St. George into the Irish Sea. It took Sumner years to perfect his work, published in 1843. Mitchell, book in hand, paused at the door when Captain MacKenzie spoke once again.

"The sea has been relatively calm but it will get rough and dangerous."

Mitchell, turned and gazed over his shoulder, responding, "I understand."

The captain shook his head. "No, you don't, but you're about to!" Captain MacKenzie paused for a moment. "Don't show them the white feather!"

Mitchell, puzzled, stared at the captain.

Captain MacKenzie responded once more, "Don't show the men any fear, regardless of how dangerous the situation!"

CHAPTER
16

SURFMEN

There was no sunset as the atmosphere darkened. Storm clouds rolled across the Jersey coast since 3 P.M. that afternoon. The January wind was blustery and blowing in a southeasterly direction. The presence of whitecaps pranced on short choppy waves as they rolled from the south to the north, moving into the Great Egg Harbor. The waves pounded the beach near Fourth Street and spray blew wildly. The low cloud cover magnified the noise emanating from the surf.

A lone figure trudged through wet sand along the coastline on this particular night. He was heading in a northerly direction from Peck's Beach Station #2. His storm coat and pants were made of brown oilskin. His hat, sitting squarely on his head, was broad brimmed, one side bending down from the wind blowing against his right cheekbone, the back brim hugged his neck. The storm brought rain around nine that evening and there were signs the intensity would increase.

Harry Young was thirty-seven years of age in 1900. He wore a patch with the number five on his sleeve, since he was appointed to this rank by John Mackey Corson, Keeper of the Ocean City Life-Saving Station #30. His service at the Peck's Beach location began on December 1, 1898.

This was a full-time position for him; his application listed him as a boatman and temporary surfman. Harry was of a slight build, yet his physical fitness and muscular strength were pronounced. He spoke to himself to toughen his resolve on this particular night. His throat was sore and he wanted nothing more than to reach home safely, remove his gear, and warm by the stove with a hot mug of drink in hand. This was the job of a surfman and he was proud of his calling.

The women were unable to restrain from staring at such an attractive man. On Sunday mornings he looked like a preacher. A laundered white shirt was buttoned to the top underneath his chin. Each side of the collar was folded over with a triangular crease pointing outward to the lapel. His coat was fully buttoned to the top with each lapel pressed tightly against his chest. His hair was medium brown, cut short with a part on the left. The curve of the hair on his forehead revealed a peak. His hazel eyes sent a message that this was a serious minded young man who displayed resolve and fortitude.

There were four watches covered by four surfmen and each required a four-hour stretch, patrolling the ocean along the beach blanketed by wind and rain. Harry's watch began at eight and would end at midnight. Sand, caking to his boots, increased his heart rate as his feet plodded along a path to the half-way house. He carried a walking staff to steady navigation. A patrol clock with a punch key was fixed to a leather strap, slung over his shoulder. He alternated between hands to lighten the load, carrying a fully lit patrol lantern. Three Coston signals were stashed inside his pockets to keep them dry.

There were numerous shipwrecks throughout the New Jersey shoreline and he knew of the history of a few. The Red House, home of the Ocean City Life-Saving Service, displayed artifacts and numerous articles of shipwrecks. Each depicted a series of events driving a captain's ship onto the beach, a fate not of his choosing. Harry was determined to persevere as he exited the half-way house, making another trip southward for his next stop at Peck's Beach Station #2. Not tonight, not tonight he repeated to himself. We don't need to see a red flare signaling a distressed ship tonight he pleaded. Let me get this watch finished so I can return to a warm bed.

This was his job and he served with a purpose and commitment. He was reminded of many ships forced to bow to Neptune's furor, wrecked off the coast of New Jersey. The years 1848 through 1871 saw numerous ships flirting with, and losing to disaster as they failed to navigate the ocean around the Great Egg Harbor.

The two-masted British brig, Huron, was dealt a fatal blow in a storm driven evening. The brig Dashaway succumbed to her demise off Peck's beach on January 15, 1863. The steamship Dawn had to be abandoned offshore on December 27, 1869, and schooners were not exempted from the occasional wrath of the North Atlantic. The Caroline Hall wrecked in a storm off Peck's Beach on March 13, 1870. In 1874 and then on March 6, 1877, other schooners, the Adelia Burley and the Adelia Hodgkins, both sunk in the Great Egg Harbor.

The surfman's job was to warn a wayward ship from the shallow sandy shoals beyond the breakers. The brightly lit red light emanating from the Coston's flare was carried for that purpose. When a ship was discovered to have run aground, the light from the flare would notify the crew a rescue effort would follow. And when a rescue was imminent, the adrenaline flowing through a surfman's veins was like a thunderstorm spewing water down a gushing creek during a summertime cloud burst.

CHAPTER

17

NEW YORK HARBOR

1901

Crossing the Atlantic was marred with cloudy days but on the morning of the 17th of January, Mitchell stood behind the wheel when rays from the sun broke over the horizon. The air was crisp and the whistle of the wind heightened, careening off the canvas. The wheel was put to a lathe and the rim and spokes were fashioned from a fine specimen of an oak tree, stained with a medium hue to allow the rich grain to seep through. It was an impressive navigational mechanism. The wheel was mounted on a wooden platform and stood six-feet-high with the girth being equal to the height. Ten spokes twelve inches long, spread equally apart beginning in the hub, protruded outward through the wooden circular hub. Mitchell noticed the stain on some of the spokes had been rubbed bare. No doubt from the weathering process and the result of wear from many a quartermaster steering the ship through calm and storm.

Mitchell's eyes, constantly scanning the sea, darted to starboard facing the southwest. Increased moisture filled the air and the smell of salt came with each passing breath. James Long drew the current watch atop the crow's nest. Bristol was his home and he completed his first year of an apprenticeship prior to setting sail. The shout of land brought Captain MacKenzie to a standstill, reaching for his long glass for a better view.

The crossing over the great ocean took a total of twenty-nine days. Anticipation and excitement filled the heart of the helmsman; this would be his first opportunity to view the Statue of Liberty. It was minutes after Mart struck the bell once for the forenoon. They were nearing the docks of

Bayonne, New Jersey, where Standard Oil Company owned 600 acres and many refineries.

"There she is, Liberty, off the port bow!" James Long's voice rang out.

A small figure rising skyward became visible to Mitchell. She was standing on a large pedestal on Bedloe's Island, one of the three Oyster Islands in the New York Harbor. They were named for their abundance of the shell. Using Mr. Wilkie's long glass, Mitchell was fascinated with her appearance, erect and tall, beckoning all a welcome to freedom.

It was January, 1901, and Sindia would dock at the wharf allowing sufficient time for the stevedores to unload the cargo. B. Ellis, acting as agent for the company, arranged for the transportation of a shipment of kerosene, lamp oil and other related oil derivatives, all bound for Shanghai. The senior officers would rely on the bosun to organize the storage and placement of cargo. A seasoned English sailor, it was his job to make sure the ship was ballasted with precision. There would be no damage to cargo, and it would be delivered in tact on his watch. Tom knew his work would impact the operation of the ship from the bow to the stern.

The day before departure the captain met with his chief officer in the chart room. The purpose was to plan a course for the next leg of their voyage. The charts were kept in large shallow drawers to keep them clean, dry and flat. Mr. Stewart, a young man of thirty-four, suffered a previous taste of the captain's displeasure when a chart was blemished. That mistake would not bare repetition. Captain MacKenzie was fastidious in habit and couldn't stand the slightest bend, crease, or marking on one of his charts. George Wilkie spread the chart on the table, preparing for the start of their voyage. The chart room was an officer's habitat where the journey of the ship and the path sailed would be plotted and adjusted.

Navigational instruments such as the parallel rule, multiple compasses, and a sextant would be conveniently tucked away in storage drawers for daily use when needed. If there was an exception to the captain's protocol, it would be charts set out for marking up, normally a task taken on by Mr. Stewart. The first mate was responsible to incorporate any of the latest navigational information into their plan. The log book was used to record an official transcript of the details of Sindia's journey.

The two conversed over the direction for the outbound route to China. The first mate suggested a passage around Cape Horn, a shorter but more treacherous route. The captain favored the easterly direction around the

Cape of Good Hope. Their return cargo, a collage of tableware, home furnishings, and decorative household items purchased on consignment, would be delivered to merchants in New York in time for Christmas. Captain MacKenzie, with numerous voyages to Calcutta, would weigh the factors including distance, provisional or repair stops, if any, and the assessment of danger sailing around Cape Horn.

CHAPTER
18

SARGASSO SEA

It was the twenty-ninth of January and the ninth day after leaving the port of New York. Mart struck the ship's bell five times for the morning watch. The port watch was on deck and John Farmer was perched 150 feet above the ocean, scared of the height but enjoying the beautiful view. Something caught his eye as he strained to see what was floating on top of the ocean. He shouted to Mr. Wilkie. His long glass was required to examine the presence of a vast element of debris floating on top of the water. The color of the matter was mixed shades of red, brown, and yellow. Sindia reached the edge of an unusual sea.

Mr. Wilkie bellowed to the lookout, "Algae, we're in the sea of algae."

Mitchell, at the wheel, was interested in the announcement. Within a half hour, the hull was knifing a path through the Sea of Sargasso. Captain MacKenzie left the comfort of his cabin to ascend the stairway to the main deck. He stood near the wheel, port side, conferring with his second mate. The ship was surrounded by free-floating seaweed, another new and interesting experience for Mitchell.

"What am I looking at, Mr. Wilkie?"

"It's the Sargasso Sea. Algae grow abundantly within the borders. It floats freely out here and consistently stays in a specific area."

Mitchell watched with amazement, it was everywhere.

"My suspicion is the algae can reproduce while living on top of the ocean --- looks the same each trip."

"If it's here each time you pass perhaps it feeds something," suggested

Mitchell.

"Keep your eyes open, big turtles and plenty of large fish abound," responded the mate.

Mitchell, hoping to see huge whales, was quick to inquire if they lived in this sea.

The third mate pondered, "Perhaps this time of the year, stay alert! You may see a white marlin surface. They love to leap out of the water. There are dolphin and shark feeding out there too." Mr. Wilkie thought again. "We could pass a humpback --- they come through when migrating --- there should be tuna as well."

Mitchell loved the study of geography and the sea.

"There is no land bordering the Sargasso Sea, Mitchell. It's the only sea in the world bordered by other bodies of water and ocean currents," instructed Mr. Wilkie.

Mitchell listened intently, learning in school while out to sea.

"The Gulf Stream is the western boundary; the current of the North Atlantic defines the northern boundary, our current position. The east side of the sea is bordered by the Canary Current and the southern portion of the sea is bordered by the North Atlantic Equatorial Current." Mr. Wilkie finished.

"How big is this sea?" Mitchell asked.

"About 700 miles wide by 2,000 miles long --- it's huge!"

The captain summoned Ian Quay and Luke Addison. Additional sail would be hoisted up the masts since the winds decreased to force two. Every captain feared the risk of being becalmed. They could lose precious time due to the lack of wind. It was the captain's job to maximize every movement of wind possible. Mr. Wilkie gave the order for the rigging monkeys to ascend the ratlines to set additional sail.

Mitchell discovered that cold and warm water masses converge in the Sargasso. It was time for the Norwegian, *Sveinung,* to make his presence known to Mitchell. Idle chatter and plenty of it was his favorite pastime.

"Keep your eye open for tuna," Sveinung suggested.

"Why?"

Sveinung responded, rubbing his belly. "Vant to eat good or vant to eat the stores Mart cooks up? Keep your eye out for tuna." He smiled at the helmsman. "Amberjack, wahoo, white and blue marlin, they all spawn out here. I'll be happy to eat any one of them. Mart's salty pork and bacon is already old and no replacement for fresh fish."

The bosun grinned during the exchange.

"Don't try to pronounce his name, it's too complicated," chimed Tom.

Sveinung, confused look on his face, responded. "Common name in Norvay!"

"Call him S, everyone else does." Tom walked away muttering to himself.

S was one of three Norwegians selected for the crew. He could talk up a storm and often did, usually when you wanted silence. So spot for fish Mitchell did, often, and for what seemed like a long time.

There were several species of birds feeding on the rich food supply floating in the Sargasso. Mitchell watched the Bermuda petrel and the bridled tern. The petrels had white bellies and a black capped head with black markings covering their wings.

"What was that sound?" Mitchell asked.

"Eerie mate, isn't it? They make a scary crying sound," S responded.

Meanwhile the bosun glanced over his shoulder in time to see Mitchell, face turning green, bending over. The helmsman's mind was playing tricks with his stomach; this could be a very long day. His stomach rumbled and rolled in tandem with the pitch of each swell. S told more than one of the crew not to focus on the waves. It was the end of January and the temperature was transitioning to balmy.

S studied Mitchell's face for one second, then muttered; "Oops, *havet syk* (sea sick)!"

There would be plenty of the blue Atlantic for the helmsman to adjust to for days to follow.

CHAPTER
19

THE ATLANTIC

Charts covered the table. Captain MacKenzie joined Mr. Stewart to plot the next course of their journey. Their sail plan would take them southeast, far away from land, deep into the Atlantic. Captains felt safer when far out to sea. Coastal areas brought risks of shoaling and wind patterns blowing off the mainland, creating dangerous conditions. Sindia was passing through the southeast side of the Sargasso. The captain's latest sextant reading confirmed they were north of the 30th parallel. The trade winds would blow steady and their chart recorded historic wind speeds to be favorable, between eleven to thirteen knots.

Mitchell stood to the right of the wheel, the wheelhouse constructed on top of the poop deck. He was amused by the term until, on a previous sail, the mate explained the word came from the French word, "la poupe." The poop was the roof formed over the captain's cabin built in the stern or rear of the ship. It was a struggle to maintain the wheel when winds increased and the path of the ocean current changed. Mitchell was struck with the beauty of the sun drenched sky, finding himself in the middle of the Atlantic.

"Tell me about the trades, Mr. Stewart!"

"They originate off the west coast of Africa."

Mitchell couldn't comprehend the distance to sail to the west coast of Africa from their current position.

"We know they blow southwest as they cross the Atlantic. They dip near the equator, then reposition and blow west by northwest along the coast of America."

"Now I know why I've been fighting the wheel all morning! What about tacking," asked the helmsman?

"It's difficult to maintain a consistent tack when we sail into a headwind. I'll be teaching you about navigation through the horse latitudes and trades."

"Ship on the horizon," called the lookout.

Mart struck one bell signaling the afternoon watch. Mitchell glanced at the card, keeping the ship to her course. The oncoming vessel was a steamship; Captain MacKenzie put his long glass to his eye and steadied himself. More time passed as he continued his surveillance.

"Looks like the Curfic," he commented to Mr. Stewart.

Mr. Stewart descended the steps to the chart room to look up the ship's details. The Curfic was a steamship launched by Harland and Wolff in 1888, one year following the launch of Sindia. The weight of the vessel was 4,689 tons. They altered course to sail close to each other and as the two ships passed, Mr. Wilkie signaled the Curfic. Each master would log the day, the time, and the position of sighting, and report this information when passing a signaling station near the coast. Lloyd's of London set up a system for communicating the location of ships. They kept up-to-date information for the owners as they monitored their progress through shipping lanes.

The captain lowered his long glass after another look. The sighting of a steamer reminded him of his days on the S.S. Gaekwar. The vessel was one of several steamships in the Brocklebank fleet, the others being Ameer, Pindari, and Mahratta. The captain commanded the Gaekwar on multiple trips from Liverpool to Calcutta. His mind drifted into another voyage. What was his wife, Christina, doing at home in Liverpool? Her husband, commanding a ship in the middle of the Atlantic, revived memories of another time. Christina was on board the Gaekwar with the captain during the 1891 census. He missed those days at sea when the two sailed together.

The sighting of the Curfic served as a brief reminder that the merchant days of shipping cargo under sail were waning. The growth in using the steam powered vessel was the future. Perhaps he should call this voyage his last sail. After all, he was sixty-two and had logged thousands of miles of sail. He would put that thought to the back of his mind for now. The beauty of the blue ocean provided a window of tranquility he savored for the moment.

Mitchell was enjoying the early days of his journey at sea and he knew there would be many more before the sighting of land. His ship, the one he was piloting, was below thirty degrees latitude. The cold air of the North Atlantic was behind and they were sailing into a noticeably warmer climate. All of the hatches leading to the main deck were opened to their fullest. The smell from the containers of case oil stored below on the third deck permeated the insides of the ship. The air was stagnant, no circulation, the odor of the oil would be with them for a long time.

Mr. Stewart approached the wheel.

"The trades, westerlies, easterlies and latitudes; what do these names mean? There are reasons for each name. Got the answers for me helmsman?"

Mitchell glanced at the amused smile on Mr. Stewart's face. It was the first time he noticed the first mate had his shirt sleeves rolled above his elbow.

"Tattoo on the left arm, sir?" he inquired.

Mr. Stewart had his initials, GS, marked on his forearm.

"We passed through the North Atlantic and we're south of the Sargasso, near the thirtieth parallel. The wind patterns will change as we near the equator." Mr. Stewart redirected the conversation.

"S told me colorful stories of becalmed ships south of the Cape Verde Islands. Is that true?" Mitchell asked.

"Certainly is! They're a group of ten islands formed of volcanic origin. Settled by the Portuguese, in fact. We use the islands as a marker, the doldrums lie south of the islands," offered Mr. Stewart. "The discovery of the wind patterns date back to the time of Columbus," he added. "The trades are a huge force that blow west over the Atlantic from the west coast of Africa. The winds blow for thousands of miles, circulating northward as they reach the Americas, moving up the North Atlantic. We call them the westerlies, short for western trade winds."

John Morley, within ear shot of the first mate's comments, was interested in joining the conversation. Mitchell was learning an important lesson experienced mates knew, and that was wind patterns.

"Why are they called the trades?" John asked.

Mr. Stewart cocked his head and thought for a moment.

"Good question! During the early 18th century a system was put in place for the purpose of increasing trade over the North Atlantic." The first mate tilted his head toward the helmsman. "The network was the result of specific forces cultivated over a period of time. Local economic conditions provided the need for trade and the prevailing wind and sea currents provided the means to transport products." John Morley listened quietly as Mr. Stewart continued the lesson. "Columbus was likely the one to discover the prevailing winds sweeping across the ocean, moving westward, and circulating in an enormous pattern eastward toward Europe. He reasoned these wind patterns would propel his three sailships to complete the return voyage back to Spain and Queen Isabella. Without them he couldn't return."

Mitchell listened with interest, dissecting the reasoning.

"Who benefitted from the trade and what did they trade?" Mitchell asked with interest.

"Assorted tropical goods, sugar and molasses," Mr. Stewart paused. "The products were shipped from Brazil and the West Indies to the American Colonies. They were also sent to places in Europe."

"What did the colonies trade?" Mitchell asked.

"They grew much tobacco and harvested furs." Mr. Stewart continued to teach. "Where do you think the dye, indigo, comes from? It's a product from the colonies. Other products such as lumber are harvested in great quantities and manufactured to be sold in Europe for building."

Morning progressed into late afternoon and nightfall erased the shadows on the deck. Mart, always in need of fresh air, climbed the stairwell to the foredeck to sound the bell for the evening watch. Three strikes signifying 17:30 hours of the first dog watch. It was Mitchell's turn to rest. Stretched on his berth in the fo'c'sle, he reflected on his new knowledge of wind patterns, their impact on his sailship, the largest sailing vessel on the oceans of the world this night.

Captain MacKenzie prepared his entry in the log. They departed the port of New York Harbor forty-two days ago. Combined nautical miles sailed were estimated near 3,800.

Sunday, March 3, 1901. Skies fair, winds west, force 4. Barometer 29.9, distance 115 miles. Curfic sighted, signaled position. Sailmaker made new fore topgallant stunsail. Two ships, unidentified, following, evening watch.

CHAPTER

20

ASCENSION ISLAND AND TRISTAN DA CUNHA

The helmsman steered Sindia deeper into the South Atlantic, far away from land. South of the equator the air mass continued to increase in temperature. The fo'c'sle was so hot the men took to constructing hammocks on the main deck, sleeping outside underneath the evening stars. The humidity increased and lighter work clothing was the order for each passing day.

It was an eerie sensation when the ship becalmed after entering the doldrums; thirty-two canvas sails covering 35,000 square feet, once full with the force of wind, now lay limp as if taken ill. Luke spoke of previous sails when the doldrums lasted as long as two weeks. This was a time to clean the ship, stain and paint the wooden areas, and grease the wire workings for the sails.

The atmosphere was clear on the eve of March 28th. Captain MacKenzie stood at the wheelhouse, scanning the heavens, waiting for the return of the wind to carry them out of the doldrums. He motioned to Mitchell, pointing to the southern sky.

"It's the Southern Cross."

Mitchell's eyes scanned the sky until he found four stars, one shining brighter than the others.

"What am I looking at?" Mitchell asked.

"A constellation named the Southern Cross --- it's an important navigational reference."

"An amazing sight, I have never seen this before," responded Mitchell.

"Two reasons --- one --- you live in the northern hemisphere --- the other, you have never sailed on a ship south of the equator."

"So we never see this formation of stars in Scotland?" Mitchell inquired.

"The cross never rises above the horizon in the northern hemisphere. The lands below the equator are the only ones that witness these stars."

"One of the stars is brighter than the others," Mitchell reflected.

"That would be Acrux."

"You know each of their names?"

"The other stars are Gacrux, Delta Crucis and Mimosa. Every captain uses the cross for navigation; it's an indicator of the position of the South Pole."

Mitchell was reminded of the many navigational tools to be studied, the elements of science, once a mystery, were becoming clearer.

Many of the crew brought or fabricated musical instruments from pieces of wood obtained from the ship's carpenter. John Massie assisted the carpenter. He knew more songs than any of them. In the evenings some of the crew would gather to play renditions of their favorite sea chantey songs. Others passed free time by hanging fishing lines over the side, hoping to catch something tasty for dinner, and Mart openly hoped for their success. Fishing with a line from a large ship was more difficult than expected.

∞

Mart climbed the stairs to the main deck and struck eight bells for the morning watch. The sun climbed over the horizon a couple of hours ago. The ocean was deep blue and choppy waves appeared. Rolvsson was assigned lookout, perched 150 feet above the deck amidship.

"LAND," he yelled loudly, "LAND!"

The first mate, amidship, was excited to get a look with his long glass. Minutes passed as he continued to study the appearance of what looked like a volcanic island. Mr. Stewart turned toward Captain MacKenzie, face in the sun.

"Ascension Island," the first mate announced.

"Where are we?" Mitchell asked.

The captain drew in a breath of walnut plug purchased from Ogden's in Liverpool. The clay pipe was his constant companion. Ascension Island was sparsely inhabited, except for a small force from the British Board of Admiralty.

"How far are we from the mainland?" Mitchell asked.

"Ascension is nearly 1,000 miles from the western coast of Africa. Pernambuco, Brazil, is 1,400 miles to the west.

"Ascension, odd name for an island," Mitchell exclaimed.

"It was discovered by a Portuguese explorer in the 1500s. This is the story; he saw the island on Ascension Day. Mr. Wilkie will signal, sending a message for the Eastern Telegraph Co."

Mitchell looked at the card.

"Finding and reporting position is critical out here, isn't it?"

The last yellow ember in the captain's pipe extinguished. "Aye, we send a wire to Lloyd's confirming our position. The Board of Trade is notified and Anglo American will be informed of our progress."

Ascension Island grew much larger as they neared the coast. Mitchell noticed the hue of the ocean changed from a deep blue to a lighter shade. S returned to his pastime of spotting sea turtles, an occupation he enjoyed. Mr. Stewart described the island as ninety square miles in size. Mitchell was impressed by the majestic rise of a mountain with two peaks, one of them, pointed in appearance, the other rounded at the top. As they sailed closer to Georgetown it was evident the island evolved from volcanic activity many years ago. Fifty-five days into their voyage, Captain MacKenzie charted their position and logged their distance, 5,000 miles sailed, Shanghai seemed far away.

∞

The crew was informed they were sailing south by southeast toward the Tropic of Capricorn. George Stewart was busy charting a new course, one that would take them near Tristan da Cunha, the most southern island near Africa. The westerlies were persistent, blowing very strong for the next two weeks. Ocean swells grew in size and force due to wind conditions. Captain MacKenzie was forced to take in sail in response to wind speeds between force five to six.

Mitchell reached for his bag of personal belongings kept in storage inside his bunk in the fo'c'sle. Aside from clothing and bits of personal food, the diary and his mother's prayer book were precious, and his most valuable possessions. The crew was respectful of the belongings of others stowed inside a bag, tucked away in the confines of their berth. Food left outside this area was fair game and disappeared quickly. His last diary entry described the sights experienced at Ascension Island. They reached day fifty-seven of their round the world voyage, and, according to the calendar it was March 3rd.

The evening sun dropped below the western horizon of the South Atlantic. Captain MacKenzie prepared the daily entry for the log.

Monday, March 18, 1901, reached Ascension, winds west 17 to 23 knots, passing rain squalls. Latitude 7.9 S, 14.4 W, barometer 29.75, distance 129 miles. The captain recorded they sailed nearly 5,100 miles since leaving New York.

∞

The sound of Mart ringing the ship's bell brought Mitchell to his feet. It was time to get to work. John Morley, now being relieved, commented on the increasing cooler weather. Sailing south of the equator meant the temperatures would begin to cool. The morning temperature was near sixty-two degrees and the high for the day would be another seven to ten degrees. The barometer reading was lower and the content of moisture increased in the air.

Mr. Stewart looked at the log and calculated their passage since leaving Ascension. The distance sailed was near 2,000 miles. Captain MacKenzie joined his chief officer in the chart room. A sextant reading would be taken at noon. The captain spent most of his career commanding ships under the Brocklebank flag. In those days his company followed the protocol put into practice by the East India Co. Every captain would navigate to the east side of Tristan da Cunha. Although his employer changed and the ship sailed under a new owner, the captain would adhere to protocol and bring his vessel within view of the volcanic island.

∞

Thomas Fitzpatrick took a turn in the nest. His desire was to feel less humidity and no rain during his watch. Mitchell eyed the card and paid attention to the wheel. S continued his usual banter drawing no one's attention in particular. No poll of the crew was taken; however, it was clear to most that the jaw muscles constructed around S's mouth were greased with oil. The constant flapping was a familiar sound all had become used to. Talk laced with wisdom would be welcome yet it was not forthcoming.

The sails were constructed of fine canvas purchased in Arbroath. They blew full with the strength of the breeze riding the westerlies.

"Land!" Thomas paused and screamed once more. "Land off the port bow!"

The captain and his chief officer were summoned to confirm location. They estimated they were nearing the next check point. Mitchell could see land in the distance. An extremely large peak ascended from the horizon, towering over the rest of the island. Mr. Stewart had his long glass trained on the island.

"Has to be Tristan," he announced. "There is no other island nearby and certainly none with a peak that towers above all else."

Later, Sindia was passed by two tea clippers sailing north by northwest in the opposite direction. It was moments like these when the starboard and port watches scurried to the side of the ship to catch a glimpse.

"Tristan has a north by south length of seven miles," Mr. Stewart commented. "There are smaller uninhabited islands in the chain. Tristan is the most remote inhabited land in the world," he added.

Mitchell was awed by the thought there were faraway islands on the sea unknown to anyone.

"We are 1,500 miles from the nearest continental land, South Africa, and 2,500 miles from South America," Mr. Stewart estimated.

Mitchell's world grew larger as he studied each day. There were times when he felt overwhelmed by the enormity and potential danger out at sea.

"St. Helena is the main island and a member of this archipelago. The island is about 800 miles southeast of our current position, but the island lies outside our sail plan," Mr. Stewart taught once more.

"Who owns all of these islands?" Mitchell asked.

"They were founded by the East India Co. in the 1600s and they continue to be ruled by the British."

The wind and current pushed them within closer sight of Tristan. A few on the starboard watch summoned the port watch to view the island. Mitchell was impressed with the size of the mountainous display of volcanic island, now covered in green. St. Mary's Peak rose over 6,000 feet into the sky. Clouds were dispersing and the sun was making an appearance over the sea. Thomas spotted a double rainbow over Tristan as they continued their pass. It was a beautiful sight, a new experience for Mitchell. Within the hour the island lay as a speck on the horizon in the path of the ship.

CHAPTER

21

CAPES OF SOUTH AFRICA

Mitchell stirred to the sound of two bells of the middle watch. It was a relief to maneuver out of his bedroll and get on with the day. He was not used to the feel of bugs crawling on his legs in the middle of the night. The fo'c'sle was dark and there was no place to hide from the ever present dampness, penetrating from the sea. In minutes he would ascend the stairwell to take his place by the wheel to guide the mighty vessel once more. He memorized the identity of the ten spokes on the wheel. At times he thought it proper to name each one. But that was at times of boredom, and there were many. He knew their individual shades and he counted them every day, watching them move left to right, then right to left, as they slid through his fingers. The movement of the wheel varied due to wind speed and currents, whenever he was required to respond to a correction in course. Today was a different morning from others. The port watch was bustling about and there was constant chatter. Certain members of the crew turned a watchful eye on the weather, wind, and currents.

S appeared on the deck, absent of a small portion of his breakfast usually stuck to his beard. Even Mitchell noticed a serious mentality to the Norseman on this day.

"Why the concerned look on your face?" Mitchell inquired.

"Time to pay serious attention to the sails," his eyes scanned aloft. "We're sailing in the roaring forties mate."

Mitchell heard the term before. He was about to experience this new phenomenon and it was time for another lesson in navigation. Mr. Stewart rounded the flybridge heading for the wheelhouse.

"Hope you slept good helmsman, we'll be busy for the next few days."

"S said we're in the roaring forties." Mitchell questioned.

"Aye mate." Mr. Stewart stared toward the port beam. "The westerlies pick up speed when crossing the fortieth parallel. Gets exciting down here; keeps you alert. Captain has the sails crowded on and the cape is ahead."

Captain MacKenzie was on top surveying the weather conditions and currents. Sea Legs, his pet dog, didn't seem to be bothered by the obvious increase in the pitch. The topgallants and the royals blew full and the ship was leaning heavy to port under the press on the canvas.

"Force five this morning," commented Mr. Stewart.

The captain nodded in agreement.

It was a good time for Mitchell to ask questions and learn. It was also a time to remain focused on the seriousness of the conditions of sail. After all, S set his usual chipper demeanor aside.

"How does the wheel feel?" Mr. Stewart inquired.

"It's tight, I feel the pressure of the current"

"It will get a lot rougher. John will be with you at the wheel as we close in on the cape." Mr. Stewart paused. "The passage around the southern part of Africa is dangerous," he said with an ominous warning.

"Who named the Cape of Good Hope and why?" Mitchell asked.

Mr. Wilkie insisted on being part of the conversation. "Answer that one mate --- I'm anxious to hear your reply."

Mr. Stewart grinned. "The cape was named by the Dutch --- I don't know why they named it the Cape of Good Hope."

Mitchell peered at both of them.

"Cape of storms, I knew that," Mr. Wilkie responded.

The morning passed quickly and by the eighth bell of the forenoon watch, the sun was covered by interspersing clouds. Captain MacKenzie, as customary this time of the day, would use his sextant to measure the angle of the sun in relation to the ocean surface to calculate distance. Mr. Stewart examined the barometer for changes in atmospheric pressure. The port and starboard watch would be on alert for the duration of the passage around the cape. Everyone knew being watchful and ready to act quickly was critical.

"This makes me feel uneasy," commented Mitchell.

Morley made the passage one other time. You could say he knew what to expect but that was only one passage. Ian Quay, assistant to the sailmaker was also in the galley. A mug of coffee in hand and a plate of beans with bread and jam sat before him.

"This is the spot with the greatest wind force along the coast of South Africa," Ian muttered. "I'd say we're at force six and the captain is hoping the wind speed won't increase beyond this. That's why he ordered the skysails and royals tightly secured," he added.

"Captain's watching the weather. Mr. Stewart's got his eye on the barometer and both are watching the currents and wind. I need another mug of coffee," commented Morley.

Mitchell passed S on deck and he was returning to his usual banter. Someone had to be responsible to pick up the slack and maintain levity among the crew. S was just the man for this purpose. Mitchell and Morley took their position behind the wheel. The pressure to maintain course increased with the change of wind and current. Both could feel the strain of the converging currents pushing the ship in the direction of the strongest current. Mr. Stewart left the flybridge to stand with them at the wheelhouse.

"Look over your left shoulder, see the point of land we passed!" Mr. Stewart motioned as he spoke.

The noise of the wind slamming into the sails was loud and the ropes and wires in the rigging resonated loudly.

"We're on the west side of the cape," Mr. Stewart added. "Agulhaus is next."

Mitchell looked puzzled.

"Agulhaus?"

Mr. Stewart looked at Morley. "Tell 'em about it, mate!"

"There is another cape, Mitchell, Cape Agulhaus." Morley strained as the force of the wheel pulled to port. "It's the southernmost point on the continent of Africa."

Mr. Stewart added, "It's about ninety miles from the cape."

"What do we expect to see at Agulhaus?" Mitchell queried.

"A striped lighthouse! It's not what we expect to see, it's what we will experience." Mr. Stewart was enjoying the banter. "Two currents converge at the same time, helmsman. The Atlantic smacks right into the western face of the Indian Ocean at Agulhaus." There was quiet. "But it's a lot more than that mate. The warm Agulhaus current meets the cold Benguela current and between the two, one of them must turn back on itself."

"Rough ocean!" Morley offered.

"Rough and unpredictable," cautioned Mr. Stewart.

Mitchell was intrigued by the change in conditions and the complications causing the captain and his chief officer to think and react to them. The bow of Sindia plunged downward then heaved upward with each passing wave.

Seafarers are often a superstitious lot. Captain MacKenzie and the first mate were thinking about such things but neither planned to discuss the reasons.

"Tell 'em about the cape doctor," Morley ventured forth.

Mitchell's interest was raised and all eyes were on the first mate. Mr. Stewart cocked his head to the left, thinking.

"It's a term used to describe a wind pattern, one that blows consistently from the southeast of the continent over the peninsula. The wind runs true during March and April," he answered. "Our sails are set to catch the doctor's blow. My eye has been on the barometer all morning." Morley listened intently. Mr. Stewart wasn't finished with another one of his lessons. "We have low pressure southwest of the cape. If the weather changes to high pressure, the wind will be gale force from the southeast," he instructed.

Mitchell studied his face. "So the situation changes from serious to dangerous?"

"That's why Agulhaus is known as a graveyard of ships," Morley inferred.

Morley froze as he said it. He had a friend who served on a ship that never made it past Agulhaus. He decided he said enough for one passing of the Horn. Silence overtook the three of them. Mitchell spent the remainder of the afternoon contemplating what he heard, thinking about the many challenges to be considered when one commands a 326-foot windjammer, especially in these waters.

The presence of afternoon clouds gave way to an evening sunset. Mitchell returned to the wheel after a couple of rests. The ship's bell was struck eight times. Captain MacKenzie, clay pipe in hand, blowing smoke in the air from black cherry tobacco, appeared on deck for an observational stroll. The pleasant aroma invaded the presence of the salt air. Mitchell pondered the change in direction as the sun began to set off of the stern. He was told their new direction would be east by northeast.

∞

Days passed and Cape Agulhaus disappeared beyond the horizon. Mitchell awoke to the ship's bell. It was time for hot coffee and bread with jam. Hope Mart made some bacon from one of those hogs we brought with us, he thought.

Mr. Wilkie was the first person Mitchell saw as he ascended the wheelhouse. The sun was making an entrance over the horizon. Rays of red and orange mixed with pink and yellow were bursting forth from the ocean's surface. In minutes S made his usual appearance and proffered to talk about all matters knowledgeable to him. It was an acceptable alternative to getting on with cleaning the third level below. All sorts of smells and disgusting debris lay below. Mr. Wilkie was content to let the Norseman dispense with his usual fodder because the bosun was below deck. If the bosun was present, of course, S would be nowhere to be found.

"You're a lucky helmsman today," S offered while casting an eye toward Mitchell.

"And why is that?"

"We're hugging the coast instead of sailing further south. The barque you're piloting is past Madagascar by now and we're navigating through the Indian Ocean."

Mr. Wilkie knew where S was going with this cerebral display of Norse nautical knowledge. He simply let S continue with his lesson. Mitchell, confused, simply peered around the wheel and watched the beam.

"We got a load of crates filled with case and kerosene oil bound for Shanghai."

"That's right," Mitchell acknowledged.

"And so it's on to Shanghai, but what if we we're going to Queenstown to pick up grain?"

S knew Mitchell never navigated the most southern portions of the Indian Ocean.

"This will be interesting," the second mate muttered.

Mitchell had a puzzled look on his face.

"If we were sailing to Australia, Mr. Wilkie would set the card for the south. We could cut off as much as 1,000 miles if we pass closer to the Antarctic. And that means we would be far below Agulhaus Banks." S explained.

S pointed his finger toward Thomas Matthewsen. "Ole Thomas, sitting up there in the nest would have his eye out for icebergs, and you might be steering around a few during our passage."

Mitchell turned his head toward Mr. Wilkie, looking for confirmation. He nodded in agreement.

"Impressive," Mitchell replied. "But too much discussion breaks my concentration."

Within a minute, Thomas panicked and screamed from the nest.

"EDDY!" He drew in a breath and shouted at the top of his lungs two more times. "EDDY! EDDY!"

He was pointing to the port side off the bow of the ship. Mr. Wilkie rushed to the rail and peered out to the ocean. Turning to Mitchell he ordered his helmsman to turn to starboard. Mitchell, without hesitation turned as instructed. A couple of minutes passed while he waited for the reason for such excitement. Mr. Wilkie turned to him and pointed out to the ocean. Sindia was approaching a huge funnel off port side. The ocean was circulating in a large clockwise pattern. He couldn't believe the size of the hole, approximately 100 feet in breadth. The funnel dropped, creating a swirling sucking noise. Another minute and they were looking at the funnel off the stern of the ship.

"Eddy," gasped Mr. Wilkie. "Rare to see but they do appear, must have dropped fifteen feet or more."

∞

At three bells of the afternoon watch Richard Parker spotted a square rigger off the starboard bow. The sight of another ship was always a welcomed event. It served as a diversion breaking the boredom that set in on a long voyage. Mr. Stewart brought his long glass to his brow as the two ships drew closer. He directed John Farmer to fetch the second mate.

The Dundee was approaching and Mr. Stewart knew Mr. Wilkie served as an apprentice on a Far East voyage. Mr. Wilkie peered through his long glass as the two ships passed.

"It's the Dundee alright," announced Mr. Wilkie. "I identified the ship's flag flying from the mizzenmast."

"When did you serve on her?" Mitchell asked.

"I signed on September of 1895 and my service ended in the same month of '99."

"And where did you sail?"

"Foreign trade, we ran routes to China and Japan. I served a second tour as an AB in September of 1899 through August of 1900."

Mitchell and Mr. Wilkie gazed at the Dundee as Mr. Stewart signaled their identification and location.

CHAPTER
22

REUNION AND
MAURITIUS

The turbulent and treacherous waters of the two capes were behind and the crew was hoisting sail. Luke inspected his newly constructed topsail secured to the mainmast. Mitchell steered while Mr. Stewart ordered the crojack set. The presence of land was gone and a northeasterly course was set. The southeast trade winds were dominant as it was now May in the year 1901.

"Tell me about the next leg of our journey?" Mitchell inquired of the ship's sailmaker.

Luke had much experience studying the wind patterns and navigating the Indian Ocean currents. His hair was dark brown mixed with many silver streaks. A sailmaker, he earned every one of them.

"We're in the twentieth parallel and will be riding the back of the southeast trades for a very long while. Temperatures will change and the air should be slightly cooler as we press further northeast toward the next set of islands."

The hot daytime temperatures were behind and the crew was experiencing moderation. Yesterday's high was near eighty-two degrees. Cyclones were still a possibility although they were more predominant during the months of January through March. The possibility of the Sindia meeting one of those dangerous storms was diminishing with each passing day.

"We'll be sailing off the coast of Reunion soon, you'll know it. Humidity will increase and there will be plenty of moisture. I've got to get below and finish sewing the stitches on a jib," the sailmaker announced.

"Can you show me how sails are made?" Mitchell begged.

"Aye!"

∞

Day 111 was checked in Mitchell's diary. Each day of the week became blurred and lacked sequence when out to sea. Events were clearer when he wrote in his journal. Time mattered to the captain since he was responsible to maintain the ship's log. This particular day was Friday, May 10. Many days lapsed since leaving the port at New York Harbor. It was even longer since he left his beloved Scotland. Life at sea was lonely and standing behind a wooden wheel, six feet in diameter, in all sorts of weather, could try one's patience.

His day began with a reading of the 25th Psalm from his mother's prayer book. The ninth verse spoke to him; "He leads the humble in doing right, teaching them his way." Verse twenty-one reminded him of Caitir Garrow, his grandmother, and her frequent admonishment, "May integrity and honesty protect me…" There was something about reading from Psalms that he treasured. How long will I be an apprentice and how long will I serve as a helmsman? A few questions Mitchell pondered as Sindia cut through the blue swells in the Indian Ocean.

The southeast trades were kind to the ship. Captain MacKenzie left the sails full and Sindia took advantage of prime conditions since passing Agulhaus. They were averaging over 100 miles per day according to the entries in the ship's log. The hatches were opened to their fullest, but the smell of the kerosene permeated the lower decks and conditions were barely tolerable.

S was quiet and it was noticed by most of the port watch. All agreed the quiet was welcome, however, there was an eerie atmosphere created by the absence of his jabbering mouth. Richard Parker, atop the crow's nest, bellowed to all on the main deck, land was in the distance. Reunion was near and Sindia was closing in on the island. The captain and first mate were on the flybridge, long glasses in hand. By their estimation they were following their intended navigational path. It was indeed Reunion in the distance.

Captain MacKenzie knew much about the foreign places encountered over many voyages to Calcutta. The island was under French control in the

1700s. The dimensions are nearly forty miles long by twenty-eight miles wide, one of the larger islands passed on this voyage.

"I wrote in my journal this morning, twenty-five days have passed since leaving Cape Agulhaus," Mitchell announced.

"Reunion is 2,200 miles from Agulhaus," Captain MacKenzie replied.

The captain switched tobacco brands. Mitchell could detect a different aroma from the usual black cherry often present in their talks. Time passed and Reunion was sighted off the port bow. Mitchell borrowed Mr. Stewart's long glass to gain a closer view of the island. He was impressed by a very large peak.

"That's a volcano," responded the first mate. "They call it the Piton." The view was breathtaking. "It rises over 8,000 feet to the eastern side of the island. The highest peak is nearly 10,000 feet, it's northwest of the Piton," he added.

Mitchell noticed the weather was changing once again. The day would be a hot one and the intense humidity suggested rain was coming.

∞

The following day another call came from the nest. Richard Parker was on watch. The Isle of Mauritius was a day's sail, 120 miles from Reunion. Mitchell inquired about the distance from the coast of southeast Africa. They were over 1,000 miles away. The terrain was altogether different from Reunion as mountain peaks were much lower. Mr. Stewart informed him the highest peak was below 3,000 feet. He was looking through the long glass at a series of inactive volcanoes. Merchant seamen characterized Mauritius as the isle of broken mountains.

Sindia was near the twentieth parallel southern latitude. It was winter in the southern hemisphere and the weather was a balmy eighty-three degrees. Mitchell couldn't help but think it was springtime in Scotland, the temperature would be in the mid-forties. It was the middle of May and Mr. Stewart instructed him to be on the watch for storm clouds. He was relieved they made it through this leg of their sail without major incidence. The beauty of the blue water and the immensity of the sea were impressive and he was enjoying his daily observations.

CHAPTER
23

COCOS AND SEAS BEYOND

Two weeks passed and S returned to his normal self, talking up a storm, and dispensing his personal knowledge as a seaman. Mr. Stewart humorously explained to a few of the port watch that his illness was behind. Most of the crew found it difficult to ignore S. Some preferred him ill, tucked away in quarantine in the lower hold of the ship.

"Why do you think his family put him to sea?" Mr. Stewart suggested to Mr. Wilkie.

By observance, it was common knowledge that even Sea Legs displayed the most ambivalence toward the Norwegian.

Mitchell recorded day 131 in his journal. Two weeks followed since passing Mauritius. There were daily sightings of ships during this time. Other barques chose to sail south of their location following the Australian grain route. According to Mr. Stewart, Sindia would continue on a northeasterly course.

"If we drew a straight line north of our position we would sail into India," blurted S, proud of his navigational acumen and anxious to share it.

Mr. Wilkie, perched on the flybridge, half-heartedly nodded in agreement.

"He's an intelligent Norseman. India has thousands of miles of coastline. Could you get your chart and be a bit more precise," queried the second mate.

The northern Indian Ocean was vast and Mitchell recorded his experiences when writing in his journal. The appearance of the water was a deep dark blue. He was informed by the first mate, two more weeks would pass before the next sighting of an island. The southeast trades continued a steady blow, pushing Sindia deeper into the Indian Ocean. Captain MacKenzie and Mr. Stewart met in the chartroom to discuss their next change in course.

"Do you plan to chart a course to the Malecca Strait?"

Mr. Stewart knew if the captain was avoiding the northern passage, then they would sail for the Sundra Strait. The second mate spread his chart on the table. The captain, clay pipe in hand, gazed at the chart while listening to his first mate's opinion.

"Malecca is far to the north, the strait is longer and the depths are more to our advantage," commented the captain.

"The Sundra Strait has the presence of sandbanks, tidal flows and shallower water," Mr. Stewart acknowledged.

The first mate was right but the captain was ultimately responsible to accept risk. Both of them had experience running ships through Sundra.

"Set our course for Sundra," the captain commanded.

The navigation of their ship would take them through a channel between the Indonesian Islands and the islands of Java and Sumatra. Captain MacKenzie was familiar with the narrow shallow passage, and aware that the time allotted to deliver the merchandise to New York prior to Christmas was a serious consideration.

According to Mitchell's journal they were out to sea 142 days, over four and one half months since departing the New York Harbor. Mart struck the bell four times, the start of the morning watch. Mitchell ascended the stairs to take his place behind the ship's wheel. His hands were rough and calloused, a by-product of countless hours devoted to a wooden wheel.

Richard Parker was sick with fever and for the second day the captain confined him to a bunk apart from the fo'c'sle. John Farmer, one of eight of the crew from Liverpool, took his watch as lookout for the morning. One island appeared followed by another. John spotted more than two of what would be a chain of twenty-four islands. Captain MacKenzie and Mr. Stewart moved to the starboard side of the bow. Sea Legs followed in close pursuit. Long glasses focused, both of the officers waited to confirm they were approaching the Cocos Islands.

Two hours passed and they were looking at multiple low lying islands. They used the sextant and chart to confirm their location. The Cocos were previously named the Keeling Islands after William Keeling. He sailed by them under the employ of the East India Company in the 1600s.

The highest elevation was only sixteen feet. The territory of Australia possessed ownership to the chain of islands, now in closer view. Mitchell inquired about the islands and S offered his usual remarks, explaining enough to sound convincing.

"They are nothing more than flat low-lying islands with coconut palms and coral reefs," he offered.

Captain MacKenzie and Mr. Stewart knew a telegraph station was to be established on Direction Island, one in the chain. It was unconfirmed if the station was in working order so they continued their course for Sundra Strait. Mitchell observed many different seabirds but he was unfamiliar with the names of the fowl in this part of the world.

∞

One week passed and the changes in the sail plan became evident. Sindia left the eastern edge of the Indian Ocean, sailing through the Sundra Strait. The first mate ordered the sails lowered for a sounding. The color of the water changed from a deep blue shade to a lighter hue. The further they sailed the lighter the shade and the captain's propensity for accurate soundings increased. By the 17th of June they sailed 650 miles from the Cocos Islands and were nearing Sangiand Island.

"Not much beach to speak of," Mr. Stewart commented to Mitchell.

The contour of the island displayed a sharp rise from the island's edge. The compass inside the binnacle pointed northeast. A short time passed and changes in the depth of the strait revealed shallower water.

"The widest distance is near fifteen miles and the depth will decrease to near sixty feet as we approach the northeast end," commented Mr. Stewart.

Mitchell stood by the wheel, waiting to change course if the first mate ordered. Mr. Stewart claimed the port watch and Mr. Wilkie manned starboard. Mitchell observed land masses barely visible, one lying to the port and the other to starboard. Mr. Stewart confirmed Sumatra was to port and the island of Java lay to starboard.

Richard Parker returned to feeling his normal self after passing the fever. Two other of the crew had similar symptoms so the captain separated them from the rest of the crew. He would not take the risk of an epidemic running through his crew, spoiling their plan to arrive in Shanghai sometime in June. Mitchell noticed tidal waters caused him to change course as the shift in the current produced drifting.

The sun set off the port side of the bow. Shades of pink mixed with lighter shades of red and blue unfolded as rays of light performed their magic show in the western sky. Mart finished serving the evening meal to the starboard watch. He ignored the usual complaints from the crew without comment.

Winds were light and sails were crowded. They passed through the strait and were near the mouth of the Java Sea. John Morley returned to spelling Mitchell at the helm. John Farmer was high above the main deck in the crow's nest. The watchman had more to observe compared to sailing in the vastness of the Indian Ocean. The Java Sea was large but shallow. The ship increased in speed as the bow cut into the calmer waters of the Java. Mr. Stewart was watchful but didn't take soundings as frequently, compared to their passage through the strait. His charts displayed depths near 160 feet. The presence of many small fishing boats was observed; Shanghai must be near.

Richard Parker didn't have to issue his usual call to confirm the presence of land to port side. The three officers were all present on the main deck.

"Must be Belitung off the east coast of Sumatra," implied the first mate.

Belitung was large in appearance compared to the smaller volcanic islands passed in the South Atlantic and Indian Oceans. One mountain peak rose 1,500 above the sea level.

"What country governs Belitung?" Mitchell asked.

"The Dutch, since the 1800s."

The cold weather by the cape was replaced with mild and agreeable temperatures. An hour passed and the sun slipped over the horizon as beautiful color gave way to a dark sky. Mitchell and Morley engaged in discussion topics about their homeland. S was warming up for his nighttime ritual. Sea Legs mastered a superior ability to focus on the art of sleeping.

All fore royals and upper topgallants were set as conditions changed. They anticipated fair weather through the north side of the Karimata Strait. The captain navigated this strait before since most of his service with Brocklebank took him to the port of Calcutta, returning to Liverpool, rounding the Cape of Good Hope.

CHAPTER
24

SHANGHAI

Sindia looked magnificent under full sail in the middle of the South China Sea. Whenever Mitchell rested John Morley readily took his place at the ship's wheel. Mr. Stewart ordered a course adjustment after conferring with the captain. A northerly course set the approach to the territorial waters of the East China Sea. The crow's nest had been manned by Albert Brother, one of eight Liverpudlians serving on Sindia, since the fourth bell of the forenoon watch. A shout below confirmed land was visible off the starboard bow. The captain and his chief officer reasoned they were passing the southern tip of the Philippines. The morning check of their sextant confirmed their suspicion.

The following day an anxious crew readied to pass through the Strait of Taiwan, west of the island. The toil of working the sails was wearing and the crew was tired and ready to dock. The narrowest part of the strait was believed to be eight miles per their chart and the body of water widened to one hundred ten miles. The prevailing wind from the Asian monsoon can bring dangerous conditions for ships. The patterns blow southerly during the months of June and July. The braces were set and the yards made fast to allow for maximum speed as the merchant vessel cut through the strait.

Mr. Wilkie informed Mitchell they would pass through the northern tip of the Philippines, and then reenter the East China Sea. Shanghai beckoned; the crew had been out to sea for more than 157 days. Less than four days passed and the canvas was stretched full as the southerly winds propelled Sindia through the calm sea, ripe enough for maximum speed. The captain logged an average of one hundred and fifty miles per day.

∞

Mart rang six bells of the morning watch as the spokes of the ship's wheel slid through Mitchell's hands. The East China Sea was behind and Sindia was approaching the mouth of the great Yangtze. Tom Wright ordered the starboard watch on deck with the port watch. Rigging monkeys were sent up the lines, lowering and securing the royals on the fore, main and mizzenmasts. The gaff topsail and upper and lower spankers were drawn in and fastened to the braces. The upper and lower topgallants were already loosed and would soon be secured as well.

Mitchell watched as mainland China appeared off port as they passed a particularly large island to starboard. The staysails and upper topsails remained set. Sindia would sail up the river with the press of the wind against the lower topsails and the three foresails.

John Farmer, perched in the nest, was the first to spot the Wusongkou Lighthouse. This was an important landmark because of the Woosong Bar. The location marks the spot where the Whangpoo River meets the Yangtze. The converging currents wash mud and silt, depositing the residue in a bar-like formation which all merchant ships must navigate. Mr. Stewart's chart recorded sufficient depth for safe navigation albeit a crossing of caution was the smart approach. No one wished to run Mr. Rockefeller's ship upon a sandbar.

The crew of thirty-three sailed up the Yangtze to enter the Whangpoo River. The final leg of the journey was slow and deliberate. Fishing boats and other merchant ships of varying sizes were present on the river. The river was more than 1,000 feet wide in most places and with the depth consistently measuring thirty feet. Sindia measured nearly twenty-six feet from the bulwark cap to the keel. There would be ample river depth to accommodate her draft, given her hull was laden heavy with hundreds of containers of kerosene and case oil, including many tons of stone ballast.

Mitchell, resting in his bunk, opened his mother's book and chose a reading. It was Tuesday, June 25, 1901. He was following an example set by his father and dictated by his grandmother years before. His feet and arms were tired and in a few minutes his eyelids would sag. Hopefully, a couple of hours sleep would rejuvenate his tired body. The excitement of docking at the port of Shanghai faded as he drifted into sleep.

The sun would be lifting over the horizon in a matter of an hour. S made another notch on a small piece of wood used for a calendar. Seamen acquired habits and superstitions passed down over the years. Being away from home for months on end wore on many minds. They were at sea for 158 days.

The morning sun pierced through the atmosphere and the heat would create taxing working conditions. Shanghai was difficult for the crew to tolerate in June while the residents were accustomed to the hottest month of the year. The breezes circulating air through the ship were gone. The temperature would climb to the mid-nineties today. John Farmer spotted the Standard Oil tug sent to tow them to port. Finally, docking in Shanghai was near at last.

Men pulling rickshaws were common on the street running parallel to Sindia's berth. This was the first time many of the crew saw someone from China, a land far away from the United Kingdom. They were curious since their appearance differed from the characteristics of their Celtic background. Sindia was a long way from home and for days she would sit motionless, docked on the waterfront along the western bank of the Huangpu River.

Captain MacKenzie was familiar with the port of Shanghai. Mr. Stewart was responsible to confer with the bosun to instruct the twenty-six members of the crew regarding shore leave. They would confine their visit within a designated area, the Shanghai International Settlement. There was a history behind the establishment of the settlement and the captain was aware of the details. Some of the crew wished to purchase tokens and trinkets from the streetside shops. S was the first to state his priority; the consumption of a hearty meal combined with more than a few drinks of distinct pleasure.

The helmsman, awake after a short rest, stood on the flybridge peering out to the street of Shanghai. The population of the city reached nearly one million by the year 1900. His ship was docked at the busiest port in all of Asia. Captain MacKenzie appeared on deck, clay pipe in hand. The change in tobacco was distinguishable. The aroma suggested he switched from black cherry to walnut plug, purchased straight from the counter at Ogden's in Liverpool.

Mitchell was able to ask questions others would not. The relationship grew between the two Scots but the captain wouldn't permit a public display of favoritism to any of the crew. To do so invited a potential problem.

"What is the Shanghai International Settlement?" Mitchell asked.

The captain struck a match, lit his pipe, drew in a breath and blew out the smoke. Mitchell looked at his steel blue eyes as the smoke lifted in the warm air.

"We are in a designated area established nearly forty years ago. The Qing Dynasty has ruled China for many years. The British military took possession of this area by force and established the settlement."

Mitchell always found their talks informative.

"The Treaty of Nanking established the settlement independent of Chinese law. According to the treaty, this designated area, and four other ports, would be open to foreign trade." Mitchell listened. "The British established the settlement along the river bank to further commercial interests," the captain continued.

Mitchell was fascinated with learning and he would study more of China's history for the first time in his life.

Thomas Wright was thirty-two years old. He was born in Bristol, England. The Agreement and Account of Crew listed him as boatswain; he was at sea for fifteen years. Tom was responsible for assignment of work detail on a daily basis for both watches of the crew. Mitchell peered at the line of dockworkers traversing up the gangplank, all coming to unload the ship's hold of its contents. He watched with curiosity, his eyes gazing at a people unfamiliar to Scots.

"Who buys all the kerosene?" he inquired of the captain.

"Chinese workers and farmers will purchase most of it."

"For lamp oil?"

"Aye -- about ten years ago Standard Oil began marketing kerosene to a large population in China -- about 400,000,000 people. They associated the Chinese name Mei Foo or American Trust to their efforts. Mei Foo eventually became the name of a lamp made from tin produced by Standard Oil."

"What price do you think they charge for the lamp?"

"Rumor is they give it away and if they do sell some, they are sold at a very low price. It's the kerosene Standard Oil wants to trade."

The unloading of the cargo stored in the belly of the ship would continue into the next day. Mitchell was fascinated by the new surroundings occupying most of his waking hours. S, on the other hand, boasted of his conquest in finding new food and drink to satisfy his desire.

The noon hour approached with the captain making an appearance on the main deck. He was dressed in a clean white shirt and business trousers. Mitchell and Morley sat nearby, playing a game of cards.

S pointed his index finger toward a man standing on the wharf next to the gangplank. Neither of them knew his identity. By observing his dress they reasoned he must be important. The captain proceeded down the plank, shook hands with the stranger, then after exchanging pleasantries, stepped into the rickshaw with him. They watched until the two were out of sight before dealing the next hand. Morley took his turn to shuffle.

"E.H. Fraser."

"What?"

"E.H. Fraser, that's who he is," asserted Mr. Stewart.

"Who is E.H. Fraser?" Morley asked.

"He's the British General Consul in Shanghai, that's who he is."

"An important title," Morley replied.

"His name is on the bill of lading for the shipment of boxes, all to be loaded after the kerosene and case oil boxes are gone."

Mr. Stewart stood, stretching the muscles of a sore shoulder.

"It will be to my pleasure to get rid of this smell of kerosene."

∞

The loading of two hundred tons of manganese ore was completed by the dock workers. Tom Wright gave instructions to the supervisor of the longshoremen to arrange the boxes on the floor of the lower hold. It was his job to insure they were arranged in a manner whereby the ship was properly ballasted. The conditions of the sea and the level of trim would dictate when adjustments were required. For now, he would use his judgment to ensure the trim of the ship was to his satisfaction.

Mr. Stewart reviewed bills of lading for shipment of camphor oil and reed matting. Mitchell and Morley watched while containers of goods were brought up the gangplank and loaded into the hull.

"How do they manufacture camphor oil?" Mitchell quizzed.

"It's made by distilling the bark and wood from the camphor tree," Mr. Stewart replied.

An imprint was stamped on each box. *Zam-Buk* was the name given to the wood extracted from the camphor laurel tree.

"They told me the tree is plentiful south of the Yangtze. These trees grow sixty to ninety feet tall. Anything else you want to know?" Mr. Stewart asked with a grin.

It was a very hot evening with the crew sacked in self-constructed hammocks strung between the rigging. The heat was unbearable in the fo'c'sle. The captain returned to his ship as the sun set, a package wrapped in paper was tucked underneath his right arm. Some of the crew occupied idle time carving objects from wood obtained from the ship's carpenter. The remainder, being more musically inclined, sat about playing a variety of Celtic songs; some remembered from childhood, others learned from seamen of foreign voyages. Mitchell stretched on his hammock, listening to the music, wishing for the nighttime air to cool. Stars lay speckled all across the sky, the quantity comparable to the sands strewn across the beach of a tropical island.

∞

Mart brewed the morning coffee and stirred a concoction of stew filling the pot. Warmed bread baked two days ago served with jam accompanied the meal. The crew was at port and complaints were minimal for the moment. Even S learned to eat quietly. It was the onslaught of heat that was responsible for sapping their strength, reducing their energy and need to moan about the food. As the sun rose Tuesday morning there was a renewal of anticipation for the event of the day. A tug would appear to tow them to a point where they could separate and hoist sail. The bosun hung the flag, signaling the crew to return to the ship. All were anxious to hoist sail. The port of Kobe, Japan, beckoned, and the return to the open sea and the fresh salt air were foremost in their minds.

Mitchell set his foot on the first step of the stairwell as Captain MacKenzie opened the door to his cabin. He and Sea Legs were heading atop. He motioned Mitchell to enter. It was the second time Mitchell was invited to visit Captain MacKenzie inside the captain's chamber. He pointed to a beautiful humidor sitting on top of the table. It was a gift from E. H. Fraser. He noticed a Foo-dog, bronze in color, attached to the lid as a handle. The humidor was crafted of tin. The background color for the lid and the base consisted of a blend of green and yellow. An assortment of leaves in varying shades of green adorned the lid. A plume of white feathers spread outward in front of the dog. A light blue pattern was painted around the circumference of the lid at the base. Green stems were painted on the base with an assortment of pink or white flowers attached to the stems. The same light blue design was painted around the entire bottom of the base. It was a beautiful display of artisanship.

"Captain, may I inquire of Mr. Fraser?" Captain McKenzie nodded, giving permission. "We noticed his name was marked on the boxes stored in the hold."

Sea Legs walked over to his usual spot by the captain's bunk and laid down, chin resting upon his crossed front paws.

"Your reference is to Sir D. E. H. Fraser, Acting British Consulate in Shanghai?"

Captain MacKenzie's humidor

"Aye." Mitchell acknowledged.

"This is the first time we had an opportunity to meet one another. His appointment is recent; however, I knew of his name and his reputation from a previous voyage. What is it you wish to know?"

"He must be between forty to fifty years old; how does one secure the position of consulate?" Mitchell asked.

"Your perception of his age is correct, forty-two to be exact." The captain motioned for him to take a seat in a chair.

"He said he arrived in China in March of 1880. He was twenty-one. Came here as a student interpreter."

"Is he a Scot?"

"Indeed. Home town is Portobello outside of Edinburgh. He's a highlander, same as me!" A grin broke on the captain's face.

"Tell me how he obtained his job!"

"He made a decision to enter the consular service some years ago. Many of his peers pursued scholarships and academic directions, not Mr. Fraser."

"Meaning, he had other interests?" Mitchell quizzed.

"I suppose."

"Why the three initials, C.M.G., after his name?"

"He was awarded the honor of the Companion of the Order of Saint Michael and Saint George."

"What is that?"

"It's a designated order of chivalry founded in 1818 by King George IV, acting as Prince Regent for his father, King George III." Mitchell, inquisitive by nature, was eager to learn more.

"We didn't discuss the matter; however, Mr. Fraser did allude to his service to the King. He referred to steering British communities through some difficult and sticky situations."

"Have you met others with the same title?"

"He's the first; the title is awarded to one who renders important non-military service while in a foreign country."

Time slipped away and Mitchell's welcome was nearing an end. Nightfall surrounded the settlement and it was time to disappear to the wheelhouse.

CHAPTER
25

KOBE, JAPAN

One week passed since Sindia set sail from the port of Shanghai. The sail to Kobe would cover nearly 800 miles. The easterly sail across the East China Sea was behind and the Osumi Islands were within sight. The island of Kuroshima was the first in a series of volcanic rock spectacles. It was dark gray in appearance with jagged peaks. All of the islands became visible off the starboard side of the vessel. Mitchell was behind the ship's wheel when the lookout spotted Takeshima. The following island, much larger in appearance, placed them in a strait between Tanegashima and Kyushu, the third largest of the island chain, all part of the empire of Japan. Their navigation continued as they left the East China Sea for the Sea of Japan. Sindia was an impressive sight, cutting the waves under a full set of sail.

It was July 3rd and their course was adjusted again, heading north to the Osaka Bay. The next vital navigation would enable them to pass between Tomogashima, a cluster of four islands. Meanwhile, Mitchell logged in his journal day 167 of the sail. Mr. Stewart barked orders to lower the staysails.

The port of Kobe was busy; it was known by captains for an increase in commercial western trade. They dropped anchor, docking in the bay, waiting for the opening of a berth and a tug to guide them to port. The conditions in the fo'c'sle remained intolerable. Sleeping in hammocks on deck was preferred by the crew, the climate being subtropical. Daytime temperatures would climb to the high eighties and the humidity was high. Nighttime lows dropped to the mid-seventies and rainfall was common this time of the year. Sea Legs slept next to the binnacle atop the main deck with the crew.

On Friday, July 5th, Japanese longshoremen began the task of loading cargo. Tom Wright inspected the contents as they lay under roof, protected from the weather at the terminal. Many boxes, packages, and containers of goods would be positioned in the hold. It was his job to figure out where the items would be stored, given the fragility and risk of breakage of many of the goods. The bosun would have to ballast his ship while protecting a valuable cargo destined for the retail shops in New York City. Everything would be systematically loaded, he would not let one of his ships sail absent of proper trim.

There were twelve separate bills of lading for individual consignees for fifty packages of Japanese matting. Each would require inspection and acceptance before written approval was granted by the ship's master. Tom labored, systematically reviewing another twenty-five bills of lading for other consignees for bamboos, curios, linseed, baskets and screens.

Delacamp and Co., with offices in Japan and New York, assumed the responsibility for the shipment of all pertinent goods to multiple consignees. Each bill of lading contained a description of cargo with the wording, "Being marked and numbered in the margin and is to be delivered in the like good order and condition at the Port of New York (*the dangers of the seas only excepted*)."

The document included a disclaimer; "Tin case camphor will be shipped, vessel is in no wise responsible for claims or damage arising from the contact, fumes or odor thereof." There was additional language below the date and signature line which bore the name of Allan MacKenzie, Master. "It is also mutually agreed that this shipment is subject to all the terms and provisions of, and exemptions from, liability contained in the Act of Congress of the United States, approved on the 13th day of February, 1893 and entitled, "An act relating to the navigation of vessels, etc." Captain MacKenzie reviewed every detail and signed all of the bills of lading. Looks like they covered themselves in all aspects, he thought to himself.

Mitchell watched with curiosity; this was his first interaction with Japanese longshoreman. The men were careful yet swift as the work of loading the merchandise was bound by a deadline. The sooner Sindia could leave port, the quicker the merchants would receive their consigned goods. Knickknacks, curios, dishware, cups and saucers, vases and a multitude of other household items would be gifted to family or a friend come

Christmas.

The bosun requested the assistance of Mr. Stewart and Mr. Wilkie; a second opinion for cargo placement was welcomed. Everything had to be secured in the appropriate location, given the hull would experience constant and changing vibration from the motion of the sea.

An accounting of the inventory followed. There were 2,900 cans of camphor oil and 1,656 tubs of camphor to be loaded and stored. After these items were secured, the 300 boxes of wax were put in place. The largest and most time consuming was the storing of 24,747 rolls of decorative Japanese matting. They were carefully laid on the beams of the lower deck between each of two tie plates. The last items to be loaded were 3,315 cases of curios containing fine china and other collectables. Once fourteen boxes of linseed and five cases of decorative screens were in place, all cargo was secured and approved by the bosun for transit.

CHAPTER
26

OUTBOUND

Captain MacKenzie, at his desk, sat in his Windsor chair purchased in southeast England. The humidor, a gift from Everard Fraser, revived recent memories of his time docked in Shanghai. He thought of the possibility he may never again visit the ports of the Far East. By the time his ship reached New York he would turn sixty-three years old. His career at sea was a long one filled with a vast array of experiences. Given the risks and perils of the occupation, he knew he was blessed to have survived so many years at sea. There were stories to share with anyone who would listen as every seaman knew they were tempting fate. Neptune was powerful and he could blow, sending a violent storm into the path of many a ship. It was said by the crew who knew the captain best, there was not a storm sent by Neptune that Captain MacKenzie couldn't tame.

The document set before him was titled, "Certificate of Discharge." The words on the next line followed: For Seamen Discharged before the Superintendent of a Mercantile Marine Office in the United Kingdom, A British Consul, or A Shipping Officer in British Possession Abroad. He picked up his writing instrument and began to fill in the categories, one by one.

	Name of Ship	Sindia
❖	Official Number	93757
❖	Port of Registry	London
❖	Registered Tonnage	3,067
❖	Horsepower of Engine	SV
❖	Description of Voyage	Kobe
❖	Name of Seamen	Thomas Burke
❖	Age	46
❖	Place of Birth	Liverpool
❖	Date of Engagement	18/12/00
❖	Place of Engagement	Liverpool
❖	Date of Discharge	04/07/01

The captain filled in the current date and his eyes dropped to the last group of words. I certify that ….. above particulars are correct and ….. are true and of good character ….. described herein. Two seals, one on the right, the other on the left, represented markers for the captain's evaluation of the seaman being discharged. The first, "Character for Conduct" and the second, "Character for Ability." Upon each seal Captain MacKenzie placed the imprint of a stamp stained with ink, "Very Good." When the document was turned sideways there was a line for the signature of the seamen. A second certificate of discharge was filled in for Thomas Newman, also from Liverpool. Chisaii, a sixteen year old from Kobe signed on as a cabin boy, desiring to make the trip to New York.

The anchor was weighed. The tug arrived to guide Sindia from her berth to make way to the sea. They would get underway with light sail until they cleared the four islands of Tomogashima, the vast Pacific lay beyond. Ewan Roland, steward, finished listing the stores for the journey to New York. They included vegetables, pigs, chickens, and other items for consumption, plus multiple barrels filled with gallons of water.

Mitchell remained on duty behind the ship's wheel on the forenoon watch on July 10th. The upper topsails and lower topgallants were set. The upper topgallants and the royals were loosed from the braces. Once all the mainsails were hoisted and set, the jibs and the spankers would be hoisted. The empire of Japan was to the helmsman's back and growing smaller as each half hour passed. He was crossing the Pacific for the first time and the pages in his journal would be filled with daily experiences. A total of 182 days passed since he left New York Harbor.

Tom Wright checked the trim of the vessel and found the ship to be off by four inches. The job of loading the cargo went smoothly; however, he would not be satisfied until they shifted ballast to obtain an even trim. The bosun chose S, John Rolvsson, and Albert Brother, to complete the task of shifting the ore to maintain the ship's ballast. Sindia answered the call as anticipated. Mr. Stewart was satisfied with the response of the wheel and the course of sail.

"What will be the first island to be spotted?" Mitchell asked the first mate.

"None for many miles. There are a thousand out there and our course will take us to deeper water where it's safe."

Mitchell had neither experience nor knowledge of the dangers that lie ahead.

"We'll ride the westerlies for a very long time," Mr. Stewart continued.

"What is our biggest danger?"

"There are many, mate?" Mr. Stewart replied. "Thousands of tropical islands for one, and there is also nighttime navigation to consider," he cautioned.

Mitchell thought for a couple of seconds; better to have a full moon.

"We sail east and most of the islands will lie to the southeast of our position. There are many shoals and reefs and all of these small islands are wrapped with shallow water. We have no need to risk fickle wind patterns that could land us in a dangerous situation."

∞

Mr. Stewart calculated they were north of the Johnston Atoll as it was day number 183, but the group of low lying islands were nowhere in sight. They lay in the vast Pacific and the atoll was marked as a reference point, consisting of only four small islands.

"How were the islands named?" Mitchell inquired.

"They were discovered by Captain Charles Johnston in 1807."

Mitchell was amazed at the references of history and the dates applied to the discovery of markers on their voyage.

"He commanded the HMS Cornwallis for the Royal Navy," Mr. Stewart added.

∞

Days passed and the noontime sun rose to the highest point in the sky. Captain MacKenzie, sextant in hand, obtained coordinates while calculating the ship's position. Mr. Stewart suggested the faint appearance of islands off starboard could be Kiritimati. His chart showed the island to be Christmas Island. Kiritimati was translated to describe the popular holiday. The island was discovered on the eve of the holiday by the navigator James Cook in the year 1777.

The weather was consistently pleasant. Day after day daily temperatures climbed into the seventies shortly after sunrise. Mr. Stewart, consulting his charts, had only one objective in mind. This ship would sail safely north of the many raised coral bed islands identified on his chart as Kiritimati. The crew simply knew they had passed below the thirtieth parallel and were heading toward the twentieth.

The entry in Captain MacKenzie's log would record the passage to the north of the Marquessas Islands. He and Mr. Stewart studied their chart, all with the intent to keep their vessel out of harm. The Marquesas were part of a larger group of five island chains. They included the Society Islands, named by Captain James Cook. The other island groups included the Tuamotu Archipelago, the largest chain of islands in the world, the Gambier Islands, a large grouping of volcanic origin and coral atolls, the Austral Islands and the Marquesas. A notation on the chart confirmed the islands were owned by the French as late as the mid 1800s.

No one begged the question, "How far to the Horn?" The consistency of the weather meant Tom Wright could extract as much work out of the starboard and port watches as possible. Each day could be counted on to bring full sun and temperatures in the mid-eighties. The crew spent the greater part of their shift preparing the main deck to be stained with a new coat of linseed oil. It would be slippery for the crew after application, but it was better to apply the oil now, and allow the drying process to cure before they approached the cape.

"Enjoy the balmy weather," S commented. "The further south we sail the colder and nastier it gets before we round the Horn."

The captain ordered the sails full, day after day the fair weather continued as his ship rode the trades, sailing over one hundred miles each day. Mitchell imagined his feet made an impression on the poop deck. He no longer thought a sailship would present quiet solitude. Noise was constant, an ever present voice, yet there was a certain sense of harmony. The wind blew between force four to five. His ship would creak and list while responding to the action of the swells. The rigging echoed an endless chatter as metal scraped against metal.

Luke was a Scot, a sailmaker, and he was born into the trade. He was ever present upon the deck, inspecting sails for wear, tearing, or adjustment. The captain relied on his knowledge to produce the efficiency of sail for his windjammer.

"Can you show me how you made the staysail?" Mitchell inquired.

"And when is your watch over?"

"Four bells."

"Then look me up in my shop and we'll put you to work."

Luke was fifty-two years of age. His voice was as thick as the fog sweeping into the bay at Arbroath. No doubt the rasp in his vocal chords could be traced to the years spent in cold weather conditions at sea. His clothing was modified due to the warm weather, yet it was typical of the man who was born and raised along the North Sea. His cloth trousers were suspended with leather braces and a waist belt. A leather sheath was fixed to his belt, holding his knife and a fid, used for making large holes in canvas. A variety of other tools consisting of a palm, a pricker used for making small holes in canvas, a punch set for making thimbles, plenty of needles, and a Bullock's horn were stored in his ditty box. His shirt was a knitted Guernsey with a harbor steps pattern. His leather boots were black and he rarely left his seaman's cap on the hook in his cabin.

Mitchell was surprised at the quantity of sail stored in the hull of the ship. Luke suspected the helmsman left the safety of his home in Glasgow to experience the glamor of life at sea. Mitchell knew nothing of a sailmaker's life. Conversations start somewhere so Mitchell simply stumbled his way into this one.

"Where is your home?"

"*Obar Bhrothaig* (Arbroath) is one of the places a sailmaker comes from lad."

"Never heard of it!" Mitchell spoke with a puzzled look.

The application of Luke's trade taught him patience; however, he wasn't patient with ignorance.

"The County of Angus, lad! My home is sixteen miles ENE of Mr.

Stewart's, Dundee."

"I see."

"If you aren't a fisherman, but better to be a sailmaker from Arbroath, it's likely you are employed at Webster's making canvas," he challenged.

"And why is that?"

Luke sat in his chair with a needle and canvas cloth in each hand.

"Because that is the home of Francis Webster & Sons, Ltd., lad."

"And they make the finest sails?"

"No," replied Luke.

"They make the finest canvas from flax and I use the canvas to make the finest sails!" Luke proudly proclaimed.

Mitchell thought a moment and then grinned.

"Of course, I spend a lot of time with the wheel in my hand watching your sails react to the force of the wind."

Luke, with patience slipping a wee bit further, decided it was time to recite the process, quickly and directly.

"Flax is linen, comes from linseed. The fibers are used to spin into strands. The unspun fibers of the flax plant are stronger than cotton but they are also less elastic. The finest grades are used for sheeting while the coarser grades are used for canvas."

He lifted his brow to see if his student was paying attention, he was.

"The canvas is shipped in bolts twenty-four inches wide. There are some common elements that I look for when picking canvas for sail. The first is elasticity, the higher the better for upwind sails. Then there is strength," he continued. "The breaking strength is important and it's measured per cross sectional area of the fiber. Next is creep; it's important to measure the stretch of the fiber over time."

Mitchell listened while Luke described his trade. He spoke of designing the shape of the sail, cutting patterns, and sewing techniques, all designed to fit a square-rigged vessel.

"And what about you lad, you learning anything since you signed on as an apprentice?"

Mitchell nodded in the affirmative.

"And where ye from?" Luke added.

"Originally, the Isle of Islay, then I moved near Glasgow to live with my grandparents," he responded.

"We have a Hebridian on board, 'eh!" Luke chided.

"Church of Scotland?" Mitchell inquired, noticing a St. Martin's Cross sitting on a table nearby.

"Certainly," the sailmaker replied.

The helmsman spent the remainder of the time conversing with and watching his mentor work. Luke described the process of cutting sailcloth into patterns and sizes, all to be sewn with precision to withstand the constant wear from the weather.

CHAPTER

27

ROUNDING THE HORN

Four bells of the morning watch sounded. The watchman, aloft in the lookout and dressed in winter attire grew uneasy as time passed. The sky in the southwest was partly cloudy and the wind blowing from the northwest off the Andes hailed the presence of a threatening predator. Sindia was approaching the headland of Tierra del Fuego, an archipelago off the coast of southern Chile. The territory consisted of a land of dark gray and black rocks with craggy looking spaces near reefs. It was a beautiful landscape, the fury of the ocean beating into cliffs, spewing salt water spray many feet in the air.

Mr. Stewart atop the poop deck, and Mr. Wilkie near the ship's bell, kept watch, long glass in hand, sailing toward the Drake Passage. They watched for Isla Norte, one of the smaller islands in the Diego Ramirez Archipelago, first sighted in 1619. The Isla Gonzalo was larger; however, they knew if this island was sighted first they were off course, sailing further south than intended. The chain of islands lay sixty-five miles west by southwest of Cape Horn in the Drake Passage.

S pointed to the hundreds of birds making their presence in this area of the passage. The black browed and grey-headed albatross used the archipelago for breeding grounds. They also spotted an abundance of southern giant petrels.

The name *Kaap Hoorn* could be traced to a city in the Netherlands. The name of the island at the point of the cape was called *Hornos*. The Horn was the northern portion of land bordering the Drake Passage. Sir Francis

Drake, a sixteenth century English privateer navigated these waters many years before. The passage was a 400-mile-wide span of sea between the converging currents of the Atlantic and Pacific. This was the place of the greatest challenge for many a navigator, the Horn being feared by every seaman. Many stories were recorded of countless ships disappearing below the icy waters without leaving a trace.

Mitchell learned it was safer to awake with caution when entering waters near the Hermite Islands. The ship ploughed directly into a twelve foot swell causing a thud and a jolt inside the fo'c'sle. There was no warning. With feet dangling over the bunk, his head shot forward and connected with the beam one foot above. A pounding jolt to the floor and seconds later blood was trickling over his brow, dripping slowly onto his left cheek.

S was the first to spot the bandage protruding beneath his cap as the helmsman strode up the stairwell to the deck. Red spots were visible on the white cloth protruding outside of his winter cap.

"So the Hebridian with the accent of the Clyde had a run-in this morning!"

He smiled as he slapped Mitchell on the shoulder. The helmsman, head aching, decided the best course of action was to take the wheel without rebuttal. Morley was looking forward to relief and coffee in the galley.

Captain MacKenzie, clay pipe tucked in his breast pocket, stood by the rail amidship. The triangular ship's flag flapped in the wind. The Anglo-American house flag and the ensign mirrored the same pattern. George Stewart, at the wheelhouse, cautiously watched the weather. The barometric pressure had fallen.

"Are we near Cape Horn?" Mitchell, forehead in pain, inquired.

"Today's the day mate. Could be rough sailing, this day won't end without all being alert." Mr. Stewart stared at the darkening sky. "Mother Nature unleashes nasty conditions at the Horn. Strong winds, large waves, converging currents from the two oceans and even possible icebergs. It's an exciting place to sail if your nerves can withstand the strain when Neptune turns for the worse," the first mate cautioned.

Mitchell didn't know what to say. S taught him if an apprentice doesn't know what to say, keep your mouth closed. Superb advice from one unable to follow his own directive.

"What is our current position?" Mitchell asked.

"Further south than Agulhaus is off the coast of South Africa. My chart has Horn at 56 degrees south and Agulhaus at 35. I'll get one of the crew to help with the wheel, watch the card," Mr. Stewart directed.

"And the wind is streaming off of the Andes?"

"The winds blow hard from west to east around here. The captain has more experience than I with passages of this sort. A funneling effect occurs between the mountains and the Antarctic Peninsula. It blows straight through the passage." Mr. Stewart's demeanor was ominous.

A half hour passed and Thomas Matthewsen, aloft in the nest, was staring at a series of huge, thick, black clouds, descending from the north moving toward the ship.

"LAY ALOFT, OP THE RIGGIN!" Mr. Stewart barked loudly to the port watch. He raced to the stairwell leading to the fo'c'sle and galley. "STARBOARD WATCH, STARBOARD WATCH, ON DECK!" he called with alarm.

The smell of rain permeated the air and within minutes, light droplets increased to bullets as rain pelted the sails. John Farmer climbed the rigging of the mainmast to lower sail. Losing his grip on the wet line he lost his footing and fell. Mitchell caught sight of him in mid-air as he bounced off the lower topgallant, blowing him leeward, landing on the deck. The power of the wind and the noise of the rigging muffled the sound of poor John as he lay motionless.

Sindia pitched to starboard as a huge wave crashed into her hull. Mitchell lost grip of the wheel while Morley tried to assist. Rain poured off the sails and washed over the deck. The ship broached to starboard and the bow pitched downward following a tremendous swell. The cold ocean crashed over the bow sweeping Rolvsson and John Massie down the main deck, knocking them up against the halyards. Rolvsson grabbed John by the arm and clung with the other, holding on to the line for safety.

Captain MacKenzie, stationed on the poop deck, watched Mr. Stewart moving about amidship issuing commands to the crew.

"NOW UP AND STOW THOSE SAILS!" Mr. Stewart yelled with a ferocious command.

Mitchell watched in amazement as fearfully, Ed Reed, Alex Kinnaird and Thomas Fitzpatrick struggled with footing on the ratlines, climbing out onto the lower leeward yards. They were suspended sixty feet in the air over the ocean, cold wind and rain beating against their backs. The wheel pulled away from Mitchell's hands as Sindia plowed through a swell, violently crashing into a trough. The leeward yard of the mizzenmast tilted to starboard, two of the crew came close to being catapulted into a hissing ocean. The ship righted and the hull began a pitching motion to the port side. The sea swelled and another wave broke over the deck, washing over everything in sight, spilling through the starboard side. Mart, tossed in the galley, struggled to his feet as water came gushing through, sweeping banging utensils and food in its path.

A half hour later the storm passed as quickly as it came. Droplets of water continued to fall on the remains of the skysails, left to hang from the braces after the crew unsuccessfully withdrew to safer places. The sky to the northwest grew brighter; however, clouds remained for the duration of the day. Mitchell remained at the wheel, shivering from the wet and cold. Hopefully squalls like the one that passed would not be encountered again.

Mitchell, following a reprieve, was back at the helm when Mart struck six bells of the afternoon watch. It was late in the day when a large mountainous shape became visible off port. The dark jagged terrain separated the middle of the island from the west side to the east. The middle portion jutted upward toward the sky, rising above the ocean floor. The whole side of the mountain was sparsely covered with patches of a green moss-like substance. Mitchell was looking at Cape Horn for the first time in his life. Captain MacKenzie, clay pipe lit, puffed and blew billows of smoke as he surveyed the site. Sea Legs lay undisturbed behind the Binnacle.

"The mountain is about 1,400 feet above sea level." the captain commented.

"Scary morning," Mitchell replied.

Captain MacKenzie, feet spread for balance, surveyed the coastline, ignoring the comment. Moments passed.

"The closer we come to the Horn, the steeper and wilder the waves become. Risk and peril come with the job when rounding the Horn. Two currents converging with the shifting winds produce a front," the captain cautioned. Mitchell listened, nervously. "The Horn's climate is subpolar, cold weather is prevalent much of the year. This crossing was one of the easier ones. Other masters have encountered the presence of rogue waves, some towering halfway up the mainmast," Captain MacKenzie recalled.

Mitchell, dumfounded, was grateful for the horror to be over.

At one bell of the first dog watch the sun broke briefly behind the clouds. The Pacific was behind and the southern Atlantic beckoned a welcome. It represented the gateway to a return to the long awaited New York Harbor. The presence of small dark islands continued to mark the ship's progress, as they continued toward the eastern pointe of *Isla de Los Estados*. Mitchell observed the presence of sea life spread amongst the far southern portions of South America. The albatross, with a gigantic wing-span near ten feet circled off the stern. Petrels dove into the sea, then lunged skyward carrying small fish with their talons. The prions, displaying a bluish gray upper body could be spotted as well. Shearwaters also made their presence known. Mr. Stewart lent his long glass to Mitchell as penguins could be spotted dotting the cliffs of the isle.

∞

Mr. Stewart knocked on the door to Captain MacKenzie's cabin, notifying him as instructed the night before.

"Captain, we're approaching Pernambuco."

The captain finished an entry in the ship's log. Sindia left New York 296 days ago. This was the morning of November 9, 1901; Sindia was passing off the coast of South America and it was summer in the Southern Hemisphere. The recorded temperature as of 7 A.M. was 68 degrees.

Mitchell took his turn behind the ship's wheel, sun glistening over the deck. Captain MacKenzie offered his usual morning greeting, passing by, striding to the taffrail. All was quiet as Mr. Stewart caught up with the captain.

"Took the calculations myself, captain. Our location is latitude 5 N., longitude 25 W."

Captain MacKenzie, standing at the stern of Sindia, stared toward the west into the sea. His face solemn, as if paying homage, remembering. As morning passed Mitchell stood beside the first mate, by the wheel, into the early afternoon.

"Mr. Stewart, may I ask a personal question?"

The first mate nodded in agreement.

"Captain MacKenzie appeared more serious than usual this morning. Is there anything wrong?"

"He was remembering, he requested he be informed of a specific latitude and longitude off the South American coast."

"Where are we?" Mitchell asked.

"North of the coast of Pernambuco, Brazil."

"And there must be some special meaning to this location?" Mitchell had permission to press on with his questions.

"We were passing latitude, 5 N., 25 W., Captain MacKenzie lost a friend at sea at that location."

"What happened?"

"It's more like a story, a sad one, very sad."

"The Talookdar was the 183rd sailship, a windjammer, built by Harland and Wolff, and purchased by the Brocklebanks for their East India trade. The date was December 12, 1890. Talookdar sank, her fate from an accident."

A sharp chill ran through Mitchell's spine. "Tell me what happened!"

"Talookdar, like Sindia, was a steel hulled square rigger. Captain A. J. Orr was in command with a crew of thirty-five. They were on a run returning home, sailing north of Pernambuco. A collision occurred with another ship."

"Do you know more details?" Mitchell asked.

"Certainly! Talookdar was in service for five years, making the Calcutta runs. The ship was commanded by a series of masters, those being Captain Ellery, Captain Orr, followed by Captain Marley, and on that fateful night, Captain Orr."

"A sinking at night!" Mitchell shuddered.

"Talookdar left the doldrums and picked up fresh breezes, catching the northeast trades on a starboard tack. They were laden with hides, jute, linseed, and wheat. It was 3 A.M. and they collided with a German ship, iron hulled, Libussa, bound for Valparaiso."

"There was a rescue made, of course!" Mitchell hoped.

"Eight of the crew saved, twenty-seven were lost, drowned, including Captain Orr. Take a good look at the size of that mainsail," Mr. Stewart pointed aft. "Their sail broke from the mast and came down, enveloping many of the crew in lifeboats in the water."

The story was told, once again, by Mr. Stewart. He left Mitchell's side, for the moment, the helmsman was speechless.

CHAPTER
28

OCEAN CITY LIFE-SAVING SERVICE
1901

There was a large sign printed in black capital letters hung on the wall facing the doorway inside the life-saving station.

"YOU HAVE TO GO OUT BUT YOU DON'T HAVE TO COME BACK!"

This was the slogan greeting each surfman when they entered the doorway of station #30. At the opposite end of the room was a second sign with two words, capital letters, all in black.

"PROFESSIONALISM AND FITNESS."

Many a surfman was asked to live by the code described in these words. Some could not so they severed employment. They never knew when an event, a mishap at sea, would require them to risk it all, to rescue a crew on a ship in distress.

A Red House was often built to the dimensions of forty-two by eighteen feet. The roof was shingled and the sides were painted in red. There were forty-seven of them dotting the coastline from New Jersey northward through Long Island and into New England by the year 1873.

On this particular morning, John Mackey Corson sat at his oak desk in the life-saving station, located at Atlantic Avenue and Fourth Street. An envelope addressed to him from Mr. Sumner Kimball was deposited in the mail box posted near his door. It was the responsibility of Mr. Kimball to supervise periodic inspections of each of the stations placed in service. He ascended to the role of general superintendent of the National Life-Saving Service in 1871.

Keeper Corson was born on March 19, 1853. His ancestors settled along the Jersey coast in the 1700s. In order to fulfill his duties as keeper he left his native Seaville and took up residence on Peck's Beach. On October 1, 1876, he secured employment at station #30 at the age of twenty-three. In his letter of application he listed his occupation as fisherman. During the ensuing years there were six from the Corson family, all from Seaville, employed at the same station.

The inlet at the south end of Peck's Beach separating Ocean City from Strathmere was named after the Corson family. It was the same inlet John Peck negotiated with his whaleboat, 200 years before. The beauty of the inlet changed as the ocean's current swept a continual stream of sand southward, sculpting the contour of the beach and dunes surrounding the inlet.

In 1901 Keeper Corson was forty-eight. He stood five-feet, nine-inches tall, his shoulders were somewhat rounded. His hair was silver and gray, a moustache of similar color was trimmed close to the corners of his mouth. His hands and arms were strong and powerful. His uniform consisted of a black waistcoat, double breasted, with eight brass buttons lined two each side by side. A black cap, circular on the top with a short rounded brim, sat on his head. His pants were matching black and hung over his leather boots. This was the traditional uniform worn by each surfman.

The crew of the Ocean City Life-Saving Service was employed to be on duty for ten months of each year. The period of service started by August 1 and concluded by May 31 of the following year. Townsend Godfrey was forty-two and came from Cape May County. He was born in 1859 and was employed at station #30 as early as 1880. The patch on his sleeve designated him to be rank #1. Francis Corson, age forty-seven, was born in 1854 and resided at Seaville. He came to the life-saving service on December 1, 1901, ranked #5. William J. Chadwick, age thirty-two, was born in 1869. He was formerly a fisherman, employed at the station in 1898, filling rank #4. Mulford M. Jeffries was born in 1866, aged thirty-five, and formerly a fisherman. He began his service in 1893 and was ranked #2.

Ralph Jones was a surfman, ranked #7, with previous service from 1898-1900 at Tathams life-saving station, located on the island seventeen miles below Ocean City. He was twenty-eight, born in 1873 and was looking for a new job. Keeper Corson offered him a position as a surfman, rank #6, on December 1, 1900. Joseph D. Norcom, age forty, was born in 1861 in North Carolina. He was formerly an experienced sailor and boatman before accepting his job at station #30 in 1897. He was ranked #3. Harry Young was born in 1863 and was thirty-eight years old. He was a former boatman and a temporary surfman. He came to station #30 in 1898 and was ranked #5.

The life-saving station was constructed of wood and built to stand two stories high. Two large sliding doors with three glass windows in each separated left and right to gain entrance inside. A white two-railed fence was built around the perimeter of the station. Sand dunes sprouting wild seagrass grew around the perimeter of the property. A twenty-foot lookout was constructed on top of the inverted V shaped roof. Glass windows provided the watchman a panoramic view of the island and the ocean, high enough to see over the dunes. A flag pole ascending higher than the building was erected next to the station, safely within the confine of the white fence. The American flag, announcing the home of the life-saving service, waved in the gentle breeze.

Shaking sand off his boots he called to the keeper as he closed the door securely behind him.

"It's a cold one John. The sun feels good so I walked down to say good morning to the surf."

Keeper Corson heard that one before.

"She's awake indeed. The wind is kicking up a northwest blow and there are plumes of spray lifting five feet in the air."

He poured his first cup of coffee and pulled a wooden spindle-backed chair closer to the desk. Townsend Godfrey was one of two surfmen to hold the rank of one, the other being Francis Corson, a relative to the keeper. Both of these surfmen were able bodied and designated to step in and fill the keeper's job in the event he could not.

Townsend noticed the envelope on the desk. The keeper, knowing his thoughts, explained.

"It's a directive from Sumner Kimball, he wants to see an updated report."

Each man knew Mr. Kimball employed officers from the Revenue Cutter Service to serve as inspectors. It was their job to ensure that all life-saving crews were well drilled and each of the stations were inspected and in good working order. The surfmen had to be skilled in flag signaling, for instance. They carried two flags, one red, one white, and they were cut to form a rectangle three feet by five feet in size. Signaling was practiced on the beach every Wednesday afternoon. A red flag represented a dash while the white flag a dot. The flags were used to communicate letters spelling words using Morse code. By raising signaling flags in patterns, the surfmen could send a message to a passing ship.

CHAPTER
29

SOUTH ATLANTIC

The captain and Sea Legs entered the chart room. Mr. Stewart was reviewing his chart covering a portion of the Atlantic.

"It's going to be close. We can make port in time for the Christmas holiday. The merchants will be short on time to receive the merchandise they wish to market to the shoppers."

"It isn't good news but it is what we anticipated," offered Captain MacKenzie. His brow dropped with concern.

"Luke has sail crowded on and if we're lucky to make eight knots, we might be at the harbor by the 14th. That is an optimistic view, my calculations suggest this is the most favorable scenario." Mr. Stewart forecasted.

Captain MacKenzie stared at the chart, head tilted to one side.

"We have to maintain full sail and hope for as much blow as we can muster. The merchants taking consignment of the shipment will be upset with any delay."

The captain was aware of the time constraint and focused on impatient shipowners. There were no excuses offered when docking at port after the expected arrival date. To do so invited a shipowner to pass over one master for another when offering a new command.

"We've got to push mate, we crowd the sails on for now," the captain added. "They knew the risks but it will fall to my shoulders."

Mart appeared on deck and sounded four bells of the afternoon watch. Word spread and there was a buzz about the ship that New York Harbor was only days ahead. Morley took the wheel so Mitchell could rest in the fo'c'sle. He was well acquainted with the rolling and pitching, depriving him of rest while flat on his back in a wooden berth, approximately eighteen inches wide. The constant presence of water and mist about the ship gave Mitchell time to relish the thought of stepping on land once more. After a brief respite in New York, he would set sail for England and return to Scotland. His father often referred to the green Isle of Islay in the native Scottish Gaelic, "*Eilean uaine Ile.*" Perhaps he would visit his mother's grave. That would have to wait, he pondered. There was a lot of sailing to complete before he could allow his mind to think of that day.

The afternoon passed and they watched the sun set off the port side. Morley, sometimes the poet, thought to himself, Red sky at morning, sailors take warning, red sky at night, sailor's delight. Clouds increased throughout the afternoon and there were no rays from the sun attempting to break through the thickening atmosphere. Morley repeated the phrase aloud as the captain appeared at the wheelhouse.

"Reminds me of Shakespeare," responded the captain.

"Like a red morn that ever yet betokened, wreck to the seaman, tempest to the field, sorrow to the shepherds, and woe unto the birds, gusts and foul flaws to herdsmen and to herds."

John Morley glanced at the captain, puzzled by his words, holding his tongue. Captain MacKenzie read the morning sky and was reflecting on the evening event too. His knowledge of analyzing weather was vast given his days at sea. They were all at the mercy of the ever-changing wind patterns. The captain lived upon the waves of the sea for many a night. Long enough that he reasoned a red sunrise suggested particles aloft in the sky were part of a force sent by nature, an indicator that a system just passed from the west. A seasoned captain, it meant make preparation, a storm system may be moving to the east. The morning sky was a deep fiery red and it could be a forerunner of high water content coming in the atmosphere. He turned from the taffrail to head for the stairs.

"John, rain is coming!"

Mart prepared the first round of the evening meal. The starboard crew was present; he would have to suffer through raggedy insults, reflections of his cooking, then the port crew would show up and repeat the process. S was reliable and known for a curt comment or two upon digging his spoon into the bowl. He didn't disappoint this particular evening, muttering to

Jim Long sitting across the table.

"Only a few more days of feed for the hogs and we can dig into real food when we get to New York!"

Everyone expected their portion of each meal to be found in the wanting, this far into the sail. Thomas Fitzpatrick purposely maintained a look of displeasure on his face, yet he picked up his spoon and said not a word.

Clouds continued to thicken and by late evening, Mother Nature produced light moisture in the air. Mitchell was watching port side for any land mass, although he knew they were simply too far out to sea for a sighting to occur. They were many miles from land yet his wandering eyes kept vigil. Silently he hoped for a glimmer of light, something to pick up his spirit, and suggest the voyage was near its end.

Mr. Stewart spoke of passing by the outermost portion of Cape Hatteras on a previous voyage. Charts were his business and he knew of the shoals spreading outward for miles from the barrier island. George was told of stories of large waves crashing the beaches of Hatteras Island. Mitchell remembered that Mr. Stewart cautioned him to watch for a change in direction and increase in speed. This would signify to an east-bound ship they were leaving the Gulf Stream and entering the Labrador Current.

The Atlantic currents made for excellent travel for sailships, except in the area of Diamond Shoals, just offshore at Cape Hatteras. The warm Gulf Stream collides with the colder Labrador Current, creating ideal conditions for powerful ocean storms and sea swells. Both Captain MacKenzie and Mr. Stewart were warned of the large number of ships that ran aground because of shifting sandbars. Mitchell, alert at the helm, waited for the prophesied response of the ship's wheel.

CHAPTER
30

BERMUDA,
COASTAL CAROLINAS

Mart's mental clock woke him up early on the dawn of December 8th. The sun was preparing to breech the surface of the horizon. Three bells sounded notifying the starboard watch they were on duty. Morley stood at the wheelhouse for the better part of fifty miles. The sun broke through the horizon off starboard. He watched the array of color as it splashed into the atmosphere, mixing orange and red to form varying shades of pink. The sky reminded him of a painter's pallet.

An hour passed when John Farmer, manning the crow's nest, detected a spot off the horizon. Spray leaped from the water spewing over the bowsprit as Sindia plunged into the trough after a swell. It was difficult for the second mate to hold fast and draw his long glass for a closer look. Mitchell's eyes fixated on Mr. Wilkie, serving as his pair of eyes looking out to sea. Any obstacle, a danger to the path of their vessel must be spotted. Several minutes passed when the lookout bellowed.

"LAND PORTSIDE!"

Mr. Stewart, summoned from sleep, bounded up the steps two at a time. A quick stumble interrupted his path to the taffrail as she pitched in a downward motion into another trough. He took hold of the edge of the taffrail, steadying himself. Sea Legs, startled, responded with a quick bark, then seconds later, lowered his head to doze once more.

"We should be passing to the east of Bermuda," Mr. Stewart announced. "My calculations suggest the Florida current is nearing an end. The current has been with us since we rounded the tip, carrying us. I think we're near the Gulf Stream."

∞

As day turned to night the ship's senior officers conferred in the chart room. All agreed it would be the force of currents, wind, and course adjustments that would propel Sindia to make New York Harbor by December 15. It was time to consider another course adjustment since the captain was pushing to make up for lost time rounding the Horn. His chart was spread on the table with rules and instrumentation within reach. Past research and records of passage suggested Bermuda was 700 nautical miles from the New York Harbor. This distance in mind, his calculations proved they could be in the harbor in four to five days. Sindia would be dockside by December 14, eleven days before Christmas. It simply wasn't enough time to have the entire manifest unloaded and distributed to the stores for the merchants.

Mr. Wilkie was making rounds, inspecting the ship. Thomas Matthewsen climbed the rigging to the nest preparing to cover the last dog watch. Between the two it was a lonely place to find oneself, out in the Atlantic on a December's eve, darkness, except for a few lit lanterns about.

Below the wheelhouse in the privacy of his quarters, the captain prepared another entry in the ship's log.

Saturday, 7th December, 1901. South Atlantic, afternoon breezes favorable, Gulf Stream, Bermuda sited during morning watch. Latitude 32 degrees, 22 minutes, N, Longitude 64 degrees, 47 minutes W. 5 P.M., heavy clouds. W.S.W. wind, increased moisture, force 4. Barometer 29.3, falling.

∞

Mart sounded four bells of the morning watch. The sun didn't break over the horizon on Tuesday the tenth. His bones reminded him that cold, damp, December air would reign for the remainder of the sail. The cook wished for the warm weather days sailing the Pacific Ocean, and he knew they escaped the hurricane season of the Atlantic. These storms were massive, covering hundreds of miles, and they spawned in warm ocean currents off the coast of southern Africa.

"An ominous warning for this morning's weather," Mart muttered to

Louis, standing nearby, swabbing the deck.

He looked up with eyes fixed on the crow's nest. Richard Parker was engaged in his own responsibility, head bent toward the eastern horizon, eyes fixated on the sea. Mart whistled to draw the attention of the ship's watchman. Sindia pitched to port and the thud of the bow slammed into the sea, startling the second mate. Mr. Wilkie was on many a voyage, his legs adjusted to the roll of a ship as she pitched with each wave. His body and mind were attuned to every present changing condition at sea.

Mitchell watched the captain as he studied the ocean current, the wind conditions, and the atmosphere.

"Bad weather coming?" Mitchell called to the captain as he turned from the rail.

"We have a front moving in, could be in for a toss, will take more time to tell," the captain suggested. The captain and his first mate conferred as customary. "Full sail for now, we'll push her for speed and keep watch on the conditions," the captain ordered.

His morning stretch and observance complete he went below to his cabin. The entry in the morning log and a study of the chart confirming their position was foremost in his mind. His calculations suggested they left the Florida Current for the Gulf Stream. Watching for a shift in the current's direction, the Labrador Current would carry them to New York.

Log entry: Tuesday, 10th December, 1901. 6 A.M. Thickening clouds, deteriorating weather, barometer 29.1, wind, 11-16, force 4.

∞

Sindia sailed in the Gulf Stream as the current increased with warm seas moving into the western North Atlantic. The plan was to tack W.N.W. toward the coastal Carolinas using the wind off the port quarter. They would take advantage of land generated wind patterns then change course eastward toward North Carolina, sailing northeast across the Atlantic Ocean. Mr. Stewart concluded the velocity of the current would be swift near the surface, the maximum speed near five to six nautical miles per hour. The average speed of the Gulf Stream was closer to four nautical miles per hour. The current would slow to a speed near one mile per hour as the current widens to the north.

Thomas Matthewsen descended using the lines from the nest. Some of the rungs were worn and one was broken. More repairs he thought to himself. The moisture clung to the wires overnight. With thirty feet to go his right hand slipped from its' grip and his body flung away from the line, swinging toward the lower topgallant. The sail formed a hollow spot in the response to the wind as he pushed off the brace. The wind, reflecting from the sail, blew his body toward the line and he grabbed hold to stabilize himself once again. Go slow Mitchell thought to himself.

The thought of a broken arm or a bent leg was not to a seaman's advantage. Had he fallen overboard, being swept into Neptune's graveyard was very real. He might have viewed his fate as easier to endure compared to the pain and suffering of mangled limbs or a broken back. Between the swift current and the speed of the ship, he would have ten minutes before going under, permanently. Once he met his fate the food chain of the Atlantic would be increased by one.

Mitchell said nothing of the descent as Thomas limped toward the wheelhouse. Paul Nolan, his replacement, climbed the rigging to the nest.

"No more sightings of islands for the rest of the journey," Thomas called.

"It's the cold air I'm thinking about, no more warm tropical days," Paul responded.

"Fifteen days away from Christmas. The shipment of trinkets, assorted housewares and fine wares may not arrive on the shelves of the stores in time for the holiday," Thomas added.

Captain MacKenzie and Mr. Stewart exchanged opinions about their position and the condition of the sea. The Beaufort Wind Scale lay on the upper left corner of the table, although they rarely resorted to it. The information contained in the scale was emblazoned on each of their minds. The wind increased from force two to five in a matter of twenty-four hours. The two were anxious because Mother Nature could spoil their plan for a safe, timely arrival in the harbor. Force two meant wind speeds between four to six knots. A light breeze and the ocean would generate small wavelets, crests a bit glassy with no breaking.

"Conditions are changing, Mr. Stewart," cautioned Captain MacKenzie.

The onset of morning brought increased wind speeds between 17 to 21 knots. Waves formed between five to eight feet.

Mr. Stewart would go up top shortly.

"What about whitecaps?" the first mate inquired.

169

"They're scattered, leave the sails in place but we maintain a watch."

Mr. Stewart left the chartroom for his own inspection of the changing weather. The foresail, mainsail, and mizzenmast sails were blowing full, all the way up to the topgallants and skysails. An artist would have a beautiful picture to paint as it was always an impressive sight. Sindia was riding westward seas off port and there was a strengthening list leeward. The repetitious backwash of waves could be seen starboard. The pitch will increase, he reasoned.

"Beginning of wild seas," S relayed to Tom Wright as he cleaned the deck below.

"Perhaps, ready for rough seas are you?" Tom questioned.

"Always, the warm tropics are behind and now, well, it's time to deal with the angry Atlantic --- feels like I'm coming home."

S was used to the shallow North Sea where weather was nasty and seas were rough. Captain MacKenzie heard the bell sound eight times of the last dog watch. He penned an update to the ship's log.

Tuesday, 10th December, 1901. Force 5 wind, 17-20 knots, pattern shifting, barometer 29.0.

∞

"Tam," as the Scots on board Sindia referred to the bosun, dispatched some of the men on the starboard watch to clean brass fittings and polish the metal surfaces. He would improve the appearance of the ship for entry into the port in New York. The cans of paint and varnish were stowed in the hull before they passed Bermuda.

Boyd McAndrew, the carpenter, was busy checking the fore, main, mizzen, and jiggermasts. He climbed the ratlines to inspect the braces to make sure there were no cracks in the wood, splinters or fissures that could spell disaster if indeed winds increased. Boyd chose to inspect the low lying braces while sending S, Rolvsson and Fitzpatrick up the rigging. They would inspect the heights he had no intention of climbing, not on this day.

The starboard watch displayed signs of restlessness. They were thousands of miles into the voyage and food supplies dwindled as fast as the morning buns at Mrs. B's bakery in Liverpool. Erickson, suspended from the brace securing the mizzen topsail called to Mr. Wilkie.

"Itchy backside mate, I'm getting an itchy backside!" George turned his head to look at John Farmer, dangling from the brace.

"We need a rough sea to liven it up," S droned on.

The port watch crowded round the galley for the mid-day meal. Chisaii sounded eight bells of the forenoon watch. Although all were hungry, but disappointed, no one dared to complain about the pea soup and bread. The bread was left over from Monday's bake and the salt air hastened the hardening to a crusty state. The soup was the weakest display of slop in a bowl that S had tasted for some time. He mused that even Sea Legs hesitated to chew on Mart's second day old bread, dropped on the deck for his consumption.

Rain moved in during the latter part of the afternoon and into the evening watch. Albert Brother, donned in oilskins, prepared to climb aloft for the first dog watch. The evening sky brought thick clouds and more rain blown by the cold December air. It felt like small particles, creating a sting on the portion of his face left uncovered by his beard and moustache.

Morley held the wheel, his eyes moving port to starboard, knowing the dullness of the task would eventually bring boredom and tiredness. Donned in oilskins and rain coat, he was alone as the starboard watch was ingesting the evening meal with hesitation. There were signs the wind speed was increasing, his hold on the spokes of the wheel, required additional effort to steady the ship's course. There were no longer any stars or an evening moon to provide reflection of light on the sea. It was a lonely place, yet a desirable place if alone you wish to be.

S couldn't resist spending an evening by the wheelhouse with a fresh breeze driving rain into his face. It was another opportunity to exchange tales with the helmsman. Sea Leg's fur was wet on the outer edges but completely dry under the layers near the skin. It was the benefit of being bred for water, a yellow Labrador was suited for weather turned foul.

"Sea Legs, down to the cabin!" Morley commanded.

Finishing his early evening walk on the deck, he sidestepped down the stairs and scratched on his master's door. It was his time to enter the warmth and dryness of his favorite place for the rest of the evening.

"Where do you think we are?" Morley elevated his voice to be heard above the wind and rain.

The Norwegian grinned and shook his head. "Somewhere northwest of Bermuda, unless this weather moves quickly, captain will be forced to rely on his judgment and dead reckoning for a while."

Morley stood by the wheel, course set, the ship plowing into waves eight feet high. Visibility was low with a cold rain beating into his stubbled face.

"Now you know why I grew the full beard," S added. "We're in for a hard blow, Neptune has a rough ride in store."

The North Atlantic was S's home, his place of employment, and at times, some decided he thought a dangerous amusement.

CHAPTER
31

MARK GRAY

It was a cold December morn as breezes swept into the bay from the ocean. Captain Peter Lynch crossed over the Maine Railroad tracks heading north toward Waterman's Wharf. The wharf was built alongside the Mystic River in the Charlestown section of Boston. His responsibility for this trip was to take command of the Mark Gray. He was very experienced and loved to sail. The wooden construction of the ship was what he loved the most.

The owner of the three-mast schooner was M. A. Osborn. One of his business ventures included procuring small shipping engagements from acquaintances and friends. Many of these were contracts for shipping goods along the eastern seaboard of the United States. Osborn purchased the vessel from J.S. Emery & Co., following a dispute whereby the owners filed claim for financial damages against Venezuela. The ship was chartered for a run to Maracaibo; however, events following the docking complicated the return voyage.

The Mark Gray was constructed in 1882, the ship being of local pride. The original launch was in North Weymouth, Massachusetts. Lynch preferred three-masted schooners and simply put, he was anxious to get underway. His mind was preoccupied with the view of the upcoming sail he knew well. They would sail out of the Mystic, down the Boston Harbor, and into the North Atlantic.

The ship was registered as #9145, the mark of a vessel specializing in mercantile trade required for identification. The length of the hull was

124.5 feet and the beam from starboard to port measured 32.4 feet. Set in the water, the three-masted vessel drafted a total of 9.3 feet. The gross tonnage of the ship totaled 308.

Captain Lynch hoisted the flag containing forty-five stars of the United States. He greeted his crew of seven by the gangplank, as they set about making preparations for their departure. The walls in the chartroom were outfitted in cherry wood. The protective stain provided a beautiful enhancement to the richness of the interior of the room. Peter and his first mate, Richard Brown, studied the chart to be used for their navigation for the initial leg. The Mark Gray would set sail without cargo, using stone for ballast, bound for the port of Brunswick, Georgia. On docking at Brunswick they would pick up their payload of molasses, rice, and sugar, and return to their native port of Boston.

SOMEWHERE IN THE ATLANTIC

Mr. Wilkie was the second officer to set foot on the main deck. Mart sounded the bell and descended down the stairs to the galley, for another round of morning breakfast preparation and dispensing hot coffee. Morley stood by the wheel, struggling to maintain the position on the card. Winds were blowing force five and the sea churned many whitecaps with huge spray.

Captain MacKenzie and Mr. Stewart studied the chart depicting the coastal Atlantic region of South and North Carolina. Chisaii delivered coffee while they discussed weather conditions and location. Captain MacKenzie pointed to the chart, speculating they could be off course by 200 miles, somewhere off the coast of North Carolina.

His morning log entry:

Wednesday, 11th December, 1901. Northwest of Bermuda, bearing NW, force 5 winds, waves 8 to 10 feet, weather conditions deteriorating rapidly.

The day passed slowly as the weather thwarted the barque's progress. Mitchell took his usual turn spelling Morley at the helm while S, occupied with duties, kept up the banter. All grew tired of his prolonged discourse for the love of bad weather.

"Do us a favor and jump off for a wee swim," invited Morley.

S grinned and responded. "I would, Mr. Morley, but would you come about to pick me up?"

BOSTON HARBOR

Morning passed and the Mark Gray departed from the dock. The helmsman turned to starboard heading down the Mystic River, passing underneath the Chelsea Bridge where the Chelsea River empties into the Mystic. Another turn to starboard and the schooner was bearing south, approaching the United States Navy Yard. Numerous wharfs came into view, portside, lining Border Street. Boston Harbor was a busy shipping port in December, 1901.

Within minutes they entered the mouth of the Boston Harbor. Captain Lynch ordered the upper sails set. The Mark Gray responded by picking up speed when the sails were braced. The southern tip of South Boston could be seen to port and the wind increased as they sailed into wider waters. The first mate watched as he piloted the ship east toward the south side of Governor's Island.

Captain Lynch wanted his ship trimmed to perfection before they entered the North Atlantic. The Mark Gray passed to the north side of Lovell Island and the helmsman adjusted course southeast, in order to put the Great Brewster Island to port. He was anticipating a series of markers known as Boston Lights, which would appear on the port side guiding their path into the ocean.

CHAPTER
32

OCEAN CITY
DECEMBER 14, 1901

"Get going old Buck, you'd think I have a lot of time but not today."

Bertram Darby was an enterprising young man fifteen years of age. He was in no mood to be sitting atop the wooden bench of his father's delivery wagon, this particular Saturday morning. Years earlier, his father founded the Philadelphia Laundry Plant. Bertram, together with his younger brother Roy, was actively engaged in working at the Ocean City branch.

The seaside community grew to a small town with more than 1,300 residents and more would follow with each passing year. There was one delivery wagon for the town's laundry business. Bertram was in charge of the care of Buck, and most importantly, anything to do with the maintenance of the business. This included feeding and brushing old Buck, and sometimes it meant scooping up road apples, depending upon where he deposited them. Asbury Avenue metamorphosed into the business district and old Buck knew one of his stops was in front of the Swarthmore Hotel. He could use a rest for a spell while his owner delivered a weeks' worth of clean laundered sheets.

"Good morning Ralph!" Bert beckoned to the surfman as he tied old Buck's rein to the metal post.

It was raining the entire morning and there were signs the weather would worsen during the day. Ralph Jones was employed by the Ocean City Life-Saving Service. He wore his uniform with pride and the number six was visible, sewn on the upper left sleeve.

"You got the last watch tonight?" Bert inquired as they met near the gate. "It will get nasty before it gets better," he added.

"Harry Young and Ed Boyd will be covering the last watch tonight." Ralph seemed anxious to get to the corner pharmacy.

"They're in for a soaker of an evening!" Bert lamented.

"Yes, I'll take to the comfort of my warm home tonight."

"Tell 'em to keep a sharp eye out tonight," cautioned Bert. "Rough ocean, rain and howling wind --- it's not a good forecast for ships on the ocean tonight, is it Ralph?"

Bertram was too young to become a surfman besides, his younger brother Roy was too young to run the branch of the family business. Ralph, his mind preoccupied, kept on walking. Delivery complete, Bertram climbed up to the bench and squawked to his horse.

"Go Buck, speed it up, let's get back to that dry barn!"

Around the corner and a few blocks later, women gathered at the First Methodist Episcopal Church. They carried colorful red ribbons and holly, all in time for Christmas decoration. Bert pulled on the rein to make old Buck turn right toward Wesley Avenue, where he would drop off the last delivery of the morning.

"Good morning Mr. and Mrs. Corson," Bert called.

The keeper of the life-saving station, his wife, and their youngest daughter Inez, were walking to the corner store. Cold damp days frequented the month of December. Visitors, enjoying the refreshing salt air and beach during warm summer months were gone, but the permanent residents remained. The shop keepers will close early this afternoon, Bert thought to himself, as he swung the last of two baskets into the wagon. He hopped to the seat and reached for the reins.

"Go Buck!" Bert jiggled the leather straps. "Let's go old Buck," he demanded again. "I can smell the hot chowder mom is warming on the stove."

Buck responded one leg at a time, as one horse shoe after another pounded the hard packed sandy street, eleven days before Christmas.

Peck's Beach required two life-saving service stations by the time 1900 came to a close. Ocean City's Station #30 took responsibility for patrolling the upper half to the midstation at 34th Street. The Peck's Beach Station covered the midstation to the lower end of the island. They combined resources any time the situation required cooperation. John Mackey Corson was in command as keeper of station #30, and Adolphur C. Townsend was employed as keeper at the Peck's Beach lower station.

The roll of surfmen acting under the keepers' command included Townsend Godfrey, who attained the rank of #1, Mulford Jeffries, listed as #2, Joseph Norcum, #3, William Chadwick, attained the rank of #4, Harry Young, #5 and Ralph Jones, #6. John Mackey's relative, Francis Corson, and Edward Boyd were employed as surfmen as well.

It was the responsibility of the keeper of each station to maintain a list of all the equipment available for life-saving and rescue operations. Each station had one galvanized iron surfboat. They maintained 180 fathoms (six feet per fathom) of hawser, 300 feet of hauling line, nearly 600 yards of rocket line, projectiles, and sundry equipment.

The keeper maintained a log of the surfmen on patrol. This included the watch patrolled, the duration of the watch, and weather conditions. The rules and regulations required all of the crew members to train consistently and become proficient with four skills. They were routinely tested for the set up and efficient use of the Lyle gun, the breeches buoy, the Merriman suit, and flag signaling.

The Lyle gun was developed by Captain David Lyle of the U.S. Army, along with the assistance of life-saving service officers. A small brass canon was used to fire a fourteen-inch bullet shaped projectile, attached to an eyebolt fastened to the rope. In practice, and as they found in rescue operations, the line could carry a distance of four hundred yards.

The breeches buoy rested on two short thick wooden planks, cross linked for strength and stability. They positioned it on the sand as the apparatus held the buoy and the lines. An anchorage in the sand was required for the equipment stabilizing process.

The crew brought shovels for each set up to be used to prepare the buoy for operation. Two tally boards were fixed to the line and sent out to the ship's crew. The boards listed the instructions to be followed. Other equipment included a hawser cutter, block and tackle, and a heaving stick. An oval shaped weight was attached to one end of the line secured to the heaving stick. The rescue concept was to toss the line to a survivor of a wrecked ship within a distance of fifty yards.

The breeches buoy consisted of a pair of short-legged oversized canvas pants, sewn to the inside of a circular life preserver. The line shot from the Lyle gun was attached to a heavier whip line, which in turn was secured over a pulley. In the event of a rescue attempt, the line, shot to the ship, would be secured by the crew and tied to one of the ship's masts. The whip line was pulled by the surfmen to bring out a heavy hawser on which the breeches buoy could ride.

The Merriman suit was a full body rubberized covering with the exception of the face. The suit could be inflated for swimming or buoyancy in cold water, if for some reason the breeches buoy was ruled out in the rescue effort.

The surfmen developed into physical specimens due to the combination of the demands placed on their bodies, their fitness training, and the nature of the drills. They would load the equipment on a beach cart and slip a harness around their chest. The harness was attached to the cart so they could haul the cart to the site of the drill or the shipwreck.

The keepers and the surfmen were well aware of the risk of a failed mission. The drills, week after week, and year after year, were planned rescue missions, all in preparation for a real emergency. The best crews were able to fire the Lyle gun, rig the breeches buoy, and haul a stranded sailor down from a wreck in a few minutes. The keeper had little time to decide if the rescue should begin with a Lyle gun and the breeches buoy, or, would a surfboat rescue begin immediately. The stranded mariner's odds of a safe rescue increased dramatically, once the life-saving service was on the scene.

In 1901 the crew for each station was employed to be on duty ten months of the year. They were paid $65 per month for service from August 1 through May 31 the following year. The number one surfman was paid $70. The keeper was required to live at the station, his yearly stipend being $1,000. J. Mackey was asked why a surfman would take on the risk and responsibility of the job. He thought but three seconds, grinned, and replied.

"They are a caring bunch, they admire and embrace professionalism --- my men know boats and beach lore inside out."

CHAPTER
33

NORTH JERSEY COAST

The seven member crew of the Mark Gray passed through the mouth of the Hudson to the New York Harbor around four o'clock in the afternoon. Signs were about, an impending change in the weather was possible; however, there was no expectation of a storm. That is, not one of a significant size, one that could impede safe passage to Brunswick, Georgia. Nightfall came early given the state of the atmosphere and it was December. The sky darkened with the advent of thickening clouds. The air was damp and the captain suspected rain was coming.

By six o'clock in the evening it was raining and by eight o'clock, Captain Lynch ordered the entire crew on deck. Wind speeds increased during the afternoon and evening, and now blew force six. A storm blowing in from the southeast brought wind speeds up to twenty-two to thirty-two knots. First Mate Brown strained to see through the rain. Seas were running heavier with wave heights between eight to thirteen feet. Spray broke from the whitecaps as they slammed into the bow. Poor visibility took over and navigation was difficult. The senior officer found it nearly impossible to rely on dead reckoning to determine position.

The force of the wind caused Captain Lynch to tack in a south by southwest direction. He ordered the braces angled to minimize the impact of the force of the wind on the canvas. Within the next hour he decided the conditions warranted taking in sail to reduce speed, maintain trim, and stabilize the 249-ton vessel. Brown went below deck to check the ballast for any shifting, increasing risk, by altering the trim of the hull both fore and aft.

∞

Ninety nautical miles south along the coastline in Ocean City, Joe Norcom was assigned the six o'clock to midnight watch at station #30. He was outfitted in oilskins and equipped with a Waltham pocket watch, four Coston flares, and the key to the timeclock, to confirm his arrival at the 34th Street checkpoint, Peck's Beach.

Joe was forty years old. Prior to accepting and training for this position, he spent most of his time as a sailor and boatman. He knew the surf and was well acquainted with bad elements on this particular evening. Head bent to the sand with his rain hat blowing in toward his brow, he patrolled near 10th Street, heading south to the checkpoint.

The wind was strong and he reasoned no one should be out in these conditions, but there were ships passing from the north to south. There were shipping routes and tacking patterns for sailships to follow, and the substantial deterioration in weather was simply another challenge. Rain set in and he sensed it would be a long time before it stopped. Patches of fog scattered the coastline of Peck's Beach. He had seen this before and the pattern of weather promised it would deteriorate before it got better.

Bill Chadwick, at the southern end, patrolled the beachfront to the checkpoint at 34th Street. At thirty-two, he was a fisherman for many years prior to enrolling with the life-saving service. At this time of the evening he was positioned approximately a half-mile north of Corson's Inlet. The wind howled and the rain pelted his back. He was barely able to keep his head up while scanning the sea. His experience taught him weather conditions would deteriorate, and he was hopeful ships navigating the seas would receive safe passage through Neptune's battlefield. His task was to patrol the beach between 34th Street and Corson's Inlet until relieved.

∞

Mitchell was given a reprieve from the ship's wheel while John Morley stood outside in the foul weather, clinging to the spokes to maintain course. He had no way of knowing if the ship was being blown off the captain's intended course. Mr. Stewart became restless due to the increased deterioration in weather. Seas were very rough and navigation had been rendered difficult. The royals were blowing full on the fore, main, and mizzenmasts.

Luke conferred with Captain MacKenzie since it was his suggestion to haul in the staysails. He estimated the wind elevated to force 7 with swells running twelve to twenty feet. White foam blew off the tops of the waves and disappeared through the darkness. Conditions changed drastically. Morley struggled to keep the wheel in line with the card, fearing the ship could shift from their intended course. Mr. Stewart ordered Frank Hudson to stand on the opposite side of the wheel, to provide Morley the stability required to maintain their heading. Thomas Fitzpatrick, donning oilskins, would stay aloft in the crow's nest until his watch ended.

∞

As the evening advanced it was clear the Mark Gray was shrouded in a serious coastal Atlantic storm. Captain Lynch was genuinely concerned for the safety of his crew and the security and ultimate fate of the schooner. The vessel was constructed with a low freeboard therefore waves crashed into the hull displacing water over the entire deck. They passed the Sandy Hook peninsula and conditions turned foul quickly. The glow from the Fresnel lens of the lighthouse was momentarily distinguishable. It, being the oldest in the United States, was in continuous service since 1764. The structure stood ninety feet high and the lens, beckoning many a captain and crew since 1857, was a constant welcoming site.

Navigation with instrumentation turned useless without visibility of the stars. Captain Lynch was forced to revert to instinct and dead reckoning. Winds were near force six with wave heights estimated between eight to fourteen feet. Plenty of white caps were visible and spray was breaking off of the waves. Lynch was a bold master and fearless in the presence of bad seas; however, his instinct told him they should have put into New York Harbor, to ride out what was to come. It was the potential duration and veracity of the unexpected that plagued his mind.

∞

The grandfather clock struck eight times on the evening of the fourteenth. Reverend Lake was situated at his desk, kerosene lamp lit, and writing instrument in hand. His thoughts turned toward Sunday morning's sermon with his notes from the book of Luke. In chapter 3, Luke, the doctor, outlined the lineage of Jesus, listing each generation by name, from Joseph back to Adam. Christmas was eleven days away. The theme to his message was, "Who brought hope?"

The church was established by the reverend and his family plus a few friends. The congregation was young yet flourishing. Newcomers representing future residents were purchasing building lots along established roads named West, Asbury, Central, Wesley and Atlantic Avenues. The new settlers of the seaside community would promise to adhere to the laws dictated by the Ocean City Tabernacle Association. Each ordinance was incorporated into their deed as a restriction when they purchased land.

∞

Joe Norcum arrived at the midstation, drenched from the rain. The wind was ferocious and his head ached from the assault upon his forehead. His hair was soaked from water seeping under the brim of his hat. Four more hours for his leg of the patrol was a daunting thought. It was time to rest in the wood sided shack and key into the clock, confirming he reached the southernmost point of his patrol.

The door to the shack blew open from the pressure of wind and rain as Bill Chadwick entered.

"We've got near gale conditions out there mate." Bill announced.
Joe nodded in agreement as he stripped a pair of wet socks from his feet, reaching in a pouch for a dry pair.

"How was it coming up from the inlet?" Joe responded.

"Heavy mist at first, increasing winds, then rain swept in; started light but its heavy now."
Joe's face was wet and his skin was red from exposure to the elements from the storm.

"Wind blew me up the beach, had to pull my feet from sinking into wet sand. It was work but not as hard as your patrol. And now the wind will blow me back to Fourth Street while you put your face to the gale," Joe chided.

"Think of the crews working the ships at sea tonight! Not a night to be adjusting sail!" Bill cautioned. "I couldn't see past the waves. Fog moved in and visibility was reduced to the second row of breakers."

Bill pulled the key from his pocket and inserted it into the timeclock, confirming he completed this leg of his watch.

"My bones have been telling me this will worsen before it breaks," he lamented.

CHAPTER
34

ISLAND BEACH, N.J.
DECEMBER 14, 1901

Wind swept up the beach blowing sand with fury. The surfman patrolling near Toms River knew a gale set in from the southeast. Nor'easters brought heavier wind damaging low-lying coastal areas. The southeasters rode in with heavy rain and often dangerous fogging conditions.

Toms River Life-Saving Station #13 was built directly on the beach at Decatur Avenue. The station was manned with surfmen beginning September 15 through the following April 15th of each year. The Atlantic was known to be fierce this time of the year. The original station was a scant twenty-foot storage shed located to the rear of the new building. It was constructed between 1898 and 1900, but the new building was a beauty.

The two story dwelling was built with wood and resembled a Cape Cod dwelling. The front of the building faced the Atlantic Ocean. There were four glass windows on the south side and two large windows next to the front porch facing the ocean. A name plate for the station hung directly over the middle of the porch. The main floor was designed to contain a kitchen with living quarters in one large room. A long wooden table was set up for feeding the entire crew of seven.

The second story of the building was shaped in the form of the letter L; a portion of the roof faced the ocean, the second section was built at a ninety degree angle facing south. The interior consisted of one long spacious room designed to house the entire crew while on duty. Each surfman had their own bed and footlocker used for storage of personal belongings.

A brick chimney extended above the second story in between the joined sections of the roof. The first floor extended past the front porch, a distance long enough to accommodate two bays with doors that swung open. The two surfboats were mounted on a wagon drawn on four forged metal wheels. The boats were stored inside the building. In between the main floor and the storage wing was a cone-shaped two story structure designed to be a lookout. Glass windows were installed on the second floor. The entire perimeter of the property contained a white slatted three foot high fence. A weathered flag of the United States flapped from the pole outside the station.

∞

By eight o'clock in the evening of the 14th, Captain Peter Lynch and First Mate Brown realized the Mark Gray was in peril. They were in for the fight of their lives. The crew of seven remained on deck to assist with the battle to survive. High winds, large swells, and driving rain impacted visibility and navigation. The captain assumed his vessel was driven off the intended course.

It wasn't long before the helmsman could feel the ship leaving the outward flow of water. They crossed through a shelf referenced on their chart, a fixed point where an undercurrent descended through the Hudson River, into the mouth of the New York Harbor, emptying into the Atlantic. Lynch thought they were paralleling the North Jersey coast however, he would have been confident of their position if the Barnegat Lighthouse were spotted.

Old Barney was rebuilt in 1859 from plans developed by Lt. George Meade, a Union Army engineer. The lighthouse rose 160 feet in the air, a twelve-foot flashing Fresnel lens was erected inside the glassed housing. Brown was watching for the beacon with the hope of confirming their location. The Barnegat Inlet had a reputation for dangerous navigation, but once inside the bay, it would serve as a safe haven for a ship waiting for a storm to pass. The alternative, fighting a ferocious storm at sea, increased the risk of wrecking a ship with potential loss of life.

The small town of Toms River rested inland approximately five miles from the coast. There were no other towns located along the coastline known as Island Beach, the formulators of the life-saving service came from the nearby town. Dangerous weather conditions required the keeper to maintain a life-saving crew at the Red House, until the storm showed signs of subsiding.

Captain Lynch ordered sail reduced from two of the masts. The helmsman could feel the force of the waves pushing them starboard. The pressure to maintain position was beyond his capacity, he slipped and was tossed when the ship quartered the rough sea.

Brown yelled profusely from the starboard side of the bow. Fog was thickening as patches would blow through. He spotted what no seaman wished to see. Spray was breaking from the top of huge following waves pushing violently to the shoreline.

"BREAKERS, BREAKERS AHEAD!" he screamed in panic.

The sound of his voice was muted by the wind. His warning caught the attention of Captain Lynch. He maneuvered along the port side grabbing onto the rail to steady himself. His heart sank and his eyes widened as he spotted what his first mate saw.

The Mark Gray heaved forward in a pitch-pole motion due to the force of a monstrous wave. The stern of the ship was caught at a sixty degree angle to the beach, then lifted by the force of the wave and pushed forward in a violent crashing manner. They were hopelessly lifted by the force of a wave so strong, the stern slammed downward, violently, with a loud resounding crack. All of the crew was thrown to the deck; the cold seawater engulfing the surface. White foam was present everywhere as the stern scraped along the bottom of the seabed.

The entire crew was catapulted toward stationary objects fixed to the ship's deck. Captain Lynch struggled to his feet and made way for the ship's wheel. Brown stood when another wave struck the ship and the force heaved the hull of the ship upward. The wave passed by and the hull of the Mark Gray struck the floor of the ocean a second time with intense force. Darkness covered everything. The crew, fearing for their lives, grabbed nearby rigging for security to raise their body above the seawater rushing over the deck.

First Mate Brown scrambled for the box containing the flares managing to locate a dry Coston. Striking the tip, he ignited the flare and held it securely in hand. Surfman Joe Smires of the Toms River Life-Saving

Service patrolled Island Beach that evening. His spotted the glow from the flare and pulled a Coston from his pocket, struck the ends, and ignited a spectrum of yellow and brilliant red-orange flame. Captain Lynch, First Mate Brown, and the crew of the Mark Gray saw the flare, realizing they had run aground near an inhabited shore.

Joe turned in the direction of Decatur Avenue to alert the remainder of the crew and initiate a rescue attempt. Station #13 was manned by Keeper Elwood Rogers. His crew consisted of two brothers, Thomas and Dillon Wilbur, and Charles Bozier, Peter Newman, James Applegate and George Everingham.

The ship stranded a distance of one-and-a-half miles south of the life-saving station. Adrenaline surged through Joe's veins --- his heart was pumping so fast he felt as though the flare had ignited inside. His senses were adjusting to what he saw, and the fact that he and his crew were about to be thrown into a rescue attempt. Everything must work according to plan. All of those days filled with hours of drills were about to be tested.

The crew sat around the table playing cards when Joe thrust the door open, bursting into the room. Each wore their LSS cap, circular, flat on the top, with a band around the perimeter located above the brim. All sported a handle bar moustache.

"We've got a schooner stranded in deep trouble south of the station!" he said, his voice quivering.

Jim Applegate stood by the stove pouring a second cup of coffee. Captain Rogers instinctively sprung from his chair while the remaining surfmen scattered from the table. All made way to the racks of oilskins hanging on the hooks on the wall.

Tom and Dillon Wilbur were the first to open the door heading to the apparatus storage area. George opened the other side of the double doors making preparation to hook up to the harnesses. The Lyle gun, breeches buoy, and the rescue apparatus were mounted on top of a wooden wagon measuring six-feet long by five-feet wide. The Wilbur brothers reached for the heavy roped harnesses and slipped them around their neck with one side hanging over their shoulders. They were quickly followed by Pete and Charlie who copied their action. The four positioned themselves in front of the cart and prepared to lurch forward in a pulling position. Jim and George stepped over the frame in the front, and bent to lift the wooden frame to within waist length. Captain Elwood Rogers and Joe Smires, already puffing from the walk up the beach, would man the rear position of the cart.

The Wilbur's led the crew of eight, proceeding across the beach toward the surf. Wind beat in their faces and rain hammered their brows, running into their eyes. They made sure the kerosene lantern was lit and positioned on the surf side of the cart, hoping the ship's crew would spot them as they moved down the beach, through the veil of fog. Tom shouted to turn right as they neared the surf within reach of the hard packed sand. The one and one quarter mile trek would sap some of their reserves. The metal wrapped around the circumference of each wheel helped to move their apparatus through the sand toward the Mark Gray. Captain Rogers checked his pocket watch noting the time advanced to 9:30 P.M. when they arrived on the scene.

First Mate Brown signaled from the bow of the ship, holding another Coston flare. The crew, having seen Joe's flare approximately one hour prior, knew help was in motion. Joe split off the back of the wagon while Captain Rogers barked orders to position the cart and setup the apparatus. The crew began the process of unloading the cannon and breeches buoy. Meanwhile Joe reached for another flare, shielding the ends from the rain, he successfully ignited the flare, producing a brilliant red-orange plume.

Captain Rogers directed his surfmen to mount the Lyle gun on the beach. Jim and George worked in unison to set up the rigging for the breeches buoy. They continued their setup for the rescue while members of the Island Beach Life-Saving Service Station #14 made way to assist. Their station was three miles to the south of the stranding. A few of their surfmen donned life preservers covered in cloth filled with cork for buoyancy. They were determined to save all of the crew in the event they were called upon to enter the surf for rescue assistance.

The crew of the Mark Gray suffered battered bloodied hands as they clung to the rigging, waves crashing over the deck. The fog drifted and they spotted flashes of light from the lanterns spread on the beach. This was the first time the crew were part of a stranding of a schooner in a coastal storm. Captain Lynch and his crew clung to the jiggermast located at the stern. Their hope was to reduce the potential of injury, even death, as they anticipated a projectile coming toward the ship momentarily.

The wind would not subside but the shifting fog provided windows where they could see the stranded ship. Darkness continued to limit visibility as the crew from Island Beach arrived on the scene. They were ready to assist in any possible manner, awaiting orders from Captain Rogers. They completed the setup of the rigging and stabilized the breeches buoy.

George was preparing the charge since the cannon was in position. Joe lit another flare to signal the crew.

"Let them know we are engaging the rescue operation!" shouted Captain Rogers.

Joe responded by igniting the flare and standing erect on the beach facing the ship, he waved the flare in an arching motion, first to the right, then to the left, stopping for five seconds. He repeated the motion waving the flare in the same direction.

Waves continued to crash over the deck. Captain Rogers ordered the cannon to be repositioned, facing toward the front of the ship. Upon signal, George lit the charge. Within seconds the crew of the Mark Gray heard the blast, watching a brilliant flash of yellow light with sparks of blue and white interspersed. The cannon boomed, yet the sound was muffled by the veracity of the wind. The projectile spewed forth from the mouth of the cannon and the line made a whirring sound as it cut through the air. The first shot landed directly across the vessel. The crew spotted the line tangled in the foremast. First Mate Brown moved cautiously to retrieve the line and attach it high on the mast.

The waves continued their assault on the port side of the vessel. With each passing swell the Mark Gray shifted as the hull was forced into the bed of sand. By the time the breeches buoy was readied, the vessel was listing at a forty-five degree angle toward starboard. The surfmen attached the breeches buoy to the line and pulled to send it out to the listing vessel. One by one the crew took turns sitting inside the canvas sack attached to the line. The crews from Toms River and Island Beach worked in unison to bring each of the seven to safety.

CHAPTER
35

THE SOUTHEASTER

Saturday's sailing conditions were difficult and the evening weather would turn foul and unfit for sailing. Captain MacKenzie and Mr. Stewart conferenced in the chart room; meanwhile, the sea continued to rage. Sea Legs curled up in the corner seeking respite from the storm. The room was dimly lit, two lanterns opposite each other hung on the walls.

The look on the captain's face told all. "Where are we?" Conjecture, estimation, and dead reckoning using best judgment were the weakest of navigational tools available. The captain studied the chart with deliberation.

"Our likely position is east, northeast of Virginia." Mr. Stewart spoke first. "But how far out to sea are we?"

"We need a break in the weather so we can use the stars," offered the captain.

They knew there was no reprieve in the offing. Captain MacKenzie raised his head and looked at Mr. Stewart.

"We may have 400 to 500 fathoms (2,400 to 3,000 feet) beneath us. Unless we are not where we think we are. We may have blown west."

His first mate pointed to the chart, locating the mouth of the Chesapeake Bay. If they were blown off course the ocean depths would decrease abruptly. Mr. Stewart suggested they alter course easterly seeking a possible change in the pattern of the storm.

"We increase risk by heading toward land but we might find relief, calmer sea, and time to take a sounding."

The captain contemplated his suggestion, his clay pipe in hand, smoke circling the ceiling.

"If the fog breaks, in time we should spot light from the shoreline," the first mate added.

Captain MacKenzie decided to stay the course and retired to his cabin, Sea Legs in tow. His confidence, wavering, he wanted their position confirmed. That evening he recorded an entry in his log book.

14/12/1901, 8 P.M. Force 8, fresh gales, thick weather, rain, increasing wind, visibility poor.

The port watch remained on deck since their assistance was required to make the necessary adjustments to the sails as ordered. The wind pressed the royals on the fore, main, and mizzenmasts to the fullest. John Morley and Frank Hudson stood at opposite ends of the wheelhouse, feet anchored on a slippery deck, determined to maintain the set course as wind and rain swept across the ship.

The eve of the fourteenth was not a night for sleep. It was impossible for a seaman to succumb to slumber in the fo'c'sle. The ship pitched with the rough seas resulting from near gale conditions. David Jackson remained at the nest, eyes set like a hawk, squinting into rain, watching for any signs to obtain a fix for position. White spray leaping off passing waves came over the bow.

At ten o'clock Captain MacKenzie took to the main deck, rain gear covering his torso and wet weather boots for traction. Mr. Stewart joined in the watch. Luke was about, surveying each of the sails for possible tears. The temperature decreased and the rain turned to snow with ice clinging to the rigging. The officers didn't want to risk a blowout of a mainsail in these conditions, since there continued to be no sign of abatement of the storm. The crossjack was taken in and secured.

Tom Wright was in the ship's hold, lantern in hand, inspecting all of the cargo bays for dryness and safety of the ship's merchandise. Albert Brother joined in the process. The bosun needed to report on the placement of the ballast and the ability to maintain the ship's trim. The boxes containing manganese ore shifted so he secured Thomas Brown and Jim Long to help with righting the misplaced boxes. Moisture was present but the lids remained secure, thus avoiding exposure to the elements. There could be no water infiltration to the ore at this stage of the journey.

Mart grumbled about the bloody weather, the constant pitch of the ship, and now the ice and snow. It was midnight when he struck the bell eight times of the first watch, Sunday morning, December 15 had arrived. David

Jackson, relieved to hear the bell, began his descent down the lines from the nest. Easy does it, careful, David spoke to himself. Broken footholds were to be avoided if he was to set foot safely on the deck. John Brown was prepared, reluctantly though, to take his place at the watch.

"Mr. Brown," Mr. Stewart called, before he began his ascent. "Be alert, no break in the weather; if visibility improves we're looking for lights and land. We need a sounding and a fix of our position and direction."

John nodded as he began to climb the line to the nest. The captain ordered lookouts to be changed every two hours replacing the customary four-hour watch. Aroused from sleep, Mitchell donned his oilskins to begin the middle watch at the helm. Morley stayed on with Mitchell while Hudson looked relieved to be spelled.

"Sailing's been rough and the wind and snow will try your perseverance," shouted Morley. "Wish we knew where we were," he added.

Mr. Wilkie, at the flybridge, surveyed conditions, while dismayed at the weather and roughness of the sea. Luke nervously finished another round of sail inspection. The captain retired below as Sea Legs followed.

The crew, following orders, backed the afteryards and braced the foreyards, preparing to round and take the first sounding in a long time. Mr. Stewart stumbled toward the taffrail and lowered the marker line with bucket attached to draw sand from the bottom. Mr. Wilkie stared as the first mate stumbled as the ship rolled.

"Amazing how the pitch makes a man look like he's had a couple of nips!" Morley remarked to Mitchell.

The first mate lowered the bucket and waited for drag, sensing the bucket grounded, he raised it to inspect the contents. He pulled the bucket from the sea, saw white sand, and counted thirty-six markers, indicating as many fathoms (216 feet) of ocean beneath. Mr. Stewart emptied the contents overboard and stumbled toward the stairs, leading to the lower deck and the chart room. He surmised that the findings aligned with their discussion on position earlier in the day. Sindia must be further east than anticipated.

His entry in the log book, 15/12/1901, 12 A.M., sounding 36 fathoms, white sand.

Their decision to sail east increased the threat of approaching shallow waters. The storm would not abate. Hopefully they would spot the lighthouse leading to the New York Harbor.

CHAPTER 36

SOUTH JERSEY COAST DECEMBER 14, 1901

Reverend Lake finished the review of his sermon and retired for the evening. Harry Young, a former boatman and newly hired surfman, left for patrol from station #30 at 4th Street on Peck's Beach. He was used to foul weather so he knew what to expect during the next four hour watch. The low cloud cover acted as a sound barrier as the surf crashed with a crescendo on the beach. His destination was the middle station over two miles down the coast. Ed Boyd arrived at the Peck's Beach Station to begin his northward patrol to the midstation at 34th Street.

∞

By one o'clock in the morning on the 15th the storm increased to gale force conditions. Mitchell and Morley were fighting the wheel to maintain a steady course, into the blackness of the night through the driving snow. Captain MacKenzie ordered the upper topgallants on the fore, main and mizzenmasts to be hauled in.

Thomas Matthewsen, secure in the nest, tilted his head away from the wind and snow. He made an occasional turn into the elements, shielding his eyes, attempting to peer through the foul weather surrounding the barque.

"LIGHT, I SEE LIGHT!" he screamed as loud as his voice would allow.

Mitchell jerked his head upward hearing his voice.

"LIGHT SPOTTED!" The words were repeated, loudly, two more

times. "LIGHT SPOTTED --- LIGHT SPOTTED!"

Mr. Stewart slipped and stumbled, rushing to the wheelhouse. Thomas, his left arm flailing, clung to the mast with his other arm, pointing into blackness veiled with passing shrouds of fog. Mr. Stewart reached inside his coat for his long glass. It was nearly two-and-a-half feet in length, covered in a circle of brass at one end, about two inches in circumference. A black band wove around one end and it was cased in brown leather.

Several minutes passed before Mr. Stewart laid eyes on the welcomed sight. The temperature moderated and mixed rain and snow turned to light rain. At last light appeared, if their calculations were correct, they crossed the Atlantic and were positioned off the North Jersey coast. Thomas spotted light from the lighthouse at Sandy Hook, the mouth of the Hudson River was near.

Mr. Stewart, thinking the depth of the sea sufficient, decided to stay the course and ordered Mitchell and Morley to follow the direction set on the card. The snow changed to rain and there was no sign of a decrease in fog. The roughness of the sea spawned whitecaps. The Atlantic routinely splashed over the bow of the ship as it plunged into the trough of each passing wave.

∞

Harry Young was the first to check in at the middle station. His legs felt like lead and he was tired from the constant barrage of wind and rain. He sat for a spell, rested, and reached for the biscuits with jam stuffed inside his pocket. The wind was gale force and it howled relentlessly, pounding against the wooden sides of the midstation. He inserted his key into the timeclock confirming he reached his destination. There was no indication Ed Boyd had checked in from his leg of the patrol.

∞

Mitchell and Morley remained steadfast at the wheelhouse. Mitchell grabbed his wrist and winced in pain when the spoke on the wheel broke his finger, slipping from his grip. A glance toward the crow's nest revealed a drenched watchman, looking for any sighting to assist their navigation into the Hudson. The temporary abatement of colder air brought slightly warmer conditions, increasing the thickness of fog. Mitchell became anxious because it was difficult to see beyond the bow of the ship. The wind remained constant and the intensity of the rain continued to drive upon his back.

∞

Edward Boyd, long departed from Peck's Beach Station slogged northward through the sand. He spotted the ghostly figure of the midstation in the distance. Harry Young, patrolling northward, completed his round arriving at station #30. He entered his progress in the log kept on the keeper's desk.

15/12/1901, 9 P.M., gale conditions, heavy seas, rain, thick fog. He would complete one more pass to the midstation and return to 4th Street, where he would wait for the arrival of the next surfman covering the 12 to 4 A.M. shift.

∞

Mitchell battled to stay on course with Morley's assistance at the wheel.

The watchman bellowed, "LIGHT OFF THE STARBOARD BOW!"

Wilkie heard his call and remained at the bow, hoping to confirm his sighting. The fog would not abate and Mitchell peered into the veiled atmosphere with a look of puzzlement on his face.

"Who could see anything in these conditions?" he called to Morley.

Both of them stared at the nest waiting for further response. Mr. Wilkie peered through the fog off starboard with an alarmed look on his face.

Thomas's voice rang louder this time. "LIGHTS OFF THE STARBOARD BOW!" he yelled again.

Mr. Stewart immediately caught a glimpse of raging breaking surf, panicked, and turned toward the wheelhouse.

"PUT THE HELM HARD TO PORT!"

The fog changed from a thick veil to a lighter shade increasing visibility rapidly. Mr. Stewart waited, his eyes signaling alarm.

"SHE WON'T ANSWER THE CALL!" Mitchell frantically yelled to Mr. Stewart.

Mr. Wilkie met Mr. Stewart at the helm, both straining for evidence of

196

location. The watchman's voice boomed and with every ounce of volume that his voice could muster, he yelled. "BREAKERS AHEAD --- BREAKERS AHEAD!" The pupils in Mr. Stewart's eyes dilated in shock. The ship's bow pointed to the south, with breakers to starboard, Sindia was pressed by the wind into dangerous shallow water. Mr. Stewart turned toward Mitchell and Morley and yelled, reacting to impending disaster.

"HARD TO PORT --- HARD TO PORT --- PUT THE HELM HARD TO PORT!" Mr. Stewart screamed in near panic.

The helmsmen grabbed the passing spokes and turned the wheel desperately. The crew could not reposition the braces and the wind caught the sails from the southeast. The force of the wind blowing on the sails pressed the ship leeward toward the breakers. The helmsmen fought the wheel to turn her into the wind, but the ship failed again to answer the call.

Thomas watched the flurry of panic below. The crew, yelling, scurried about; a wave washed saltwater over the bow, Mr. Stewart and Mr. Wilkie screamed orders, the men of the port watch rushed toward their stations. The fog momentarily dissipated and more lights were visible. Not one light but many more, a series of lights lined in a row. Where were they --- where was the mouth of the Hudson?

His heart sinking, Mr. Stewart realized they were nowhere near the entrance to the New York Harbor. He hastened to the stairs leading to the lower deck, yelling as loud as his voice could carry.

"ALL HANDS ON DECK --- ALL HANDS ON DECK!"

The crushing blow of a wave struck the port side causing him to lose balance and fall. His feet were swept from underneath him, the pitch of the deck caused him to stumble as his head struck the side of the doorway to below.

Mitchell and Morley continued to steer to port but to no avail. The braces shifted causing the blow from the storm to push the ship leeward. Mr. Stewart and Mr. Wilkie persisted, beckoning all hands from the starboard and port watches to man positions and await orders. Sea Legs, excited, barked loudly, waking the captain from a brief slumber. Captain MacKenzie heard panic outside his cabin.

"BREAKERS --- BREAKERS IN SIGHT --- BREAKERS AHEAD!"

He rose rapidly considering the darkness and pitch of the cabin. He stumbled and fell as he reached the second step from the top. Ewan bent to lend him a hand but he fell backward tumbling down several steps. His left leg flung outward, catching and entangling in the railway against the side of the stairwell, while attempting to break his fall. Struggling to his feet he grabbed his leg, agonizing in pain, and limped to the deck to find Mr. Stewart in the malaise of bodies moving about the ship.

Mr. Stewart yelled to be heard above the crew, the noise of the wind, and the onslaught of the surf.

"LIGHTS SPOTTED OFF STARBOARD FOLLOWED BY BREAKERS, CAPTAIN!"

Sindia was pushed in a westerly direction by the force of the wind. Mitchell and Morley struggled in their effort to guide the ship away from the breaking surf into deeper water. Captain MacKenzie barked orders to back her off with the yards. His eyes locked with Mr. Stewart's and they read the fear in each other. The thought of an impending shipwreck so close to New York was unthinkable. The captain considered dropping anchor but reasoned there was a high degree of risk the ship would drift over top of it.

Mr. Stewart passed the order to back the yards of the royals and upper and lower topgallants. They would attempt to position the sails to take advantage of the force of the wind to turn the ship to deeper water. The violent surf assaulted the hull pushing her leeward. A ferocious wave caught Sindia broadside, the hull began to heave and drop with a thud as the wave forced the bow downward on a sandbar. A loud grinding noise could be heard from the depths of her hull. Some of the crew were catapulted from their feet. White foam swept over the deck and water drenched the struggling seamen, tossing them about like clamshells being rolled on the shoreline during an incoming tide.

The keel of the ship dug into the sand and most of the hull lay upon the shallow bottom of a shoal. She began to list to starboard as the wind continued an assault on the sails and the sea pummeled her from port. S rose to his knees and grabbed hold of a belaying pin to pull himself to his feet.

"DAMN YE NEPTUNE --- DAMN YE," S roared with frustration. "YOU'LL NOT WRECK US," he wailed. "OFF THE BAR --- WE'LL GET 'ER OFF THE BAR."

Luke watched hopelessly as a couple sails blew out of the bolt from the intense pressure mounted by the wind.

∞

By 3 A.M., Harry Young, head down, pressed into the wind and darkness. Rain beat on the brim of his hat. Somewhere near 14th Street he paused, lifted his head, noticing breaks in the fog. Shifting his gaze seaward he couldn't believe his eyes. Several lights flickered as the wind and wild sea battered the hull of the ship causing Sindia to list leeward.

The fog passed and patches of gray gave way to improved visibility. Harry watched as the huge sailship lay stranded between the pounding surf and the blackness beyond. Mortified, he couldn't believe what his senses confirmed. His hands shaking from the cold, he reached into a pocket and retrieved a Coston flare. Several strikes later the flare lit and spewed forth a brilliant red orange flame in the blackness of night. The flare was held as high as he could, waving it in a half-moon pattern from his right to his left. He felt a surge of adrenaline and slowed the motion of his wave, hoping a ship's officer would respond. Five minutes passed and his flare burned out. Edward Boyd, nearing the midstation, stood motionless, feet planted in the wet sand at the edge of the surf. Looking northward he spotted the glimmer of a flare. Seconds later, the light extinguished and the blackness of the night returned.

∞

Thomas climbed down from the lookout, slipped, and fell on the deck. The lines were wet and his hands were cut and bleeding. He saw the red orange plume of light from the Coston flare.

"LIGHT ON SHORE!" he screamed. "I SPOTTED A FLARE FROM THE SHORE!"

He repeated his words, looking about to find one of the ship's officers. Captain MacKenzie, reeling from the injury to his leg, didn't see the light before the night extinguished the glow. Mr. Wilkie was the first to retrieve a flare. He ignited the fuse and held it skyward with an outstretched arm. A trailing flame of bright light glowed into the nighttime sky.

Harry Young slugged southward, now standing on the beach between 16th and 17th Streets. Edward Boyd was surfside south of the midstation. Both spotted the flare offshore. The image of a huge merchant sailship with several lights aglow was stranded, engulfed in the breakers and rough sea. Harry struck another Coston flare, signaling until it extinguished, and proceeded to station #30 to mount a rescue. Ed Boyd, over a mile south, watched the response to the ship's signal from the edge of the surf. He turned to head back to the Peck's Beach Station, notify the keeper, and gather a crew for what he hoped would become a valiant rescue attempt.

∞

"SHIPWRECK AT 16th STREET!"   Harry screamed as he burst through the door to station #30.

A light glimmered on the first floor but no one was present. He raced up the stairwell to arouse Keeper Corson and the rest of the crew, attempting to sleep through the howling wind and rain.

Townsend Godfrey was born and raised in Cape May County and hired at station #30 in 1880 at the age of twenty-one. He was the first to wake, followed by Keeper Corson, after hearing the news of a ship stranded off the 16th Street beach.

The keeper upon learning of the size of the sailship realized the rescue would require additional men. Townsend set out on foot to round up every available member of station #30. He ran to the homes of Mulford Jeffries, Joe Norcum and Ralph Jones. Harry rushed about the station, gulped a second round of coffee, and grabbed a biscuit before donning his gear to proceed to the rescue. J. Mackey was hoping that Ed Boyd, located at the Peck's Beach Station saw the signaling. They could use added assistance given the size of the ship and the ferociousness of the storm.

∞

The captain, his mates, and the sailmaker stood on the flybridge and the main deck, overseeing efforts to adjust sail to dislodge their ship from the shoal. Each passing wave thrust intense pressure on the hull, causing the grinding of metal on the sandy bottom. The hope of sailing Sindia off the bar grew dimmer after each passing wave.

A rogue wave sent water crashing over the deck, requiring many of the crew amidships to scurry, or holding on to the yards. The alternative was to risk being swept leeward, riding the wave over the rail into the sea. The ocean was cold, all hands were cold, and the pain from the cuts and bruises were difficult to ignore. Each wave struck port side causing the list of the vessel to increase toward starboard.

By 4 A.M., Keeper Corson and seven members of the Ocean City Life-Saving Service trudged through the sand to get to the beach at 16th Street. Godfrey and Joe took lead positions in pulling the wagon containing the breeches buoy and rescue apparatus. Harry spotted a flare from the south end of the island. J. Mackey knew the crew from the Peck's Beach Station would respond.

By 5 A.M., two-and-a-half hours elapsed since Sindia's crew mistook the inlet at Great Egg Harbor for New York Harbor. They were aground in a shoaling area off the New Jersey coast and the angry Atlantic breached their ship onto a sandbar. The eight member crew of station #30 arrived on the scene sometime later. Keeper Frank Corson and Ed Boyd joined with a second crew from the Peck's Beach Station.

Townsend and Mulford unloaded the breeches buoy while the supporting platform was set up by Ralph, Joe and Harry. The two keepers and Ed Boyd unloaded the Lyle Gun and readied its position. All 600 yards of line were available if needed. J. Mackey ordered another Coston flare to light up the dark sky, notifying the ship's captain they were initiating a rescue attempt.

Townsend inserted the projectile and charge in the mouth of the cannon and quickly moved to the rear for safety. J. Mackey lit the fuse, a flash of white and yellow light preceded a loud boom. The first shot careened upward into the air hurtling toward the ship. A whirring sound accompanied the heavy line speeding through the air. Frank spotted the line moving on a plane toward the rigging aft of the ship.

They waited for a response for what seemed like many minutes. Who were they? Where did the crew come from? These were the primary questions racing through the minds of the surfmen. Visibility diminished as fog moved in once more. Turbulent seas accompanied by cold rain beat upon the ship, sending the crew to the rigging to escape the ebb and flow of the ocean. The sound of the wind, the clanging of the rigging, and the voices from the crew muffled the sound of the incoming line. No one from the ship's crew saw or located the first shot.

J. Mackey ordered his crew to position the cannon to prepare a second shot. Townsend and Mulford prepared the line, loaded the projectile and charge in the cannon, and stood to the rear as the fuse was lit. A loud boom followed a flash of light. The projectile and line rocketed, ascending into the air toward the bow of the ship. The rescue line was spotted careening off the foremast, but the deflection caused the line to fall hopelessly overboard into the sea.

Frank Corson sensed the men were experiencing a rush of adrenaline and the futility of two failed shots was unacceptable. His lungs, filled with cold salt air, burnt within.

"PREPARE THE THIRD SHOT --- WE CAN DO IT --- WE'LL HIT THE RIGGING AND GET THESE MEN TO SAFETY!" he screamed.

The line from the second shot was hauled in and recoiled while Godfrey and Mulford readied the cannon for a third attempt. The charge was loaded a third time and they stood rear of the cannon as J. Mackey lit the fuse. Another bright flash of light was accompanied by a boom and the third line arched into the air. The wind caught hold of the line and carried the hook toward the stern of the sailship. The hook hit and lodged, tangling in the rigging of the mizzenmast.

Mitchell and Morley heard the whirring sound as the rope flew above their heads. A loud clank followed as the projectile hit the mast and tangled in the wires securing the mizzenmast. Joe and Ed, standing ashore, proceeded to haul the hawser tight but were unable to complete the task. The ship pitched and the waves pushed Sindia into a list. Repeated attempts to secure a taut rescue line seemed near impossible. The third attempt failed and J. Mackey realized a rescue with the breeches buoy would meet with failure. He shook his head in disgust and motioned to Frank. Visibility was poor, waves continued to assault the ship, and the crew were clinging to the rigging. It was time to focus on the most important decision a keeper of a life-saving crew must make. At what point do you risk the potential loss of life, ordering your crew to navigate a surfboat in heavy dangerous seas?

"YOU HAVE TO GO OUT BUT YOU DON'T HAVE TO COME BACK!" The words on the sign hanging on the wall at station #30 took on a new meaning. The moment was now upon him and he could feel the pressure and the weight of the impending decision.

CHAPTER
37

16TH STREET BEACH

The population of Ocean City numbered less than one hundred residents prior to 1880. A boardwalk was built on the sand extending from 1st Street to 16th Street by 1883. The year 1887 marked the completion of construction and grand opening of the new Excursion House. The founder's plan to develop the island was underway, and an increasing number of investors realized there was an opportunity to employ their own capital in the growing resort. Purchases of residential building lots were secured from the Ocean City Association. The census for 1900 confirmed the year-round population increased to 1,307. The appointed managers and officers of the association included Rev. William B. Wood, Honorable Simon Lake, Charles Matthews, Rev. Ezra Lake, William E. Boyle, Charles Matthews, Jr. and Rev. James E. Lake.

∞

The break of day arrived and residents woke in the early morning hours on Sunday, December 15, 1901. The fog disappeared because a fast moving front bringing cold air moved in during the early morning hours.

Robert Duffield rushed to his front door responding to a rapid knock. Mrs. Prescott Lake Cadman stood on the front porch dressed in winter garb and in an excited state. She was a descendent of the Lake family, founders of the seaside community. Robert was employed as a typesetter for the Ocean City Sentinel Ledger.

"Get a warm coat and grab a hat and come down to the 16th Street beach!" she barked loudly.

Robert, startled, couldn't get a word in before she blurted out the news.

"What kind of a ship and where is it from?" Robert inquired.

"A sailship --- a huge one --- I have no idea --- someone mentioned the English flag --- if you want a great story better get down to the beach! You're the newspaper man --- should make an interesting story," she exclaimed, gasping for air.

Reverend Lake was looking forward to preaching his message about hope since it was Sunday morning. Word was spreading all over town about the big news. Young Bertram Darby stood behind a boardwalk piling near 14th Street, sheltering himself from the howling wind. The ship listed toward shore and appeared to be stranded.

The surf remained wild and the temperature was falling. Clouds brought snow showers turning the beach to patches of white. The remaining sails, hoisted by the crew in an attempt to get the vessel off the sandbar, were blown out of the bolt ropes. The noise from the canvas resounded like cannon fire. The force of wind reaped havoc on Luke's work as some of the sails began to tear into strips of canvas.

Amy Duffield was ten years old and lived with her father, mother, and her sister Mary, at 1126 Simpson Avenue. Both of the girls got dressed in warm winter clothes and accompanied their father to the beach. Ed Voss, fourteen years of age, rushed to the beach with Bert's brother, eight year old Roy Darby. All were overwhelmed by the immensity of the ship. The wind continued to rip through the sails imitating the sounds of reports from multiple gunshots. As residents gathered a rescue attempt by the life-saving service was in process.

Mrs. Leona Morey and sister, Miss Daisy, scampered down to the beach. The news generated huge excitement and everyone congregated at the beach to satisfy their curiosity. Mrs. Beryl Adams Scull decided to forego her usual church attire, opting to leave the morning message behind, to take in the excitement unfolding at the beach. By the time Reverend Lake's grandfather's clock chimed eight, the boardwalk was lined with people braving wind and snow.

Word spread quickly that J. Mackey Corson and Adolfur Townsend succeeded in catapulting a rescue line, lodging it in the ship's rigging. Luke and S were able to retrieve the rope and secure their end of the line. Ian Quay climbed into the breeches buoy and was hauled toward shore.

Midway through the ride the line began to sag and large waves continued to pummel the port side of the ship, causing a list toward shore. The line dipped and Ian was immersed into the cold Atlantic. Tom Wright saw the angry ocean would scuttle the rescue attempt and assisted the crew to pull him back into the ship. J. Mackey and Adolfur saw the buoy fail and decided to abandon the rescue line. The time had come to assemble a crew to man the surfboat.

Chatter spread among the townspeople standing up and down the beach, and back to those gathering on the boardwalk. Everyone gazed in awe at the four masts stretched toward the sky. Young Morgan Hand of 140 Pleasure Avenue gripped his father's hand from the time they left the boards until they arrived at surf's edge. The sailors appeared small from a distance as they clung to the rigging of the ship, avoiding the waves slashing through the port side.

"Where did they come from?" Bert Darby asked, speaking loudly to anyone within hearing distance.

"England," a man with a baritone voiced replied.

Bert was standing next to Joe Champion, Mayor of Ocean City.

"Look at the flag flying from the mast at the stern of the ship, Bert. It's the Union Jack, the flag of England."

Bert's eyes searched until he saw the flag.

"Who knows their port or where they sailed, but one thing I know, this ship is from England. The mast at the stern of the ship is the jiggermast, Bert."

George Adams, a town councilman, stood nearby, listening to the conversation. Nathaniel Smith, a friend of Ed Bowker and Maylin Robinson, were among many young boys who made their way to the beach. Marian Lake, her brother Harvey, and their sister Estella, stood next to them. Inez, daughter of J. Mackey Corson, also made the trip to the surf's edge to watch her father direct the rescue of the crew.

Some stared at the masthead, puzzled by the image of a figure of a man with a turban wrapped about his head. A full body attached to the masthead hung directly beneath the bowsprit. They could only speculate who or what the figure represented. Those who braved the wind, snow, and cold, didn't realize the ship's crew and they as eyewitnesses, were about to be catapulted into history. They would represent the nucleus of townspeople who witnessed the historic event, the shipwreck and rescue of the captain and crew of the S. V. Sindia.

∞

Bill Chadwick and George Lee, members of station #30, made their way to the beach to assist with the rescue. Everyone, in spirit, wanted to be part of history. The first trip in the surfboat was manned by Keeper Corson, sitting in the stern of the surfboat barking orders to the four oarsmen. The pounding surf was relentless, waves were coming ashore at a dangerous angle. The light snow showers thickened and increased in intensity with more snow accumulating on the beach. The oarsmen rowed into each wave at a forty-five degree angle to avoid capsizing. The fore of the surfboat heaved at the crest of each passing wave, and slapped the surface as it bounced on the ocean. Upon reaching the stern of the ship they tied two lines alongside Sindia.

Keeper Corson stood in the stern of the surfboat noticing Captain MacKenzie peering over the leeward side of the taffrail. The surfmen were surprised by his age as they anticipated a younger sea captain. He wore a thick wool waistcoat buttoned from the bottom to the top, fitting snugly underneath his chin. Oilskin boots covered his trousers over the kneecap halfway up each thigh. A wool brimmed cap sat squarely and tightly on his head. A silver moustache lined the upper lip, and horn-rimmed spectacles sat on his nose. J. Mackey Corson was staring into the eyes of a captain of a foreign vessel. He was amazed by the immensity of the ship and the massive towering fore, main, and mizzenmasts. The Union Jack defiantly flapped from the jiggermast.

Harry Young pointed to the ship's flag, "Sindia", flying in the shape of a pennant atop the foremast. The heads of the four man crew turned toward the officer standing next to the captain, most likely the first mate. He was dressed in a heavy pair of dark wool pants with boots that ran fourteen inches above the ankles. A black belt circumvented his waist and he wore several layers of shirts beneath an outer layer of heavily woven wool. Both were rough shaven, testifying to the length of the ordeal they faced at sea. The first mate donned a black cap shaped differently from his captain. Both were equal in height, standing five-feet, eight-inches tall. The younger of the two appeared to be in his late thirties.

"Captain," J. Mackey yelled to the older of the two.

He was interrupted by a loud stern voice laced with an accent acquired from the highlands.

"Allan MacKenzie, Master of the S.V. Sindia --- my First Mate, George Stewart!"

Harry thought the captain spoke as if he had something lodged in his mouth.

"John Mackey Corson, Keeper of the Ocean City Life-Saving Service, Station #30."

The captain stood erect, his voice exhibiting authority and command, though inwardly he was thoroughly embarrassed. It was his ship lodged on a sandbar, somewhere along the eastern shore of a country not his own.

"Ocean City?" Captain MacKenzie quizzed, bracing his hurting leg.

"Ocean City, New Jersey," the keeper responded.

J. Mackey studied the captain's face and in particular, his eyes. He felt as though he was peering through a window, the person on the other side was weary, mentally exhausted, physically beat up.

"My four crew members," the keeper introduced each to the seamen stranded on his shore.

People watched from shore while a discussion between the keeper and the captain ensued for minutes. Captain MacKenzie refused to dismiss his crew to be transported to shore. Mitchell watched as the keeper urged him to abandon ship. Captain MacKenzie adamantly refused to allow his crew to go ashore. He was determined to employ one final effort to dislodge the ship from the sandbar. There was much water in the ship's hold therefore, floating her to sail once more would be daunting.

The keeper persisted by combining his knowledge of the coastal waters and the condition of the ship, to persuade the captain to permit some of his crew to be taken ashore. Reluctant but relenting, Captain MacKenzie gave the order for twenty-six of the crew to make preparation for transport to the shore. He, along with five of his officer's plus the cook, would remain on board. Tom Wright had four of his men lined up and ready to board.

On the second trip the keeper ordered Joe Norcum, an experienced boatman and sailor, to man the stern. He appointed four oarsmen to replace those in the first crew. Four more crew from the ship were rescued and brought to shore safely. As soon as each boat landed, the crew members were sent to the life-saving station, very wet, cold, and suffering from lack of food and exposure.

A total of seven trips rotating four crew members per trip were required, bringing twenty-six of the crew safely ashore.   Captain MacKenzie remained on the ship with Mr. Stewart, Mr. Wilkie, Tom Wright, Luke Addison, Mitchell and Mart. He reasoned there was one last opportunity to remove his ship from her plight, and the remaining crew would be required to accomplish the task.

By 2 P.M. that afternoon, a heavy snowfall blanketed the entire town. The keeper ordered one last trip for the purpose of loading personal effects salvaged by the crew. The trip included Sea Legs as well. He made a last attempt to persuade the captain to put ashore but Captain MacKenzie refused the keeper's request. With the eighth trip completed by 5 P.M., J. Mackey and Adolfur returned to their stations with their crews, all greatly fatigued.

∞

Snowflakes fell lightly over the ocean on the morning of the 16th. The arrival of afternoon clouds was typical for mid December. News of the shipwreck spread rapidly via telegraph.   Word was buzzing throughout neighboring Atlantic City and the Free Press dispatched a reporter to Ocean City to investigate the facts and write a story.

The Western Union Telegraph Office was opened on Monday by W. J. Maloney. News of the event circulated widely after J. Mackey Corson directed a message to be sent to the General Superintendent. It was received at the Wyatt Building located at 14th and F Streets in Washington, D.C.

"Life-Saving Service --- tank steamer Simbia --- cargo of oil from Japan to New York ashore at Ocean City, N.J. Bad conditions --- crew safe." Neither the name of the ship, the description of the ship, nor the cargo content was accurately reported to the life-saving service offices in Washington.

Monday brought waves of visitors to Ocean City. The West Jersey and Seashore Railroad transported passenger cars from neighboring Atlantic City. People braved the piercing northwest wind lining the boardwalk and the beach. News spread that a large sailship bearing a flag from England lay stranded on the shoreline of Ocean City.

The news of the shipwreck was delivered a day earlier, Sunday, at the offices of Anglo-American Standard Oil Co. in New York City. Management was shocked and quickly contracted the services of the tug, "North America." The tug was moored in Somers Point, a very short distance from the Great Egg Harbor Inlet. The directive was simple, the task formidable. Hook up with Sindia located south of the Great Egg Harbor Inlet, and dislodge the ship from the sandbar. Two lighters were dispatched to the scene. If the tug was successful, Captain MacKenzie could commandeer a well fed crew and set sail for the New York Harbor. If the tug could not dislodge the ship from the bar, the workmen aboard the lighters would unload salvageable cargo. There were many customers awaiting their consignment of inventory. Mr. Rockefeller wanted the manganese ore for use in his drilling operation.

The next day's weather turned cloudy and cooler. Additional light snow fell on Tuesday the 17th. Captain MacKenzie conferred with his officers after it became clear the tugs failed to dislodge Sindia from the sandbar. They signaled ashore their intent to abandon ship. The workmen from the lighters were busy removing cargo deemed accessible and salvageable. They measured a depth of twelve feet of seawater in the ship's lower deck.

The keeper and his crew hauled the wagon with the surfboat through the snow to 16th Street by 3 P.M. the same afternoon. The oarsmen cut a different path through each passing wave. With the storm subsided, the ocean felt asleep, even tranquil. One by one, four of the officers grabbed the rope and swung over the taffrail, lowering themselves to the surfboat. The captain remained on board with Mr. Stewart and Mr. Wilkie. The rescue crew landed safely on the beach and immediately set course for their final trip.

Harry and Joe maneuvered alongside the stern of Sindia and secured lines with Mr. Stewart and Mr. Wilkie assisting. The personal effects of each were tied to a line and lowered to Joe for storage. Mr. Wilkie lowered himself followed by Mr. Stewart. The captain remained on board, standing at the wheelhouse. Minutes passed slowly as the keeper and his crew awaited the ship's master. Overcome with emotion, Captain MacKenzie stood behind the wheel, gazing at the masts, sails shredded; remnants of the ship he commanded for thousands of miles. Reality set in despite his denial that a ship's master never ends a voyage in a manner not of his choosing. He knelt on one knee with the other leg still in pain, paying homage to Sindia, the ship he commanded on her maiden voyage, accepting Neptune had destroyed his prize and possibly his profession. He bowed his head momentarily and stood to look up to the foremast. The Union Jack, the house flag of Anglo American, and the ship's flag were taken down by Mr. Wilkie. He turned his back to the ship's wheel, walked toward the taffrail, grabbed hold of the rope and lowered himself into the surfboat, never again to set foot on a square-rigged sailship.

Darkness came quickly as winter clouds hung low over the barrier island on Tuesday. The heroic efforts of the Ocean City and Peck's Beach Life-Saving crews would be remembered for years. Upon returning to the station, the keeper employed Henry Reinhart to use his horse to haul the surfboat from 16th Street. A light layer of snow fell while the entire crew returned to the station, thoroughly exhausted from the task at hand.

CHAPTER
38

THE NAVAL COURT

On Wednesday the 18th day of December, 1901, Parker Miller, Ocean City's first permanent resident passed away at the age of seventy-six years. He and his wife Louise resided at the 700 block of Asbury Avenue. He was preceded in death by one of the original founders, Reverend Ezra B. Lake, having passed away on August 7, 1900 at the age of sixty-six years. The passing of Parker came one day after Captain MacKenzie decided they had done everything humanly possible to rescue their ship. Due to a storm, the captain's plan to arrive portside in New York on the 15th, the 342nd day of their round the world voyage, would end in despair.

Captain MacKenzie secured a room at the Swarthmore Hotel at 9th and Wesley Avenue. The remainder of his crew of thirty-two were housed and fed twice a day at station #30, between the days following the rescue until December 22nd. Wesley Avenue was a wide road running parallel to the beach. The base consisted of hard packed earth and sand. An electric trolley appeared on the scene July 4, 1893, with one car running between 1st to 17th Streets. Five years later the line was extended to the end of the island near 59th Street.

The crew wandered about their temporary home acquainting themselves with the town and the residents. Some of them attended church services at the First Methodist Episcopal Church. They looked a bit peculiar wearing the donated clothes and head garb previously worn by the town's residents. The people of Ocean City spoke English; however, the crew found their accents amusing. A few of the residents inquired if Mitchell would speak in Scottish Gaelic. It was obvious the residents were baffled by his pronunciation of English, combined with a Gaelic accent from the

Hebrides. No words were remotely recognizable when he spoke in Scottish Gaelic.

In keeping with the laws established by the association there were no businesses dispensing spirits. The town had one pharmacy and the druggist had a good laugh one day. Luke and Mart accompanied S to the store, feigning bad coughs and requesting something strong to cure their illness. The sailors otherwise appeared as seamen of good health and the druggist promptly turned them away.

Captain MacKenzie received a telegram from the British Consulate in Philadelphia, requesting the appearance of the entire crew. The message confirmed what the captain suspected and deep down within, dreaded. In keeping with The Merchant Shipping Act of 1894, a Naval Court would hold a hearing to investigate the facts leading up to the shipwreck of the S.V. Sindia. All were ordered to appear before the court held at the British Consulate in Philadelphia on December 23rd. The stage had been set by the proper authority to ascertain the facts. What happened? Was fault to be found and who would be held responsible? There was an owner who lost a ship and a suitable penalty based upon an examination of the facts would be applied in court.

Anglo-American Standard Oil Co. was responsible for liability associated with the stranding of the ship. The Board of Trade at London was the designated legislative body, who in accordance with maritime laws and rules, would have to be satisfied with the outcome of the court's findings. Lloyds of London, insurers of the cargo, would require a written copy of the testimony and outcome of the court's findings. Lloyd's Register of Captains was a reference compilation of all British and Commonwealth Masters and Mates. They would log the relevant details pertaining to the names, dates of birth, location of birth, and resident status of the officers. The Port of Registry for S.V. Sindia was London. The flag of the country determined the origin of laws and regulations to be applied to the operation of the ship. Anglo-American Standard Oil Co., registered in England, would require the hearing be officiated and regulated in accordance with British legislation. Thus the closest place to conduct the inquiry would be the British Consulate, Philadelphia, Pennsylvania.

∞

On Sunday afternoon, December 22nd, the entire crew boarded the West Jersey Line bound for Philadelphia. The order of business for all on Monday morning was to appear before the naval court. Mitchell nervously sat next to Tom Wright for the journey to the city, his mind filled with questions.

"Have we committed an offense? Did we violate a law?" Mitchell quizzed Tom.

"My first experience with a naval court, mate," responded the bosun.

"Who will be there? Will they ask me questions? How do I respond?" Tom looked at Mitchell and shrugged in reply.

"Don't know anything about the court. Yes, you might be asked to tell them what you know. The truth, be truthful," he added.

On Monday the 23rd the crew walked up the concrete stairs, entering their appointed destination with history. The old oak floors creaked under the weight of the seamen. A tapping sound resonated from sixty-four feet proceeding down the center aisle. They took their seats on chestnut benches to the left side of the chamber. Minutes later Luke slid into the last row next to Mitchell. Several newspapers purchased from the vendor at the corner of the street were tucked under his arm.

A three member panel would comprise the authoritative body. They would ask questions, inquiring of all aspects leading up to and including the eventual shipwreck. Sir Wilfred Mansell Powell, acting in an official capacity, introduced himself to the captain and crew. He would preside over the affairs of the naval court. The other two members were experienced mariners. Adam Smith was Master of the British barque, Calcium. The third member was Leonard M. Coffill, Master of the British barque, Athina.

Preliminary affairs and procedures were reviewed, discussed, and presented to Captain MacKenzie, his officers, and the crew. President Powell then called for a brief recess prior to initiating the first phase of the court proceedings. The captain and his first and second mate huddled in the hallway, a place they preferred not to occupy at this time in their lives.

"What do we know of this man, Powell?" Mr. Stewart inquired.

The captain paused then responded.

"Captain Daniel Cochrane and I met at Brocklebanks years ago. We

213

passed the tests and obtained our certificates near the same time. He sailed with me when I was appointed master of Sindia on her maiden voyage."

His officers listened, motionless.

"We met in Liverpool before I agreed to sign with Anglo-American to captain this passage. Cochrane told me a story of a wreckage presided over by Powell."

"What did he tell you?" Mr. Wilkie asked.

"There was a substantial and dangerous collision at sea on the first of October, 1900. Two British steamships, the S.S. Biela and the S.S. Eagle Point met in disaster. Each ship was registered in Liverpool."

The captain paused, drawing on his recollection of the story before continuing. He had the full attention of his senior officers.

"The S.S. Biela was built around 1870 and she was a 2,170-ton passenger and cargo ship. The vessel was passing from New York to Manchester, carrying a supply of general cargo when she met her fate. The ship sank as a result of the collision."

"What about the Eagle Point?" Mr. Stewart was curious.

"The Eagle Point was a very large vessel, 5,222 tons. The ship was owned by the Norfolk & North America Steamship Co."

"Who built a vessel of that size?" Mr. Wilkie asked.

"J. L Thompson of North Sands, Sunderland. The smaller S. S. Biela was owned by Liverpool, Brazil and River Plate Steam Navigation Company, Ltd. The ship was built by Leslie Shipyard at Hebburn on Tyne." Captain MacKenzie continued.

"Did Captain Cochrane address the details?" Mr. Stewart queried.

"Fault was assessed to Eagle Point. The ship was crossing the Atlantic around eight knots in very dense fog."

"What mistakes were made?" Mr. Stewart responded.

"Biela sank and Eagle Point survived with damage. The master of Eagle Point was fined and his certificate suspended for six months. The second mate of the Biela was sighted for failing to maintain a proper lookout," Captain MacKenzie responded.

Mr. Wilkie, third mate, jerked his head backward after hearing the latter.

"The court ruled no avoiding action was taken after it became obvious the ships were on a path to collide," the captain concluded.

Luke ran down the hallway, arms filled with pages of newspapers in disarray, motioning to Captain MacKenzie.

"WE WEREN'T ALONE OUT THERE!" Luke exclaimed. The senior officers, puzzled, listened. "A newspaper headline," Luke reported. "Movement of Vessels Greatly Hindered at Delaware Capes due to Storm."

All eyes were on the sailmaker. "The American liner, Noordland, commanded by Captain Doxrud left the dock for Liverpool. Fog in the bay was so thick the pilot was forced to anchor." Luke, catching his breath, continued. "The fruit steamship, Admiral Sampson, Captain Higgins, was forced to anchor at 10 P.M. Saturday night, the 14th, outside the Capes until 8 A.M. Sunday morning, unable to find their way due to fog and the storm." There was more. "The American liner, Tropic, Captain Barber, was bound for Hamburg, Germany. He was forced to lay up at port in Philadelphia."

A few of the crew watched the officers confer from a distance.

"Here's another headline," Luke continued. "Storms Fury Felt at Sea." He read on. "Reports received by shipowners indicate many vessels damaged with several driven ashore. A German ship loaded with china and clay washed ashore at Monmouth Beach."

Luke, fingers moving through the pages was just getting started. Mr. Stewart, noticing a headline, pulled the copy of The Press from Luke's arm.

"Listen to this! Two schooners, Edith Dennis and Mark Gray, stranded. The crew of the Mark Gray was rescued by Toms River Life-Saving Service. The ship was a total loss."

Another headline followed. "Incoming Captains Reporting Wrecks on Ocean and Injuries." Mr. Stewart read anxiously.

Mr. Wilkie also read from an article. "The four-masted schooner Francis C. Tunnel, carrying a cargo of railroad ties, arrived in Philadelphia on December 17 from Brunswick, Georgia. The schooner fought a stormy passage and seaman, Leonard F. Grant, was washed overboard and drowned. The captain of the ship, also named Tunnel," was quoted. Mr. Wilkie continued, quoting Captain Tunnel. "December 10, we ran into a hurricane, blinding rain storms and mountainous seas. A tremendous wave swept over the vessel breaking the stanchions on the lee flyrail. It was night and Grant was swept overboard. The night was very dark. When the vessel righted Grant was missing!"

More stories poured forth from Luke's collection of papers. The British bark Baldwin, Captain Dalling, arrived at Lisbon, Portugal, after leaving Philadelphia. They faced a tempestuous passage of forty-six days, losing their entire deckload of rosin. The schooner Thomas G. Smith from Fernandina, bound for Philadelphia with a cargo of lumber grounded at Marcus Hook on the seventeenth. The ship was refloated by the tug, Hartley. Another schooner, Danenhower, from Georgetown, lost their entire load of lumber. The ship arrived at Delaware Breakwater on the night of the 17th.

"Listen mates!" "Spanish Steamship Cut in Half," Luke reported. "The Amesti from Bilboa, Spain, bound for Philadelphia, sank in a collision with a British steamship, Isle of Kent." "Sounds like the storm continued up the coast impacting many." Luke read further. "Here's another headline." "Collision, 328 miles east of Cape Cod on Saturday." "All hands were saved by the crew of the Isle of Kent. The British ship landed in Boston on the 17th. Captain Lezema of the Amesti telegraphed news of the loss to the agents in Philadelphia. The collision occurred in the early morning. The lookouts sighted each other but it was too late. The Isle of Kent cut halfway into the Amesti. The ship began to fill and sank within twenty-five minutes. The Kent was loaded with cotton from Savannah bound for Bremen. The Amesti left November 27 from Bilboa for Philadelphia loaded with iron ore. Amesti was 1,838 tons, 314' in length, 40.5' breadth and 21.75' deep. The ship was built in West Hartlepool, England in 1894."

Mr. Wilkie, pulling a paper from Luke's arm, found another article and began reading aloud. "Eight tank steamships --- total capacity 12,000,000 gallons, detained at port due to flooding of the Schuykill River. The conditions existed since Saturday the 15th. Ships keep coming but there are no loading berths due to flooding from the storm. The current was reported to be so swift it would be difficult to put the ships up the port."

"Any names listed?" Mr. Stewart inquired.

"Detained ships included British steamships Henri Reith, Kinsman, Oilfield, and Tonawanda. Other ships included the Dutch ship, S.S. Charlois, a French ship, S.S. Villade Douai, a German ship, S.S. August Korff, and a Spanish ship, S.S. Cadagua."

The reporting of wrecks continued to grow. Captain MacKenzie noticed a headline containing Sindia in one of the papers. His eyes widened as he read the account to his officers.

"Per the Maritime Exchange, Re: Sindia. Twenty-two feet of water in hold --- will be a total loss --- cargo ruined. Tug North American, Captain Gibbons and the tug Sommers N. Smith, Captain Mimford --- loss of

$500,000 to the underwriters and Standard Oil Co."

The captain continued reading but refrained from verbalizing any further details to his officers. The words in the article continued. "Master given inaccurate soundings by the man who was heaving the lead. Depth reported to be thirty fathoms before she struck --- captain had not a sight for some time, running obscured and on dead reckoning --- had Captain MacKenzie known position, he could have saved ship by letting go both anchors --- with a full scope of chain the vessel could have held on until the storm abated." He folded the paper and placed it inside the pocket of his coat.

President Wilfred Powell opened the session with remarks describing the purpose and reason for the presence of the entire crew of S.V. Sindia. A disaster had befallen a vessel sailing under the British flag carrying a cargo of merchandise consigned to multiple companies. The cargo was insured by Lloyd's of London and the naval court of inquiry must convene under British law.

Captain MacKenzie sat in the first row, facing Masters Smith and Coffill. Mr. Stewart, Mr. Wilkie and Thomas Wright sat alongside the captain. The remainder of the crew occupied five rows of wooden bench seats with five to six seamen sitting shoulder to shoulder. This was the first time Master Allan MacKenzie found himself in appearance at a naval court. He displayed solemnity and sincerity, all while his mind reverted to the night of the shipwreck. If there were two people who were more unsettled, it was the captain and his first mate.

President Powell lifted his head and glanced at the captain, his officers, and the rest of the crew.

"Captain MacKenzie, the members of this court realize the depth of feeling that you, your officers, and crew, must be experiencing. Given your circumstance you were so close to your port of destination, and what would have been the completion of another successful voyage. It is most unfortunate we must meet under these circumstances." The crew sat on the benches, quiet, eyes forward, motionless. "The events of the shipwreck must be reviewed and history will record what we say in these proceedings," he paused. "My responsibility is to oversee the matter at hand. My position is a formal state appointment. My role is one of presiding, not judging. The latter will be the responsibility of your peers, Masters Adam Smith and Leonard Coffill."

The captain, his officers, and crew were unaware of the background of the members of the consul sitting before them. Sir Wilfred Mansell Powell was forty-eight, born in 1853. His travels were extensive throughout the Pacific as well as New Britain. He was formerly consul for the Navigators Islands in 1885 and Deputy Commissioner for the Western Pacific. In 1888 he was appointed Consul at Stettin, and in 1889 was invited to attend a conference on Samoa at Berlin. His transfer to Philadelphia took place in 1898 when he was appointed Consul for Pennsylvania, Ohio, Indiana and Michigan.

The inquiry continued as directed by President Powell. The master, his first mate, and second mate would provide the court an accounting of the night of December 14, following into the wee hours of the morning of the 15th. Each would present their own versions of the events leading up to the shipwreck of the vessel. Individually, each would provide a description of orders given and actions taken, in an attempt to dislodge the vessel from the sandbar.

Masters Smith and Coffill were obliged to ask all pertinent questions to insure all the facts were accounted for and entered into the court record. President Powell called for a break after the session ending December 23rd, to provide time to observe the Christmas holiday.

∞

The court reconvened on Thursday, December 26th. Masters Smith and Coffill continued with questions based on the testimony provided by the three officers. The sessions continued on the 27th and proceeded into Saturday, the 28th. Mitchell listened intently, held spellbound by the proceedings which were new to him. The members of the court questioned the crew in detail, anytime they reasoned their input would shed light on the matter at hand.

The 30th of December was reserved for final questioning and a reading of a statement prepared by Master Allan MacKenzie. President Powell, positioned behind the bench, looked down over the top of his spectacles at the three officers.

"We have questioned many of you and there has been much information brought before us pertaining to the matter."

Mr. Stewart sat motionless, pale in the face.

"The proceedings have been uncomfortable for all of us. Masters Smith and Coffill have much maritime experience. To think for a moment that we have enjoyed this undertaking would be a mistake." he continued. "The process must focus on the events leading to the shipwreck of the Sindia." There was another pause. "Captain MacKenzie, you have as much time as needed to lodge your protest which will be recorded within the record."

All eyes of the crew shifted to their captain when President Powell asked him to stand and deliver his protest. The captain rose from his seat to address the court. His black leather shoes were shined and without blemish. Dressed in black pants, a pressed white shirt was covered by his double-breasted waistcoat.

His recounting of events began with a brief description of the journey around Cape Horn. His mind was focused, his voice unwavering, his presence commanded the respect of all in attendance. In spite of the events the captain's integrity remained unquestioned. He was a master mariner, one who sailed among the elite with thirty-five years of seamanship to his credit. He was a man of resolve, a Brocklebank captain, cut from a mold that produced the finest of seamen in his day. Allan MacKenzie was a highlander of good character, built of integrity shaped by his father and his father before, a Scotsman through and through. He concluded his comments with a depiction of the condition of the ship after the grounding. He followed with orders given and actions taken by all, to employ a means to escape the clutches of the wind and ocean current, relentlessly pushing his ship toward shore.

Mitchell sat motionless, hanging on every spoken word to be entered into the official testimony. The room was quiet. Masters Smith and Coffill, located perpendicular to the captain, sat erect, their demeanor exhibiting respect for a fellow master mariner. Captain MacKenzie concluded his comments.

"And the deponent further says that if any loss or damage has accrued to the said cargo, that it was caused by the severe storm and weather, and not through lack of skill, or negligence upon this deponent's part, nor of that of the crew."

With remarks concluded he took his seat. Silence enveloped the room until President Powell responded. The Court would evaluate the entire testimony and render their opinion and decision to be announced to the officers and crew on the 31st of December.

∞

A patch of light snow dusted the ground on Tuesday morning, New Year's Eve, 1901. The three members of the British Naval Court, Captain MacKenzie, and his crew of thirty-two met at 10:00 A.M. Clouds blanketed the sky over the city of Philadelphia.

Sir Wilfred Powell, Adam Smith, and Leonard Coffill, resolved a task had been given them that fit the category of an undesirable burden. The previous afternoon they met to review, discuss, and formulate their opinion of the facts presented. President Powell sat in his usual place behind the bench, with Masters Smith and Coffill located behind an oak table, perpendicular to the three officers and their crew.

President Powell, in solemn form, proceeded directly to the point at hand. The document from which he read referenced, "The Merchant Shipping Act, 1894." Centered upon the line above was one word, "Sindia."

The President read through the FINDING portion of the document and proceeded to the description of the "Sindia." The third paragraph previewed the final leg of the voyage leaving Japan for New York.

All sat quiet and motionless, waiting for the next phase. Mitchell, his head cocked in the direction of the captain, remained silent, locked in his memories, thinking of all he had seen, drawing on experiences while being schooled at the side of a fellow Scot, a man he grew to admire immensely.

President Powell resumed the proceedings.

"The Court having regard to the circumstances above stated finds as follows:"

"The Court finds that the Master of the ship "Sindia," official number 93757, of London, Allan MacKenzie, the number of whose certificate is 30124 O.C., failed to exercise proper and seamanlike care and precaution on approaching land on the night of the 14th and the morning of the 15th of December, 1901."

1. "The Court decides that the "Sindia" was under too great a press of canvas in approaching a shelving coast."
2. "That the Master should have either taken the sounding himself or have been with the mate when it was taken, in order to verify the correctness of the sounding, and to convince himself that a correct sounding was obtained."

3. "That there were not soundings enough taken, considering the nature of the coast and the thick state of the atmosphere."

"The court finds, therefore, that the certificate of the Master, Allan MacKenzie, should be suspended for six calendar months, from the date of the finding of the Court; but recommends that a Mate's certificate be granted to him during the period his Master's certificate is suspended."

"In respect to the First Mate of the ship "Sindia", official number 93757 of London, George Stewart, the number of whose certificate is 027439, O.C."

1. "The Court finds that he was in fault in giving a wrong depth of water or sounding to the Master at midnight on December 14, 1901, being at the same time under the influence of liquor."

2. "The Court further finds that the certificate of George Stewart, First Mate, should be suspended for three calendar months, to be reckoned from the date of the finding of this Court; and recommends that a Second Mate's certificate be granted to him during that period."

"The Court returns to George Wilkie, Second Mate of the ship "Sindia", official number 93757, of London, his certificate, and finds that no blame attaches to him for the stranding of the ship "Sindia." The Court has also decided that the men who left the ship on the day of the stranding did so under the sanction of the master, and that the maintenance of the crew shall be paid by the owners or their agents until the crew finally arrived at the British Consulate in Philadelphia, and the Court in pursuance of the powers vested in it by Section 483, of 57 and 58 Vict. C. 60, orders the crew to be paid off and their balance of wages to be paid to them up and to the day of the stranding of the "Sindia," viz., December 15, 1901, the following being a list of the wages due to each man as agreed to by him with the exception of any officer or man detained on board the ship for the service of the ship by the master, whose wages shall cease at the time that the service upon which they are detained by the master ceases, and not before."

"The expenses of the Court fixed at L28, 8s. 7d. are approved."

Dated at British Consulate, Philadelphia, 31st day of December, 1901.

Wilfred Powell,
President of Naval Court

Members

Adam Smith, Master British Bark "Calcium"
Leonard M. Coffill, Master British Bark "Athina"

Masters Smith and Coffill shifted their eyes toward Captain MacKenzie, and then stared at the stained oak floor. Trained to serve on the sea, they lived and survived in weather fair and foul, seas becalmed or blown by wind, sometimes producing raging waves as big as houses. This was what they knew, this was their place of business, their livelihood. Neither of them was comfortable with their assigned lot on New Year's Eve, 1901. Judgment had been rendered and the sentence passed down. The pit settling in their stomachs would take up residence for the next couple of days. The feeling would ease with the passing of time. Both understood the trials and perils faced by a master of a ship. But this wasn't their ship. The owner invested of their funds for enterprise. A conclusion must be drawn from the matter and indeed their work was complete. One of their own must find the resilience to go on with life in spite of the circumstances.

The gavel hit the block square on the surface and the crack of wood meeting wood resonated through the room. Captain MacKenzie sat in the first row, head bowed, motionless. Mr. Stewart and Mr. Wilkie sat next to their captain, staring ahead and beyond the wall behind Wilfred Powell. George Stewart, embarrassed, and George Wilkie, without penalty, understood the consequences, yet they were out of their element. Days ago a tempest raged upon the sea they sailed. Days later, a tempest raged within as they sat on a wooden bench, landlocked in Philadelphia.

Mitchell stared at the back of his captain, able to see only the cheekbone on the left side of his face. Moments passed, he stood slowly and with caution, then walked to the end of the row, turned the corner and approached his captain. Mr. Stewart parted from his seat and motioned Mitchell to take his place. The helmsman sat beside the man who had become a fatherly figure. Captain MacKenzie, forehead resting on his right hand, hadn't moved. Quiet was in control of the moment.

The captain spoke softly. "I could stand it for myself, but my two sons who hold high positions as sailing masters, will suffer keenly for the disgrace which has befallen their father."

Mitchell remained quiet. It felt as if the air had been sucked out of the chamber. Each of the officers waited for their captain to rise to his feet. And when he did, they surrounded him and walked through the courtroom door, down the hallway, through the heavy wooden door leading to the city streets, and into the cold winter air.

CHAPTER 39

FIFTY YEARS LATER

It was a gorgeous day in mid July and the temperature warmed to eighty-five degrees. Mitchell and Ailsa Graeme spent a relaxing half hour in rocking chairs on the front porch of the Swarthmore Hotel. Their plans included a short stroll from 9th Street and Wesley Avenue to the corner of 8th and Plymouth Place. Dinner for two at the Sindia Restaurant was the order for the evening.

The year was 1951 and the Graeme's itinerary included a one week stay in Ocean City. The first leg of their trip was complete after a departure from Southampton on the Cunard liner, Queen Mary. She was built by John Brown & Co. at Clydebank, Scotland, in 1936. The vessel was 1,019 feet long, weighed 81,237 gross tons, and carried nearly 2,000 passengers in first class, cabin, and tourist accommodations.

Lady Liberty greeted them on their arrival in the New York Harbor. Fifty years prior, Mitchell could visualize James Long, above in the nest, calling attention to the statue welcoming the crew to New York. A ninety-minute bus ride down the Garden State Parkway to the bus terminal at 9th and Haven Avenue left them at their destination. Mitchell was seventy-five years of age and Ailsa would turn seventy-two come October. They booked their room at the Swarthmore Hotel and upon check-in; the owner suggested they try the nearby Sindia Restaurant for dinner. It seemed a fitting recommendation given their plan to walk down memory lane.

Mitchell and his wife of forty-five years were going to savor every day and enjoy their seaside visit. It was the first time Ailsa left Scotland to set foot on American soil. It was the second time Mitchell sailed on a large vessel, this one being grandly appointed with the size overpowering his memory of Sindia. The helmsman's heart was racing due to excitement and his mind was drifting back in time. He was looking forward to dinner, but he couldn't wait to join the thousands of people who strolled down the boardwalk on a warm summer's eve. Ailsa was as eager as her husband and perhaps moreso. Mitchell's stories had intrigued her and stimulated her imagination. Frequent fireside chats over the years helped pass the evening during the cold damp winters in Scotland.

The description on the menu hinted to a portion of the dinner fare they would experience this particular evening. The chef offered a blend of traditional American cuisine with a touch of Pennsylvania Dutch fare. The latter consisted of delectables, unbeknownst to the Graeme's. The Sindia was a seasonal restaurant and their clientele featured an array of vacationers from neighboring states, including Pennsylvanians raised with a Germanic ancestry. The remainder of the menu was topped off with a savoring assortment of freshly caught flounder stuffed with crabmeat, sea bass, grouper, crab cakes, oysters, shrimp, scallops and clams.

Mitchell sipped a cold glass of iced tea and eased back in his chair momentarily.

"I can see it in your eyes dear, you can't wait to get up on the boardwalk," observed Ailsa.

She knew about the excitement and anticipation building inside her husband. It was the whole reason for taking the trip. His grin broke into a smile as he nodded in agreement.

"It's been a long time since this old mariner laid eyes on the shore of Ocean City," he replied.

Mitchell perused the tab and paid the bill as Ailsa waited by the front door. They stopped at the corner to take in the sights of a pleasant evening in the New Jersey resort. The two of them turned south toward Ninth Street then left as they proceeded toward the boards. The hearts of the two were filled with anticipation as they readied to enter the threshold of history.

Shriver's Salt Water Taffy Shop, located at Ninth and the Boardwalk, was the first store they passed. Mitchell looked at Ailsa as she pointed to the sign in the store window, "Since 1898."

"Does this bring back any memories Mitchell?"

The business was founded three years before his historical landing on the beach but there was no memory. The boardwalk was located elsewhere so Shriver's must have been somewhere in town. Too much time had passed; or, was it the combination of anxiety and the complexity of the event that may have dulled his memory?

The evening sun shifted behind the storefront shops on the boardwalk. Ailsa was glad she took the advice of the desk clerk as she slipped on her sweater. The air was beginning to cool as the sun continued its descent behind the Great Egg Harbor Bay. The two turned south as their goal for the evening was to complete the seven block walk to the 16th Street beach.

"The scent of the salt air is fresh and invigorating," whispered Ailsa.

Her eye caught the motion of descending herring gulls. A few of them landed on the metal railing fixed to the side of the boardwalk. Mitchell took in the postcard like picture of the gulls dressed in light gray feathers, changing to pure white on the breast, neck, and head.

"Look at the bright golden bills," commented Mitchell.

"Beautiful, they are distinct and graceful in flight," responded Ailsa.

She was happy to be with her husband and she couldn't wait to complete the final stretch of four blocks on the boardwalk. While passing 13th Street, Mitchell caught sight of "The Smuggler's Shop." He was fascinated with the name while the exterior of the building drew his attention. Fish netting adorned a portion of the exterior and there were old ship's lanterns fixed on each side of the doorway. He knew this was a place where he would spend more of his leisurely time during his stay in the resort.

Ailsa continued the stroll with her left arm locked in her husband's arm. The smell of the salt air subsided when the aroma of heated popcorn drenched in caramel, engulfed their senses as they passed Johnson's Popcorn. Words on the sign proudly announced, "Quality Popcorn Since 1940." Ailsa gently tugged at her husband's arm.

"We're stopping at Johnsons after we turn around to go back to our hotel," she mused.

A short stroll and a few minutes later, Mitchell veered toward the railing bordering the boardwalk. He came to a halt. They stood peering into the greenish hue of the ocean, watching the spray from a wave lift into the air. Each passing wave would curl over and lay upon the shoreline. Seconds later Mitchell lifted his arm to point to a metal stern post, anchored in the sand, protruding ten feet into the air.

The hair on Mitchell's arms bristled, his heart swelled. Ailsa was keenly aware of his emotions.

"This is the place Ailsa. That metal object is the stern post from Sindia."

Ailsa hooked her left arm into his.

"The only visible remains of Sindia. What is left of Captain MacKenzie's ship lies beneath her cover of sand."

Ailsa nodded with reverence. Mitchell remembered with solemnity.

"The grave of the Sindia lies beneath --- there were thirty-three of us --- fifty years ago I was the helmsman --- we survived the storm and the wreckage," he lamented.

Mitchell watched in silence as the setting sun cast rays over the sand and into the breaking waves. Within a few minutes Ailsa tugged at her husband's arm, motioning for the two of them to sit on the wooden bench facing the site. Mitchell sat in silence, eyes staring out to the sand and into the waves and beyond.

His mind left the present as he embarked on a slow but deliberate journey back in time. Fifty years ago at the age of twenty-five, he was the helmsman on a British merchant vessel. She was one of the largest four-masted windjammers sailing the seas. His mind metamorphosed into a collage of distant memories he thought long gone. A brief walk on the beach and below the sand lie Sindia.

He never forgot the look on Captain MacKenzie's face the day he agreed to leave his ship. It was the look of deep despair shown when someone has been irreparably wounded. When the wind enveloped the thirty-two sails the ship became a magnificent display. On that day, Sindia lay on a bed of sand surrounded by water, battered and badly bruised.

Mitchell's heart was heavy. Somewhere below in the hold covered by sand, lay the memory of a beautiful young woman of twenty-eight years. Many years ago she was full of life, happy, and in love with his father. Her son would never be afforded the opportunity to gaze at her auburn hair or into her soothing blue eyes. Perhaps it was fate that Shona Graeme's prayer book found a resting place never before imagined. The helmsman missed the mother he never knew, and mourned the loss of her prayer book.

Dark had fallen and the Graeme's finished their walk up the boards, returning to the Swarthmore Hotel. The porch was adorned with white wicker rockers and they sat for a while, resting their sore but happy feet. The night hostess opened the screened door to inquire if they desired refreshment. The custom created by guest homes and hotels was to set a table filled with beverages and a light snack. Mitchell thanked her, speaking with his Scottish accent acquired from the Firth of Clyde.

"So you are the couple --- our new guests from overseas," she inquired curiously. "First visit?"

The Graeme's responded with a nod.

"What brings you to Ocean City?"

Mitchell paused for a second and Ailsa intervened.

"Our first vacation to the states, this is a special treat for both of us."

The hostess extended a plate filled with baked goods.

"You might say we're walking down memory lane," Ailsa continued.

The hostess grinned as she glanced at her guests. Mitchell's eyes focused on people across the street.

"Is it too personal to inquire of your memory?" she asked.

Mitchell sat in the rocker, motionless, his mind drifting back in time. Back to an era obsessed with sail and his failure to meet the test Neptune engaged each and every helmsman. He demanded they employ their skill, knowledge, and endurance, in order to survive.

Ailsa responded first, "My husband was the helmsman onboard the Sindia, the night of the shipwreck. Fifty years ago, matter of fact!"

The mouth of the hostess dropped in astonishment. "May I sit?" she requested.

"Of course," replied Ailsa.

She looked at Mitchell, then pulled a rocking chair toward the two.

The conversation continued for thirty minutes more. It was obvious the Graeme's had a long eventful day, but this was the highlight of the summer for the night hostess.

"It's time to rest these weary old bones," declared Ailsa. "We're going to the First Presbyterian Church tomorrow morning."

The hostess excused herself after wishing them a comfortable nights rest. As residents and vacationers turned in, one by one, Mother Nature stirred the sea. A warm front would bring humid air into the coastal community. The store lights on the boardwalk became less visible as fog moved in and continued to churn.

Mitchell was the first to wake as the dawn of the day swept gently over the island. Ailsa would follow him to the porch in due time. Dressed in pressed black pants, white shirt and tie, he strode down the stairs to the guest room, to find a fresh pot of coffee on the table. Pouring a cup, he opened the screen door to find the same wicker rocker and wait for Ailsa to appear.

The walk to church was a brief stroll away. They noticed a young boy about twelve turning the corner at 7th Street. A dirty gray canvas bag hung over his right shoulder. He pedaled a Schwinn bicycle as he beckoned in a slow deliberate mantra.

"Bulllllletin, get your Bulllllletin, Sunday Bulletin."
The aroma of doughnuts, pastry and cinnamon buns, fresh from the oven, drifted through the doorway of the bakery on the corner.

Reverend Fischer was pastor of the church for the past eleven years. He made it a special point to stand by the front entrance this Sunday morning. A phone call and a tip from the nearby hostess were foremost in his mind on this particular day. It should be a simple task to separate his visitors from the recognizable faces of his flock. He contained his excitement as Mitchell and Ailsa Graeme ascended the steps.

"Good morning to you, Mr. and Mrs. Graeme!" He greeted them with a warm smile on his face. Mitchell, surprised, returned a puzzled look. "It was the night hostess who tipped me off," the reverend told him warmly. "Forgive my invasion of your privacy, having a survivor of the historic Sindia with us is indeed an honor."

Smiles grew on the faces of the Graeme's as they exchanged brief pleasantries with the pastor. Parishioners filled the pews as the choir took their seats behind the pulpit. Minutes later the director motioned them to stand, initiating the service as everyone sang.

Reverend Fischer offered opening remarks followed by the usual announcements featuring upcoming events. Dispensing with the details, he transitioned with the following.

"Fifty years ago, Ocean City made the news in a significant historic manner. An event unfolded that drew the attention of the entire town and people from miles around. The month was December, the day was the 15th, and the year was 1901. The largest sailship upon any sea at the time intended to pass by the Jersey Shore." People listened without understanding how the subject matter fit in with his sermon to follow. "Battered by a storm with the crew led astray by wind, rain, and fog, this magnificent ship came to rest on a sandbar off the 16th Street beach, nevermore to grace the seas she so proudly sailed on." Quiet in the congregation prevailed. "The officers and crew, a total of thirty-three, were rescued by the valiant efforts of John Mackey Corson and his crew, all members of the Ocean City Life-Saving Service. The ship's crew were members of a society, merchant mariners, most of them drawn from the countries of England and Scotland. This morning we have in our presence a surviving member of the ship's crew from that ill-fated day. Please extend a warm greeting to Mr. and Mrs. Mitchell Graeme!"

Everyone in the sanctuary applauded. Glancing to his right and nodding toward the ninth row, the pastor acknowledged the Graeme's presence. Mitchell leaned forward in the pew and nodded, it was the only gesture required for the moment.

CHAPTER
40

THE BOARDWALK

The stroll from the Swarthmore Hotel to 9th Street and Ocean Avenue passed quickly. Ailsa tucked her right arm into Mitchell's as they crossed the intersection, spotting Watson's Restaurant on the corner. Never had they witnessed a seaside community like the one that continued to unfold before them. Minute by minute they became mesmerized by life at the shore, South Jersey style.

Ailsa was amused by the bike rack located to the side entrance of the restaurant. It was filled with ten Schwinn bikes. They gestured at the coaster brakes and wide balloon tires. Multiple colors adorned the frames and a vinyl grip covered each end of the handlebar. It was at this moment when something clicked inside Ailsa's mind. She discovered why she witnessed pretty young girls near the ages of seventeen to twenty, dressed in one piece white uniforms with an apron tied around their waist. These were the girls she spotted riding their bikes about town. The beach was their afternoon playground. Early evening found them in transit to the local restaurants. Many a visitor would find them waitressing tables into the evening hours. By the time September rolled around there would be many empty savings accounts at Cape May County National Bank, all in preparation to pay the coming semester's college expenses.

The pieces to the puzzle became clearer. It was Mitchell's comment that put things into perspective.

"Makes me think of breakfast!"

Ailsa's facial appearance turned to a puzzled expression.

"I noticed the pennants thumbtacked to the walls. We flew a pennant on the jiggermast. Every ship we passed knew who we were when their long glass was focused on the top of the mainmast."

"And you think those pennants at the inn are the names of ships? Is that your point?"

"No Ailsa, it's similar though. I went to school at sea, it was my college, and Allan MacKenzie was my professor."

The picture he painted helped Ailsa to understand. "The names on the pennants are the colleges the girls attend," she interrupted with excitement.

"That's it!" Mitchell exclaimed. "We should ask someone where these schools are located. I remember names like Penn, Villanova, Temple, LaSalle, St. Joseph's and Penn State. I thought to myself. Why is one of them blue with red letters and another blue with white letters? It makes sense to me now."

They walked up the steps to Watson's, their senses filled with the aroma of freshly baked seafood. The windows to the restaurant were open and the enticing aroma spilled onto the sidewalk. Both of them ordered flounder stuffed with crab meat and enjoyed side dishes of French fries and cole slaw. The plates containing small warmed dinner rolls with tiny packets of butter were so tasty, they asked for another serving. The passing of an hour enjoying a pleasant dinner signaled it was time for an evening stroll on the boardwalk. The Music Pier caught Ailsa's fancy but Mitchell was anticipating a visit to the Smuggler's Shop.

A little boy in the corner of the store stood in front of Iron Mike, the diver's suit display. His eyes were locked on the metal helmet atop the suit of canvas. Mitchell spotted him as he walked through the door, turning to his right.

The Smuggler's Shop was located between 13th and 14th Streets on the boardwalk. Expensive displays of scrimshaw were enclosed in glass cases. Carvings on ivory colored whalebone depicted scenes of sailors, whale-boats, seamen with harpoons in their arms, and many other interesting details. After the artisan's knife cut into the bone, a black line appeared after dye was carefully applied. Mitchell was enamored with the attention to detail, intricate artwork, spawned from the hands of an artisan, or, perhaps sailors over a hundred years before.

He guessed the young boy was seven or eight years of age. He wore a light brown pair of shorts and a faded blue T-shirt. A pair of white socks extended above his canvas black and white high-top shoes. Mitchell noticed there were no boots such as these laced on the feet of the boys in Scotland.

"Fancy boots lad," he said, pointing to his feet. "What do you call them?"

"Keds, they're my sneakers," the young boy announced proudly.

"Oh, I understand. Tis an interesting name for a pair of canvas boots."

The boy stared at him, fascinated with the man's pronunciation of words. He never heard anyone speak in a manner as this man spoke. He wasn't sure he understood every word spoken by Mitchell. The boy's hair was light brown, cut very short in a butch crew. Mitchell noticed his green eyes as he studied the lad's face. There has to be Celtic blood in this young lad he thought to himself. Where else would the color of the eyes come from?

"And what is your name, lad?"

"Buddy!" responded the young boy.

CHAPTER
41

THE SURPRISE

Monday morning came quickly and the rays of the sun burst forth over the northeastern shore of the tip of Ocean City. The sun would bring warmer temperatures as it made its appearance on the floor of the porch. Mitchell was the first to rise and venture downstairs, to pour the first cup of coffee of the morning. His favorite white wicker rocker was the last one on the left in the corner. Gently rocking, he took his first sip, allowing the aroma to awaken his senses, while the mix of sugar and cream tasted good.

A half hour passed and a thin frail woman with silver hair turned onto the walkway to the Swarthmore. She climbed each stair slowly and deliberately, a red pocketbook clutched in her left hand. She reached for the screened door, placing her hand on the handle. On hearing a creaking sound made by a rocker she turned to her right. She looked his way and walked toward the gentlemen with the cup in his hand.

"Good morning Mr. Graeme," she spoke with a frail soft voice.

Mitchell, not recognizing her, raised his head to gaze into the woman's face. She reached into her pocketbook and grasped a very old book.

Holding it out to Mitchell, she inquired, "Is this yours?"

He looked at her face. It was the reflection of one pleased to give a gift, a very special gift. He lowered his eyes to the book she held in her hand. His jaw dropped and with a surprised look, he extended his hand, took hold of the book and stared at the woman. She began to disappear through a moist veil covering his eyes. Blinking, he gently turned to the page before the back cover. Two words, one in Scottish Gaelic, *"Maoilmhichill"* was inscribed on the upper half of the page. The second, long forgotten, he remembered over fifty years ago.

Glancing back to the woman's face, he being stunned, she commented, "I was standing behind you when you spoke to Reverend Fischer yesterday after church. My mother gave your prayer book to me many years ago."
The woman paused, "She purchased the book at the Sindia store, which opened on the boardwalk following the shipwreck in the early 1900s."

∞

On Tuesday, Mitchell and Ailsa walked the familiar path to the First Presbyterian Church. They were greeted by Reverend Fischer as they were seated in the chairs facing his desk in the pastor's study. The walls of the room were lined with beautiful cherry bookcases. Each of the shelves displayed delicacies written by theologians throughout the ages. Mitchell spotted three volumes, one authored by Thomas Guthrie, another by Robert Smith Candlish, and a third penned by Robert Murray M'Cheyne. All of them were theologians and preachers, well known Scots.

Mitchell handed his mother's prayer book to Reverend Fischer, explaining the sequence of events resulting in the return of his cherished personal property, fifty years later. He opened the book with great care and leafed through the initial chapters, turning to the last page before the back cover as instructed. The handwriting was old and there were hints it was written under stress. The name Maoilmhichill (Mitchell) was scrawled on the page. Below was another word, *Shamar*.

Ailsa, unable to contain herself, broke the silence. "What or who is Shamar? Can you help us with the meaning please?"

The pastor placed the book on his desk and stood to peruse the books lining the shelves behind him. He reached for a thick volume, pulled it from the shelf, and turned to take his seat.

"By whose hand were these words written?"

"His mother wrote both of them, we think on the day she died." Ailsa paused, "According to Mitchell's father."

The pastor's hand stopped at a page and he lifted his head, glancing at Mitchell. "Did your mother know multiple languages?"

"She spoke only Scottish Gaelic," he responded.

Reverend Fischer glanced at his commentary one more time. "Shamar is a Hebrew word. It's a derivation from the word Shomer, another Hebrew word for "guard". The word Shamar means to be a guard, to keep, and a watchman."

Mitchell, lost in thought, gazed at the bookshelf behind the pastor.

Reverend Fischer inquired, "How did your mother die, Mitchell?"

"During childbirth, my birth," he lamented.

"Was your father present during her passing?"

"He was not. He was returning to our home with Anna McCall, a midwife and neighbor."

"Who picked your name, Mitchell?"

"My father did."

Ailsa interrupted, "His father told me he got the name from his mother's book, discovering the page soon after her passing."

Revered Fischer remained silent for moments, reflecting on the responses to his questions.

"Someone may have spoken to her on that fateful day." He looked at the two, considering the possibility of divine intervention. "Your mother was a Presbyterian, a woman of faith. She was in the process of delivering her first child, she passes away. Your father discovered a name inscribed in the back of her book together with the word Shamar."

He paused and reflected again. "You embark on a round the world journey and are shipwrecked during a storm."

Mitchell's eyes were locked on the reverend's face.

"You're protected during a dangerous voyage to the other side of the world and back." Reverend Fischer paused once more. "Mitchell, Ailsa, there are angels. Perhaps an angel with an association of Shamar spoke with your mother that day."

The Mitchells were speechless. While satisfied with his comments, yet surprised, they rose to leave.

"One final question --- what was your mother's first name?"

Ailsa swiftly broke in once more. "Shona, it's the English version of a Scottish Gaelic name."

The pastor stood and reached for another book. Leafing through the pages, he stopped near the end and looked at the Graeme's once more.

"Shona is interpreted, God is gracious!" There was another paragraph and he read the description aloud. "The best person you can ever hope to meet --- she is kind --- passionate --- and loving in every perfect way --- beautiful," he concluded.

CHAPTER
42

TRIBUTE

The Graeme's woke early as fresh rays from the sun filtered through the bedroom window. Tomorrow they would leave for New York for their sail to Liverpool, then their journey home to Scotland. An hour passed and Ailsa knew where to find her beloved. She walked down the stairs through the lobby, opened the screen door and turned to the left, looking toward the end of the porch. Mitchell turned, smiled, and greeted her, his morning coffee steadied on the painted arm of the wicker rocker.

"Mitchell, what do you wish to do with your last day in this beautiful seashore community?"

She could read her husband's thoughts.

"Ailsa, I have been thinking, might ye mind if we took one last stroll down the boardwalk?"

"Of course not Mitchell, I knew the answer to the question before I asked. I did want to hear your reply though."

The mid morning stroll rekindled the now familiar seaside sounds as the Graeme's made their way down 9th Street toward the boardwalk. The sun was shining through thick scattered clouds and humidity was high. The same young boy of twelve pedaled his bike along the side of the street, his gray canvas bag draped over his right shoulder, partially filled with unfolded Philadelphia Bulletin newspapers. A man dressed in a blue T-shirt and white baggie swim trunks, wearing flip flops, hailed the lad for a paper, his daily read for the beach. Several seagulls cackled loudly as they surrounded a piece of scrap left on the blacktop by a passerby.

Turning south on the boardwalk they were greeted with a sudden burst of wind flowing in from the ocean. The morning would bring a beautiful beach day, but the afternoon might produce thunderheads, signaling the onslaught of a storm. A young girl was cleaning the windows at Shriver's. A host of vacationers were riding their bicycles on the boardwalk. People were enjoying a stroll, the presence of salt air filling their lungs with renewed energy.

Several blocks later they passed the Smuggler's Shop, approaching the gray bench facing the ocean. The sternpost of the Sindia, visible in the distance, signaled the historic event of fifty years before. They sat and rested, faces tilted toward the golden sun. Minutes passed and Mitchell dropped his head. The memory of another era in his life was clear and present. He could see the ship passing through the fog, and then the breakers, amidst the rain, wild sea, and raging surf.

The smuggler unlocked the door to his shop, turned and paused, recognizing Mitchell resting on the bench facing the ocean. He wandered over, stood behind the Graeme's, unnoticed, in time to hear Ailsa's question.

"What's wrong Mitchell?"

He was quiet; his head hung low for seconds, the look of sadness on his face never changing. Slowly, lifting his head, he peered out to sea.

"We let him down!"

Ailsa began to speak but Mitchell responded once more.

"We let him down. We mistook the lighthouse at Cape May for the lighthouse near New York Harbor, we had lost our way."

"But there was heavy fog and what about the raging sea and the violent storm?" Ailsa protested.

Mitchell lifted his head and glared toward the ocean. He felt the palm of a hand, one strengthened from years of toil, placed squarely on his shoulder. Glancing out of the corner of his eye he realized it was the hand of the smuggler.

"Mr. Graeme, describe him for me, please!"

Mitchell paused and drew in a breath.

"He was stern, serious in demeanor, fair-minded, a student of the sea and his calling." Ailsa listened intently. "Captain MacKenzie was intelligent, a self-educated man, he obtained his master's certificate at the age of thirty-two, a significant accomplishment in the days of sail."

The smuggler's blue eyes were locked on Mitchell's.

"He knew the ways of the sea as well as any captain does, given

Neptune's unpredictability and what he could do to his ship on any given day." The smuggler nodded. "The captain was fearless, yet he was humbled by the occurrences and episodes of near peril that could befall a crew."

Ailsa sat silently, admiring her husband.

"In his prime he circulated among the best of seamen. His father was a master mariner too. The captain was born and raised in the beauty surrounding Inverness, he was a proud highlander." Ailsa watched the smuggler's expression of fascination. "He stood tall. The days of mighty sail have disappeared over the horizon of time. They were shipbuilders, merchant mariners, and skilled navigators. He walked among the elite at the prime of his life."

The smuggler listened intently, his head turned toward the ocean. "And what became of him after the hearing?"

Mitchell dropped his head once more, paused for seconds, and turned toward Ailsa and the smuggler.

"The answer to your question is buried within the heart and soul of Captain MacKenzie. Sixteen days passed from the day he commanded a ship owned by Anglo-American and John D. Rockefeller, to the date of the pronouncement by the court. He ordered his officers to stay on board Sindia for three days, hoping we could sail her away from the shoal after the tugs dislodged her."

A few more seconds of silence passed as they thought about Mitchell's comments.

"He endured a lot of questioning. The presiding officials grilled him thoroughly with purpose, not letting up. In the end they took his master's certificate for six months. He was demoted to the level of first mate for that period of time."

Mitchell paused, reflecting on the emotional toll on Captain MacKenzie.

"He was disgraced, his fate undeserved."

Ailsa noticed his lower lip begin to quiver. She took his hand in hers.

"It was an insulting act. He so feared, not for himself, but for his reputation, built over many years, and the potential damage the shipwreck could inflict upon the careers of his sons, Allan Alexander and Ralph."

The smuggler shook his head and continued to gaze toward the ocean.

"And then he returned home to Scotland?" the smuggler asked.

Mitchell drew in a deep breath.

"After the hearing we walked together, down the stairs, out to the street in Philadelphia. It was cold and the air was still. A light snow was falling on the ground. Christmas passed and the New Year was upon us. Captain was dressed in black trousers and his Livingston winter waistcoat was buttoned to the neck. A black cap covered his gray hair. He looked exactly as he did the day I met him in Liverpool. He shook my hand and wished me a Happy New Year. Then he apologized for the sad manner in which my first and only voyage had ended. He wished me fair seas and calm winds for the rest of my life. The captain was on his way to the hotel to meet his wife, Christina. A streetcar passed by as I walked a block and turned to look over my shoulder. As he turned the corner, I could see the smoke from his Black Twist tobacco circling above his head."

The smuggler peered down the beach to the sternpost of Sindia, reflecting on the days of sail, an era gone and forgotten.

"Did his sons pay dearly for the unfortunate circumstance that befell their father?"

Mitchell, contemplating, turned his head toward what was visibly left of Sindia.

"Some years passed and I stumbled upon Morley in Ruggleys Staff. He saw the captain's eldest son, Allan Alexander, in Liverpool. He told me his son was a first mate at the time of the wreck, his younger brother Ralph, was certified a second mate, seven months before that fateful night."

Ailsa, puzzled, was hearing this part of his story for the first time. "Both sons were later certified as masters, and, like their father, at a young age." Mitchell continued.

The smuggler, silent, grinned and nodded.

"Morley told me the incident impacted his sons greatly. They were emboldened by their father's instruction and the magnitude of the event."

"In what manner?" the smuggler questioned.

"Allan Alexander displayed a tattoo, in Latin, on his left arm."

"What was it?" Ailsa interrupted.

Mitchell turned to face them. "Two words, nil desperandum! Never despair!"

THE END

AFTERWORD

The endeavor of researching and writing this novel, historically based, was dependent on gathering and interpreting as many facts as possible. My goal was to formulate a descriptive story; one that portrayed events as they may have occurred. The characters in this story lived in my heart and my head. I thought about them all the time.

The Ocean City Historical Museum has numerous newspaper and magazine articles pertaining to Sindia. One day, while researching, I found a sentence buried in a newspaper article referencing the captain. The quote was offered by David Jackson, from Dundee, Scotland, one of the surviving crew. He took residence in Philadelphia and became a citizen of the United States, following the shipwreck. He described the captain. "He was a nice old man from northern Scotland." David was sixteen in 1901.

His comment provided the nugget that lead to my search to obtain anything and everything available regarding the captain. I was able to match his master's certificate number provided by Lloyd's of London Masters and Mates Register, with the identical number listed in the British Naval Court Hearing. I knew I had found my man, or should I say captain.

A genealogical search uncovered much about the MacKenzies. Allan MacKenzie's father, John, was born in northern Scotland in the year 1806. He was a ship's captain and married Janet MacLeod. Together they raised two daughters and three sons along with Catherine Mathieson. Most likely a relative, she was fifteen years of age when she lived with them in Inverness in 1841.

Allan MacKenzie, born in 1839, was the youngest of three sons. His master's certificate opened a door, an opportunity for employment with Brocklebanks. Allan commanded Sindia before 1901 along with other square-riggers. In later years he commanded a few steam propelled ships purchased by the Brocklebanks. The 1891 census confirms he was captain of the S.S. Gaekwar and Christina accompanied him on the voyage. The census reported his location as Victoria Docks, London, in the county of Essex and a registration district of West Ham.

Allan married Christina in the county of Lancashire, England, and together they raised two sons and one daughter. Christina's maiden name was also MacKenzie and her father, Alexander MacKenzie, held a Master's

Certificate of Competency #71977, obtained on February 10, 1852.   She was one year old at the time.

The eldest son of Allan and Christina was named Allan Alexander (DOB July, 1878) after his father and maternal grandfather. Their second son, Ralph, was born on April 13, 1881. A daughter, Isabel, followed in the year 1885.

The inquiry of the British Naval Court was a rigorous and arduous process. My guess is the three member panel didn't relish the process of an inquiry of the fate of the Sindia. They didn't desire to place a fellow master through this process; but they had no choice, they had to.   Allan MacKenzie expressed remorse in his own words, upon sentencing, describing how he greatly feared for his two sons. They were accomplished mariners, busy building careers, and there could have been negative fallout from the hearing that might have impacted their future.

Allan Alexander MacKenzie obtained his certification as a second mate in 1898, before the shipwreck in December of 1901. Ralph obtained his certification as a second mate on May 13, 1901, six months prior. Following the shipwreck, Ralph passed the examination administered by the Board of Trade, London, and was certified a master on August 1, 1905 at the Port of Liverpool.

Life provides anyone an opportunity to leave a legacy to children and grandchildren. The legacy can be a composite of experiences, traits and beliefs. The lives of John MacKenzie, his son Allan, and Allan's father-in-law, Alexander MacKenzie, were no exception to this rule. All of them were experienced ship commanders who passed many of their experiences to each other and Allan's two sons, Allan Alexander and Ralph.

It was an exciting day when I located and viewed copies of original documents, filled in and signed by Allan Alexander. They sent a compelling message, adding to the story. In my opinion, it's a clear, loud message; one that would have been overlooked by most, had they not been involved with the research undertaken to that date. It lends credence to my comment that building legacies are very important.

Allan Alexander resided at 17 Empress Road, Liverpool in 1901 when he was not at sea. He passed the examination to be certified as a master on March 11, 1907. What I found influenced my opinion of the impact of the findings and pronouncements of the court, on the psyche and lives of Allan and Christina MacKenzie, and each of their two sons.

Allan Alexander was required to respond to specific questions, accompanied with official documents, comprising his original Master's Certificate of Competency. The bearer of the certificate had to testify to a question. The form of the question was very long, beginning with; "Every person who makes or procures to be made, or assists in making a false Purpose of obtaining for himself or any other Person a Certificate either of Competency, or Service, or who forges or assists in forging or fraudulently alters any Certificate......"

There was a line following the above statement requiring the applicant's signature. Located to the right of their signature was a rectangular box. Above the box is a question, beginning with, "Has any of your licenses ever been suspended or ......?" I inspected many applicants who filled in the rectangular box with one of three responses to the question. Their responses included (1) the rectangle was left blank or (2) they wrote "NO" inside the rectangle or (3) they drew a line in the form of a dash inside the rectangle signifying a "NO" response.

Allan Alexander, filling in his answer to the question, was most assuredly making a statement. He took his writing instrument and starting at the lower left corner of the rectangle, drew a heavy line through the middle to the upper right hand corner, thereby dividing the rectangle into two triangles of equal proportion. In the upper triangular space he printed the word, NEVER. In my opinion, in his response, he was making a statement, one that was based on his interpretation of his father's fate at the hands of the British Naval Court.

Allan Alexander stood five-feet, eight and one-half inches tall and had dark hair and blue eyes according to this document. He spent a total of thirteen years at sea by 1907 prior to signing the certificate. There is another point of reference, a line contained in the document for "complexion" and next to that line is a space for "specific identifying marks." He had a tattoo on his left arm displaying "Nil desperandum," Latin, for "never despair."

It's the author's opinion the message in Allan Alexander's tattoo was born out of a love for and a profound respect of his father's accomplishments. It was also an act of defiance. His response and handling of the aforementioned statement was a reaction to the sentence and fate bestowed upon his father. My guess is Allan MacKenzie suffered from self-inflicted wounds of an emotional nature, following the shipwreck.

Let's examine the life of Ralph Brocklebank, one who would have known Allan MacKenzie personally. He was a guiding force in building and shaping the family enterprise. Ralph was active in administering the business affairs of the Mersey Docks and Harbour Board for thirty years. He worked to improve dock conditions and was involved in charitable giving, especially to those providing for seafarers and their bereaved families. The firm of Thos. & Jno. Brocklebank, Ltd. evolved into the premier and world renowned shipping firm. If you were employed as a Brocklebank captain you were among the elite of your time. Allan MacKenzie was a Brocklebank captain for many years. Accordingly, he wore a pair of shoes few men in his time could walk in.

The author's conclusion, after sifting through much research, the Mackenzie's were proud Scots, they revered and protected the family name, they mastered their trade, and they were determined to conduct themselves in a professional manner from the moment they gave the order, "Lay aloft and set sail!"

AUTHOR'S NOTES

Shipwrecks at Peck's Beach

Numerous historical records document shipwrecks off coastal New Jersey. The website of the Museum of New Jersey Maritime History maintains a long list including any researched details. The Sindia came to rest on top of two previous wrecks. The ribs of an existing ship were confirmed by a diver upon inspecting the hull of Sindia a few days after her stranding in 1901. The "Rhine" (approximate date 1840) was carrying approximately 300 Irish immigrants. The ship was abandoned near Corson's Inlet after springing a leak. The Rhine was left to drift and in several days washed ashore between 16th and 17th Street. On December 17, 1866 the British ship Huron, was wrecked and was reported to lie beneath Sindia.

John Peck and the Unalatchtigo

John Peck was a whaleman who used the island as a rendering operation for his whaling business. Artifacts of the Unalatchtigo are displayed in the Ocean City Historical Museum. The names of the whalers and property owners referenced in the first chapter were the result of research obtained from the Cape May County Historical Museum. There is a picture of a whale on display at the Ocean City Historical Museum, beached at 8th Street in 1911, the dimensions of which were fifty-eight feet in length, weighing nearly fifty tons.

Harland and Wolff

More than ten years following the shipwreck of Sindia, Messrs. Harland and Wolff, owners of the famous shipbuilding company, launched at Queens Island, Belfast, Ireland, a large luxury liner on May 31, 1911. The ship was 883 feet in length and weighed 52,310 tons. The ship bore the name Titanic.

Brocklebanks

There are three generations descending from Captain Daniel Brocklebank, listed for purpose of documenting family members instrumental in building the shipbuilding and subsequent shipping empire.

Captain Daniel Brocklebank – 1741 – 1801
Thomas Brocklebank – 1774 – 1845, son of the captain
John Brocklebank – 1779 – 1831, son of the captain
Thomas Fisher Brocklebank – 1814 -1906, 1st Baronet, and nephew of Thomas and John, his mother being Anne Fisher, a sister to his uncles
Sir Thomas Brocklebank – 1848 – 1911, son of Thomas F. Brocklebank
Harold Brocklebank – 1853 – 1936, son of Thomas F. Brocklebank

In 1887 the launch of Sindia represented the 184th ship built by or purchased by the Brocklebanks. Holkar, delivered in 1888, marked the 185th and last sailship to be built for the Brocklebanks.

The number of ships owned by Thos. & Jno. Brocklebank, Ltd. reduced over the years following the shipwreck of Sindia, to the point where the shares in the business were sold to the Cunard Line in 1911. The National Museum, Liverpool, owns a collection of many accounts and documents detailing the business affairs of the firm, including original stores books of several voyages of Sindia.

The MacKenzies

Allan MacKenzie

Allan and Christina left New York City and returned to their home in Liverpool in the county of Lancashire, England, following the shipwreck. A newspaper article claimed Christina arrived in New York to meet her husband upon his return from Japan. No record has been discovered indicating he served on or commanded another ship after Sindia.

They witnessed their son, Allan Alexander, wed and obtain his Certificate of Competency as a Master #033784 on March 11, 1907. Their younger son, Ralph, earned his Master's Certificate in 1905.

In the year 1908, Allan MacKenzie resided at 41 Fazakerley Road

Fazakerley, England, the northern portion of Liverpool in the county of Lancaster. On the 7th of October, 1908, having been diagnosed with nephritis uremia, a disease of the kidneys, he died at the age of sixty-eight, with Allan Alexander at his bedside. Six years and ten months prior, Sindia, the windjammer he commanded on her final voyage lay shipwrecked on a shoaling coastline of Ocean City, N.J. He was buried along with other master mariners in Anfield Cemetery, 238 Priory Road, Liverpool, Merseyside, England.

The basis and foundation for the portrayal of Allan MacKenzie

First, the collage of research collected pointed in this direction. Allan MacKenzie was born into a Presbyterian family and he became a Brocklebank captain. Second, let's hear from quotations from the author's research assistant, Angus MacKinnon, of Troon, Scotland.

"He was a professional man and leader of men, a product of a country at that time led the world in shipping, shipbuilding, and seamanship --- he had two sons, both mariners with certificates of competency --- losing a ship under any circumstance would be anathema to his calling and the tradition of his proud profession --- he would sooner cut both of his arms off --- being a highland Scot, Allan MacKenzie was certainly a very religious man, strict Presbyterian, and these men whilst hard of necessity, had a very strong moral and disciplinary code."

Excerts from the Obituary of Allan MacKenzie --- The Nautical Magazine A Technical and Critical Journal --- 1908

- Died at Liverpool – 1908 - veteran thirty-five years at sea
- Joined Brocklebanks 1874 as chief officer of one of their clippers
- Commanded most of their fine sailing ships
- Took charge of their second steamer
- Younger days, joined the Naval Brigade under command of Captain Peel at Calcutta during the Indian Mutiny
- Among his fastest sailship passages --- commanded the Majestic, ninety-eight days from the East Coast to San Francisco

Alexander MacKenzie – father-in-law to Allan MacKenzie

The father of Christina was born in 1812 at Inverness, Scotland, the same village where Allan MacKenzie and his siblings were born and raised. Christina MacKenzie was born in 1851 and her father and mother (Mary MacKenzie) had her baptized on October 5, 1851 at St. Peter's Church (Church of England) in Liverpool. Years later, according to the 1891 Census, Alexander was seventy-nine and a widower. He resided at 7 Cathedral Road, West Derby, Lancashire, with his two grandsons, Allan Alexander, age twelve, and Ralph, age nine. His Ecclesiastical Parish was listed as the Church of Saint John the Baptist (Anglican) located at the corner of West Derby Road and Green Lane in Tuebrook, Liverpool. In the year 1937, Christina was residing at 5 Beechwood Ave. in Kew, Surrey, England, when at the age of eighty-five, she passed away on January 3.

Allan Alexander MacKenzie – eldest son of Allan MacKenzie

The eldest son of Captain MacKenzie was born in July, 1878 in West Derby, Lancashire, the same year Sindia was launched. He was designated a second mate at the age of twenty on December 17, 1898 at the port of Liverpool; three years prior to the date of the shipwreck. On July 12, 1902 at the age of twenty-four, Allan Alexander was designated a first mate, and he received his master's certificate at the age of twenty-nine, both issued at the port of Liverpool.

Allan Alexander at the age of twenty-eight married Emma Catherine Bell, age twenty-nine, on December 19, 1906 at Christ Church, Kensington near Liverpool. Officiating at their wedding was the Rev. W. R. Rhys.

He set sail on the S.S. Magellan, ship #102114, a 2,320-ton vessel, port of registry, Liverpool, on November 26, 1901, nineteen days before the wreck of Sindia. His service on the Magellan ended April 18, 1902.

During WWI, Allan Alexander served in the capacity of a sub Lieutenant in the years 1914-15 on the HMS Cambria in the Royal Navy, UK. He later served in the Royal Engineers, employed by the Inland Water Transport Corps, constructing waterways in Belgium and France. He rose to the rank of major and died of an illness on November 3, 1919 (age forty-one) in the UK, while in service to his country. He was buried in Abergele Cemetery, Denbighshire, grave location N.E. 21.

Alexander James MacKenzie – grandson of Allan MacKenzie

Born in Holyhead, Wales in 1910, he was the son of Allan Alexander and Emma Catherine MacKenzie, and the only grandson to Allan and Christina MacKenzie. In this year Allan Alexander and Emma Catherine were living at 6 Plas Hyfryd Terrace, Holyhead in the county of Anglesey, Wales. His occupation was a master at a marine shipping office. Emma Catherine passed away at the age of sixty-five on October 27, 1942. In that year her address was Gogarth Minymor Road, Holyhead, Wales.

Alexander James MacKenzie, grandson to Captain MacKenzie, married Elizabeth Rees. He was promoted to Lieutenant Commander in the Royal Navy, United Kingdom, serving on the HMS P222, an S Class Submarine, built by Vickers Armstrong and launched on September 20, 1941. The launch date was September 20, 1941 and the sub was commissioned on March 4, 1942. Displacement, 872 tons surfaced, 990 tons submerged, length 217', breadth 23' 6", draught 11', speed 14.75 knots surfaced, 8 knots submerged, armament, 6 forward 21" torpedo tubes, 1 aft, 13 torpedoes. Complement, forty-eight officers and crew.

P222 left Gibraltar for patrol off Naples on November 30, 1942. The ship sent messages on December 7 but was never heard from afterward. P222 failed to arrive at Algiers on her due date and was reported overdue on December 21, 1942. An Italian torpedo boat, Fortunale, claimed to have sunk a submarine with depth charges on that date, southeast of Capri.

Lieutenant Commander MacKenzie was thirty-two at the time of his death, listed as December 21, 1942, the date P222 failed to arrive at Algiers. The record reports Alexander James died during war service. The complement of officers and crew serving on the submarine numbered forty-eight. Burial: Portsmouth Naval Memorial, Hampshire, England - Plot: No known grave; name is listed on panel 61, column 3.

Ralph MacKenzie – youngest son of Allan MacKenzie

Born on April 13, 1881 in West Derby, Lancashire, England, was the second son of Allan MacKenzie. His hair was dark and he had gray eyes, standing five-feet, nine-inches tall. He obtained his second mate's certificate #036054 on May 17, 1901, age twenty, and his first mates certificate on March 25, 1904, age twenty-three. The Master's Certificate of

Competency was awarded to him on August 1, 1905 at the age of twenty-four. Each certificate was issued at the Port of Liverpool.

New York passenger lists confirm he entered the United States at Boston in 1904, while under employment. On July 9, 1912 his port of arrival was New York. He was thirty-one, employed by a cruise line, serving on the ship S.S. California. His stated purpose for entry was to join the S.S. Burgen of the Prince Line, Ltd.; owners were Knott & Co. of Newcastle, England.

On May 1, 1918 Ralph arrived at the port of New York, serving as third mate on the S.S. Themistocles, a 500-foot, 11,200-ton ocean liner of the Aberdeen Line built by Harland & Wolff. On June 3 of 1918 he returned to New York once again on Themistocles, serving in the capacity of a second mate.

Ralph and Kathleen M. Thursby were wed in Derby, England in 1918. In the second half of the same year he became a merchant seaman during WWI and died at the age of thirty-seven on December 18, 1918. He was awarded a Campaign Medal to WWI Merchant Seamen by the United Kingdom.

George Stewart, George Wilkie, John Morley and David Jackson

George Stewart, First Mate, George Wilkie, Second Mate and David Jackson, Cabin Boy, each from Dundee, Scotland, were original members of the crew.

John Morley, then of 72 Hagley View Rugeleys Staff, England, thirty-five years following the ship-wreck (1936), addressed a letter to the Chief Officer of the OCLSS. The life-saving service was merged into the U.S. Coast Guard; therefore, Mr. Morley's letter was delivered to Captain Christopher Bentham, Commanding Officer at the Ocean City station.

Mr. Morley confirmed he was a member of the crew and according to Captain Bentham, he recalled many specifics of the storm, the shipwreck and rescue, even inquiring if the Sindia had been refloated. He assumed she had. He referred to Ocean City being a dry town and indicated several of the crew visited the chemist (druggist) feigning colds, seeking something strong. Their gag didn't work.

David Jackson remained in Philadelphia and became a U.S. Citizen. According to an article in the Ocean City Sentinel Ledger dated December

15, 1964, there were two other members of the crew who remained in the U.S. The names were not mentioned in the article and their identity is unknown. It was the only publication referencing the possibility of more than one crew member remaining in the U.S. following the wreck.

The Agreement and Account of Crew of the Sindia

Many hours and countless attempts were undertaken to uncover the original ship's log of the Sindia, including the original Agreement and Account of Crew. The purpose was to identify each member of the original crew of thirty-three, participating in the ill-fated final voyage.

The website of The National Archives, Kew, England, offers details explaining the keeping of these documents, indicating that approximately ten percent of merchant ship agreements have survived. Many of them were transferred to the Memorial Museum of Newfoundland in Canada.

A search to locate the crew agreement for the last voyage of Sindia (1901) was unsuccessful. The museum in Newfoundland has the original Agreement and Account of Crew for the Sindia, for a voyage dated 1892/1893, the departure being Liverpool to Calcutta. The ship's master was Captain Daniel Cochran, one who would have been well known to Captain Allan MacKenzie.

On February 1, 1888, Captain MacKenzie and a crew of thirty-six departed Liverpool for Calcutta on Sindia's maiden voyage. Other masters serving under Captain MacKenzie on the maiden voyage included W. Peterkin, R. Heyburn and Daniel Cochran.

Given the original Agreement and Account of Crew for Sindia's final voyage of 1901 was not locatable, the author borrowed from many of the names of the crew listed in the original document for the 1892/93 voyage, incorporating them into the story. One example is Ewan Rowland, steward for the '92/'93 voyage. He became the steward of Sindia for the final voyage also. Aside from the Japanese cabin boy whose real name has not been uncovered, the identities of the remaining crew of twenty-seven remain unknown.

The details used for the weekly pay for the members of the crew, stated in pounds, shillings and pence, were extracted from the 1892-'93 agreement. The ship's log has not been uncovered. It may be in a museum in the United Kingdom, waiting to be discovered, or, it may be underneath many feet of sand in the captain's cabin or chart room of Sindia.

Lake Family

A historical account of the many activities and interests including pictures of the Lake family and their relatives can be found in the Ocean City Historical Museum. Their beliefs, heritage, and identity, continue to breathe memories of a passing era in Ocean City to this day.

Ocean City Life-Saving Service

John Mackey Corson and Adolfur Townsend, keepers of the life-saving stations, and the identities of each member of the Ocean City Life-Saving Service in 1901, were extracted from a publication which is the property of the Ocean City Historical Museum and referenced in the bibliography. After the shipwreck Keeper Corson filled in a very detailed report of the events leading to the rescue of the entire crew of Sindia.

Ocean City Residents

Specific references to the actual names of the residents of Ocean City in 1901 were based upon publications researched at the museum.

British Naval Court

The names of the three members of the British Naval Court were secured from a copy of the court findings contained within the report entitled, "Merchant Shipping Act, 1894, #6310." The pronouncements from the hearing were taken from a copy of the original transcript.

The Prayer Book

Among the artifacts donated to the Ocean City Historical Museum is a Book of Common Prayer published by the Church of England, purchased at C.C. Walmsley, Bookseller and Stationer, 50 Lord Street, Liverpool. The book was salvaged from the Sindia, purchased by a resident of Ocean City following the shipwreck, handed down to a relative, and later donated to the museum. The identity of the original owner of the book is unknown. Integrating Shona Graeme's prayer book in the story was born after reading of the donation in a newspaper article and upon viewing the artifact.

The Captain's Humidor

Allan MacKenzie's cloisonné (a term used to describe an ancient technique for decorating metalwork) humidor is on display at the museum. Signage next to the humidor describes it as brass with a Foo Dog for a knob attached to the lid. The captain gave his humidor as a gift to Daniel and Caroline Lake, decendants of the Lake family and parents of Marion Lake Ross, when they lived at 1628 Asbury Avenue. The gift was an act of appreciation for their invitation to him to lodge at their home following the shipwreck, before the naval court hearing.

Holkar, Sindia's Sister Ship

Holkar was registered as ship #93772, gross tonnage 3,072. The ship was 324' in length and 45' in breadth. She was built by Harland and Wolff and identified as Hull No. 205. The ship was launched February 11, 1888, one year after Sindia, and delivered to Thos. and Jn. Brocklebank on April 30, 1888. In the year 1901 Brocklebank sold Holkar and her name was changed to Adelaide. The ship was sold again in 1913 and the name changed to Odessa. In 1915, A. Meling purchased the ship and the name became Souverain. Eight years later in 1923, E. Knudsen purchased the ship and the name changed to Hippalos. In 1924 Holkar, having sailed for thirty-six years, went for breaking, a marine term for dismantlement.

S. V. Candahar

The sailship was captained by Allan MacKenzie from 1875 - 1880 on voyages to Calcutta and was sold, then resold to Norwegians in 1890, renamed Almeria and shipwrecked near the island of Nomee, near New Caledonia in the South Pacific in 1905.

S. V. Khyber

Commanded by Allan MacKenzie from 1881 – 1883 on voyages to Calcutta, was built by W. H. Potter & Sons, shipbuilders of Liverpool. Yard No. 93, Khyber (274' length, 45' beam) was launched on August 21, 1880. The ship was sold in 1898 and shipwrecked near Porthgwarra (Porth Gorwedhow – Cornish, meaning much wooded cove), a small coastal village in the Parish of St. Levan, Cornwall, southwest England on March 15, 1905.

The ship was caught in a gale, the sails were ripped and anchors dropped as she approached shore. The ship dragged and broke the chains and was blown ashore in a full gale. The master and twenty-two of the crew perished in the disaster, only three of the crew survived.

S. S. Gaekwar

Captain Allan Mackenzie listed the Gaekwar as his place of residence during the 1891 census. The ship (396' length, beam 45') was propelled by triple expansion steam reciprocating engines. Brocklebanks sold the ship in 1911 and the vessel was subsequently resold in 1914, again in 1929, and went for breaking in 1934 at Tonsberg, southern Norway.

The Smuggler

The Smuggler's Shop was located at 1312 Boardwalk and owned and operated by Sam McDowell, who is considered to be one of America's premier folk artists. He was a former art teacher at Princeton High School and Princeton's Institute for Advanced Study. At one time a local Ocean City businessman, he became very talented in painting, sculpture, and internationally recognized for his artistic work as a scrimshander. In later years he sold The Smuggler's Shop and the new owner renamed the store, Old Salt, continuing to offer the public a similar line of merchandise through the 2014 season. Old Salt on the boardwalk was closed in 2015.

College Grille

The College Grille was established on the boardwalk at 13th Street in Ocean City. The business was relocated to 605 E. 8th Street in 1970 and the name changed to the Varsity Inn. The interior décor is decorated with numerous pennants depicting the names of universities and colleges, many located within the tristate area of southern New Jersey, southeastern Pennsylvania and northern Delaware. The flag bearing the name Sindia flew from the jiggermast. The triangular shape was similar in appearance to the pennants displayed on the walls in the Varsity Inn today.

Historical Landmark for Sindia

On December 15, 1967, sixty-six years following the shipwreck, signage was erected on the boardwalk next to the pavilion at 17th Street. The Department of Interior of the United States and the State of New Jersey officially recognized the resting place of the four-mast barque, Sindia, as a historical site, the first in Cape May County. David Jackson, age eighty-two, one of the original crew was in attendance along with multiple Ocean City dignitaries and residents, a number of which were still alive and had witnessed the historic event.

The Graeme's, family and friends

Ross and Shona Graeme and Mitchell and Ailsa Graeme, together with the grandparents, Ronan and Caitir Garrow, (Shona's parents), and Keitha (no last name) and Anna MaCall are fictitious characters.

News Reporter

Nigel Harris, the English news reporter, was a fictional character created to enhance the story. The Liverpool Post was an established newspaper in operation during the dates referenced in the story.

Sea Legs

Sea Legs, while a fictitious name, did accompany the crew along with a cat and the captain's canary on the final voyage. The breed of the dog is an unknown.

SAIL PLAN

Outbound	Nautical Miles	Cumulative
Dundee to		
Liverpool to	733	
New York Harbor to	3,100	3,833
Bermuda to	633	4,466
Ascension Island to	4,500	8,966
Tristan da Cunha to	1,300	10,266
Cape Agulhaus to	1,800	12,066
Reunion/Mauritius to	2,325	14,391
Cocos Islands to	2,257	16,648
Direction Island/Sangiand Island to	650	17,298
Karimati Strait to	300	17,598
Shanghai to	525	18,123
Kuroshima Island to	500	18,623
Tomogashima Island to	425	19,048
Kobe, Japan	35	19,083

Inbound	Nautical Miles	Cumulative
Kobe to		
Johnston Atoll to	1,080	
Kirimati (Christmas Island) to	3,275	4,355
Marquessas Islands to	1,407	5,762
Cape Horn to	4,400	10,162
Recife to	3,200	13,362
Bermuda	3,100	16,462
Carolinas to		
Cape May, NJ to	650	17,112
Ocean City, NJ to	30	17,142
New York Harbor	80	17,222

The locations in the sail plan were developed though research of merchant sailing routes in 1900, research pertaining to Brocklebank routes, and in consulting, for further discussion and evaluation, with my colleague, Angus MacKinnon, Troon, Scotland. The distances are estimates provided through calculations derived from Google Earth.

SHIP'S BELL PATTERN

NO. OF BELLS	MIDDLE WATCH	MORNING WATCH	FORENOON WATCH
One bell	0:30	4:30	8:30
Two bells	1:00	5:00	9:00
Three bells	1:30	5:30	9:30
Four bells	2:00	6:00	10:00
Five bells	2:30	6:30	10:30
Six bells	3:00	7:00	11:00
Seven bells	3:30	7:30	11:30
Eight bells	4:00	8:00	12:00

	AFTER-NOON WATCH	FIRST DOG WATCH	LAST DOG WATCH	FIRST WATCH
One bell	12:30	16:30	18:30	20:30
Two bells	13:00	17:00	19:00	21:00
Three bells	13:30	17:30	19:30	21:30
Four bells	14:00	18:00		22:00
Five bells	14:30			22:30
Six bells	15:00			23:00
Seven bells	15:30			23:30
Eight bells	16:00		20:00	0:00

In the days of sail a watch was timed with a thirty minute hourglass. Each time the glass was turned the ship's bell was struck the amount of times to coordinate with the name of the watch. The bell was not struck with the turn of the glass at noon, because the captain or officer on deck would take a read by the sun, using his sextant.

OCEAN CITY HISTORICAL MUSEUM

Over one hundred fourteen years have passed since Allan MacKenzie, Master, George Stewart, First Mate, George Wilkie, Third Mate, and their crew of thirty seamen, unsuccessfully fought Neptune's wrath and wrecked Sindia on the shore of Ocean City.

The Board of Trustees, the Executive Director, and an enthused staff of volunteers have used their resourcefulness in assembling an impressive display of information and artifacts, commemorating that fateful day, whereby Sindia has been remembered as a significant historical event in the annals of Ocean City's history.

Visitors will be fascinated by historical photographs including the original founding fathers of Ocean City, pictures of historical buildings, and places of interest, a beautiful scale model of Sindia, the original carved wooden head of the Maharaja Mahadji Scindia, removed from the ship following the wreck, and a carved replica of the figurehead of the Maharaja as it may have appeared, attached underneath the bowsprit of the ship.

Included in their nautical display is an original ship's binnacle and the captain's long glass and sextant. There is a magnificent display of a portion of the ship's cargo, salvaged from the wreckage and ultimately passed down through the years via multiple sources, including dishware consisting of varied cups and saucers, plates of varying sizes, and richly multi-colored artistic works of vases, products of Japan, one standing nearly three feet high. Together with these artifacts is a humidor, used as the subject in the story for the gift from Sir D.E.H. Fraser, Acting British Consulate in Shanghai, to Master Allan MacKenzie. A visit to the museum will be well worth the while and effort, enriching one's experience.

GLOSSARY

Afteryards – The yards in the mainmast and mizzenmast.

Amidship – In the middle part of a ship.

Beauly – Stems from a French word inferring, "What a beautiful place," in Scotland, denotes a body of water.

Beggared – cut off, destitute, devoid, dispossessed.

Belaying pin – A short round bar of metal or wood, inserted in a pinrail to which a rope is tied or fastened.

Binnacle – A waist-high case on the deck of a ship, mounted in front of the helmsman, containing the magnetic compass, mounted to keep it level while the ship pitches and rolls.

Blighter – A person regarded with contempt, irritation, or pity.

Bowsprit – A spar extending forward from a ship's bow used to attach forestays (supporting a mast).

Bullock's horn – A horn from a ram that could have been used to contain grease or needles, items used by a sailmaker.

Capstan - A vertical-axled rotating machine used on sailships to apply force to ropes, cables, and hawsers.

Card – A mark on the compass in the Binnacle for staying on course, direction.

Croft - A small rented farm in Scotland, comprising a plot of land attached to a house with a right of pasturage held in common with other such farms.

Crojack – Also cross jack; a square sail set on the lower yard of the mizzenmast.

Ditty box – A bag or box used by the sailmaker to store all of his tools of the trade.

Eddy – A circular movement of water, counter to a main current, causing a whirlpool.

Fid – A conical tool made of wood or whale-bone, used by a sailmaker to work with rope and canvas.

Fo'c'sle – Forecastle; a partial deck, above the upper deck, at the head of the ship, traditionally the crew's living quarters.

Foreyards – Lowest yard on a sailship's foremast.

Halyards – Lines used to hoist a sail, flag, or yard.

Hebridian – One raised on one of the islands in the archipelago of the Inner or Outer Hebrides, off the western coast of Scotland.

Horse Latitudes – Subtropical latitudes between 30 and 38 degrees both north and south, known for calm winds and little precipitation. Many years ago, some sailships, becalmed (no movement) lightened weight by discarding livestock, sometimes horses, over the side.

Jack staff – A flagstaff at the bow of a vessel.

Jibs – A triangular staysail set ahead of the foremast, secured to the bow, deck or bowsprit.

Leeward – The side of the ship where the wind is blowing toward.

Lighter – A flat bottomed barge used to transport goods.

Palm – A protective device made of leather strapped to a sailmaker's hand.

Pinrail – A rail on the side of a sailship used to insert belaying pins.

Port – Left side of a sailship.

Ratlines – Lengths of thin lines tied between the shrouds of a sailship to form a ladder.

Spankers – A fore or aft (rear) sail set on the after side of a ship's mast, especially the mizzenmast.

Spars – A thick strong pole used for a yard on a ship.

Stanchions – Lines used to secure cargo on a ship.

Starboard – Right side of the sailship.

Taffrail – An aftermost railing around the stern (back) of a ship, sometimes ornately carved.

Yards – A cylindrical spar attached to a ship's mast where a sail is hung from.

BIBLIOGRAPHY

WORKS CITED

Books, Booklets, Pamphlets, Misc.

Baker, Kimbal. For Those in Peril: A History of the Ocean City Life Saving Service Station. December 2011.

Dorwart, Dr. Jeffrey M. Cape May County New Jersey: The Making of an American Resort Community 1992

Gibson, John Frederic Brocklebanks 1770-1950 Vols. I & II Henry Young & Sons LTD. Liverpool 1953

Hollett, David From Cumberland to Cape Horn, The Sailing Fleet of Thomas & John Brocklebank of Whitehaven and Liverpool 1770-1900 Fairplay Publications Ltd. London 1984; Sea Chantey, "Blow The Man Down," P. 81.

Hoskins, Paul M. The Immigrants. Xlibris Corp. P. 97, 2013.

Lamphear, Alberta. The Saga of the Sindia.

Lee, Harold. "A History of Ocean City" The Friends of the Ocean City Historical Museum.

Lubbock, Basil Coolie Ships & Oil Sailors Brown, Son & Ferguson, Ltd. Nautical Publishers Glasgow 1955

Mathewson, Craig First Presbyterian Church Ocean City, NJ 100th Anniversary 1896-1996, A Century of Progress.

Mowen, Sarah G. "The Cape May County NJ Magazine of History and Genealogy, June 1951, Cape May County Historical and Genealogical Society.

Beaufort, Sir Francis. Beaufort Wind Scale, U.K. Royal Navy 1805.

Corson, J. Mackey. LSS, Washington, DC, Horace L. Piper, Acting General Superintendent, May 29, 1902.

Corson, J. Mackey. Townsend, Adolphur C., Wreck Report, January 4, 1902 and January 7, 1902, United States Coast Guard, National Archives and Records Service, Washington, D.C.

Darby, Bertram. "The Ocean City Story."

Rosenberg, Matt. "Trade Winds, Horse Latitudes, and the Doldrums."

Delacamp & Co., "The Bill of Lading."

London Board of Trade British Consulate, Philadelphia, PA, "Sindia" (NO. 6310) The Merchant Shipping Act, 1894, February 7, 1902.

M. Magnus, Foreign Market Reports Agency "Copy of Manifest."

Newspapers and Magazines

DeVries, Ray E. "Sindia Pioneer resident: Came to town 30 Years Ago" Ocean City Sentinel Ledger April 14, 1931.

Gant, Lee M. "After 70 Years, Only a Mast Protrudes From Ship's Watery Grave" The Brick Town Reporter January 5, 1972.

Gilmore, Christopher Cook. "The Saga of the Sindia."

Hoffman, Luther. "Glow Ashore Taken for N.Y. Harbor" Atlantic City Press 1929

Lee, Harold. "British Sailor, Aboard Sindia When It Grounded Here 35 Years Ago, Writes to Coast Guard Chief Ocean City Sentinel Ledger December 22, 1936.

McCall, John. "Lies and Entertainment, Treasure of Wrecks May Still Await" Philadelphia Inquirer October 6, 1981.

Pollock, Michael. "60 Year-Old Copybook Yields Vivid Account of Wreck" Ocean City Sentinel Ledger June 1, 1979.

Randall, O.S. "Sindia Adds to its' 66 Year Renown-State's First Historic Wreck" The Sunday Bulletin December 17, 1967.

Sakolic, William H. "Prayer Book Donated to OCHM" Courier Post.

Salvo, Nicolas F. "True Treasure" p. 21 October 1974.

White, William. "Sindia's Wreckage on Ocean City Beach" June 2, 1961.

"Bark Sindia a Wreck" Ocean City Sentinel Ledger December 19, 1901.

"Caught in Blizzard" Ocean City Sentinel Ledger 1921.

"Dreadful Tragedy on a Liverpool Ship" Liverpool Post November 26, 1878.

"Obituary – Allan MacKenzie" The Nautical Magazine a Technical and Critical Journal July-December 1908 Issue.

"Ocean City Remembers the Sindia Excitement" Sunday Press Atlantic City, NJ December 17, 1972

"The Wreck of the Sindia" Ocean City Sentinel Ledger 1902.

Ocean City Storyteller July 16, 1970

Sure Guide June 1984

Websites

Steele, Mark. "He Recreated the Sindia, Ian Hunt, Bldr. of Replica of" *Sindia Duckworksmagazine.com* Auckland, N.Z. 2009
http://www.duckworksmagazine.com/09/projects/sindia/

Sumner, Thomas Hubbard. 1870-1876 "Celestial Navigation, Sumner Line" *Wikipedia*
https://en.wikipedia.org/wiki/Thomas_Hubbard_Sumner

"Agreement and Account of Crew, Sindia, 1892-93" Maritime History

Research Collection *Memorial University of Newfoundland St. John's, Newfoundland*
https://www.mun.ca/mha/holdings/searchcombinedcrews.php
"Brocklebank Collection" *Merseyside Maritime Museum Liverpool, UK.*
http://www.liverpoolmuseums.org.uk/index.aspx
"Celestial Navigation," "Sailors Skills," *Mystic Seaport Mystic, CT.*
http://www.mysticseaport.org/
"Certificate of Competency" *London Metropolitan Archives*
https://www.cityoflondon.gov.uk/things-to-do/london-metropolitan-archives/Pages/default.aspx
"England, Marriages and Banns (Proclamations), 1813-1921," "UK and Ireland, Masters and Mates Certificates 1850-1927" *Ancestry.com.uk*
http://search.ancestry.com/search/category.aspx?cat=34&geo_a=r&o_iid=62817&o_lid=62817&o_sch=Web+Property
"Index to Captain's Registers of Lloyd's of London" *Guildhall Library*
http://www.history.ac.uk/gh/capintro.htm
"News Accounts, Documents, Treasure Hunt" *RaisetheSindia.com*
"1900 Era Clothing" *Gentleman's Emporium UK*
http://www.gentlemansemporium.com/mens_victorian_outfits.php?gclid=CNXGxNT__MkCFY-PHwod36gI7w
Bureau Veritas of Paris, The
"Norman B. Leventhal Map Center" *Boston Public Library*
https://bpl.bibliocommons.com/search?q=Norman+B.+Leventhal+Map+Collection&t=smart&search_category=keyword&commit=Search&submitsearch=go&se=catalog
Exxon Mobile Europe
Google Earth
"Historic Town Bank," *Historic Town Bank.com*
http://www.historictownbank.com/Town_History.html
Liverpool Nautical Research Society
http:/liverpoolnauticalresearchsociety.org/
Mitchell Library Glasgow, Scotland
http://www.glasgowlife.org.uk/libraries/the-mitchell-library/Pages/home.aspx
National Archives.gov.uk http://www.nationalarchives.gov.uk/
National Maritime Museum London http://www.rmg.co.uk/national-maritime-museum
National Museums Liverpool Maritime Archives and Library
http://www.liverpoolmuseums.org.uk/maritime/archive/
Somers Point Historical Museum, Inc. http://www.somerspointhistory.org/
Ulster Folk & Transport Museum http://nmni.com/uftm
Wreck Site http://wrecksite.eu

Museums

Swope, David. "Mark Gray" Museum of New Jersey Maritime History
Boone, David. "The Age of Sail" "Newspaper Articles-Shipwrecks"
Independence Seaport Museum, Penns Landing, Philadelphia, PA.
Ocean City Historical Museum, Ocean City, N.J.

REVIEW'S

"It was humbling and emotional to read your words regarding dad in your "Dedication" - Oh how he would have enjoyed reading the whole book - You have the Clan MacKinnon seal of approval and major thumbs up!"
Stella McMillan, M.D. Glasgow, Scotland (daughter to and in memoriam to research assistant, Angus MacKinnon, Troon, Scotland)

"How fortunate for us that Harry Allen Wenzel allowed his childhood memories to inspire this highly researched historical novel. The Sindia was, in 1887, the largest cargo carrying sailship afloat. The author takes us into the lives of the British Captain, Allan McKenzie, and his family, and we learn of the challenges to gaining maritime certifications and the career path needed to command a large vessel like the Sindia. The final voyage, which this work highlights, ended in a four day gale on Dec. 15, 1901 off the coast of Ocean City, New Jersey. Stories have circulated of a possible controversial cargo. Even today, the shipwreck, now buried beneath twenty feet of sand, is ever alive in the annals of shipwreck lore and the imaginations of all who have wandered along the ocean's shores. I so enjoyed reading this work."
Oliver St. Clair Franklin OBE British Honorary Consulate, Philadelphia, PA

"This historical novel is an insightful, fact filled, journey, recording one of coastal New Jersey's most historic dramatic events. After a powerful storm raked the coast on a cold December 1901 weekend, the 1300 residents of Ocean City awakened to discover a large four mast sailing vessel, shipwrecked off their shore. It was a Sunday morning and the preachers of this island town must have had a hard time holding the attention of their congregants in the pews, as news spread about the wreck off of 16th Street beach. The author spins a fine yarn as he traces the history of the globe circling, the British flagged Sindia, her young helmsman Mitchell Graeme, and her finest captain, Allan MacKenzie. These two men, born and nurtured in the highlands of Scotland and imbued with the strong moral formation of its Presbyterian Church, weather one of life's greatest challenges. This book will delight all who love the history of Ocean City."
John S. Sheldon, Senior Pastor First Presbyterian Church of Ocean City, NJ

"The age of the sailing ship overlapped the introduction of steamships by a full century. With the opening of the Suez Canal in 1869, owners and builders of sailing vessels were forced to innovate in order to remain competitive. In the last decades of the 19th century, sailing vessels were designed and built to compete for merchant trade with the increasingly economical steamers, well into the 20th Century.

"Sindia" was one such vessel, with steel hull, wire rigging, steam winches to handle the heavier lifting operations involved, and with cargo capacity many times greater than only a few decades earlier.

It is not always easy to splice together into one account the result of extensive nautical research together with some fiction. The author has done a commendable job in bringing together two very different sources into a coherent and seamless whole. The book is a very good read and the report of the inquiry into her stranding on the coast of New Jersey in 1901 is absolutely gripping."

David White, Liverpool Nautical Research Society, Maritime and Archives Library, Merseyside Maritime Museum, Liverpool, UK

"The facts surrounding the stranding and demise of the SV Sindia are well known to maritime historians. Even though her stranding caused no loss of life, the ship became famous for her long journey around the world, and coming within hours of reaching her destination. Another historical recital of the facts would only be redundant. This author chose to bring the captain and crew to life by telling their story and their journey. The duties of every crew member, from master to cabin boy, is described, not in boring detail, but through the eyes of that crew member. While the personalities assigned to each crew member are admittedly fiction, they reflect the dreams and fears of other sailors in those positions, who have documented their adventures before the mast. This book adds a fresh human look at a maritime disaster."

David Swope, Trustee/Secretary and Research Volunteer, New Jersey Maritime Museum, Beach Haven, NJ

FROM THE AUTHOR

Thank you sincerely for your interest and purchase of Sindia, the Final Voyage. Your comments and questions are welcome and appreciated.

Contact Information

E-Mail
harry@harryallenwenzel.com

Website
harryallenwenzel.com

Publisher

Yellowtail Snapper Publishing
Harleysville
Pennsylvania

Contact Information

E-mail
Yellowtailsnapperpublishing@gmail.com

ABOUT THE AUTHOR

A business graduate of the Pennsylvania State University, Harry Wenzel pursued a lifelong career in the financial services industry.

Harry is an avid reader of autobiographical, nonfiction and historical works. He enjoys writing; "Sindia, the Final Voyage," is his first historical novel.

An avid outdoor enthusiast, he enjoys landscaping and gardening. If the subject is travel, his frequented destinations include the beaches in Florida and South Carolina, the Rockies in Colorado, and golf courses in his home state, Pennsylvania. He is most at home when by the ocean, on the beach in Ocean City, New Jersey. As a sportsman, he actively participates in golf, biking, and hiking.

Harry was raised in the Indian Valley and resides in Pennsylvania with his wife. Together they have four children and twelve grandchildren.

Made in the
USA
Middletown, DE